A Seat at the Table

Food and Feasting in the Islamic World

A Seat at the Table

Food and Feasting
in the Islamic World

QATAR MUSEUMS   SilvanaEditoriale

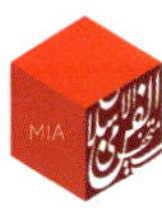

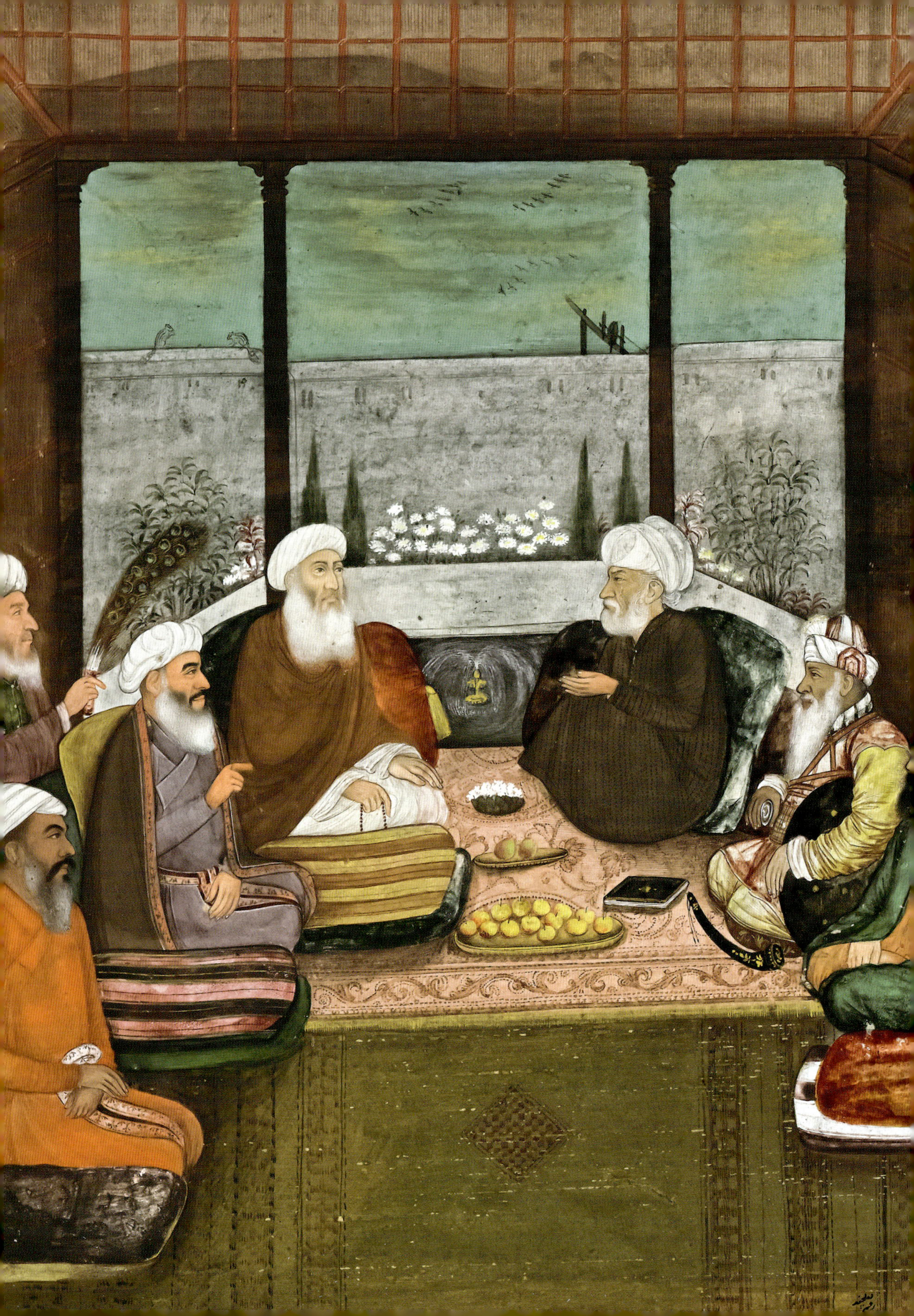

Contents

*Six Wise Men Including
Mian Mir and Mullah
Shah in Discussion*
(detail), folio from the
Ardeshir album,
attributed to La'lchand
India, Mughal period,
11th century AH/
mid-17th century CE,
opaque watercolour,
ink and gold on paper,
55.9 × 35 cm. Museum
of Islamic Art, Doha,
MS.826.2012

Her Excellency Sheikha Al Mayassa
bint Hamad bin Khalifa Al Thani

Chairperson, Qatar Museums

Foreword

This impressive catalogue, which accompanies a major
exhibition at the Museum of Islamic Art, opens new perspectives
on Muslim communities everywhere, past and present, and on
the history of Islamic art. It does so by exploring what happens
when an individual's most basic necessity, food, becomes a
vehicle for sharing with others. *A Seat at the Table: Food and
Feasting in the Islamic World* reveals with fascinating insight
how dining in Islamic cultures has built community, forged
relationships among people from diverse backgrounds, and—
not least—inspired a multitude of art.

A legacy of the 2021 Qatar-US Year of Culture, *A Seat at
the Table* builds upon an important earlier exhibition, *Dining
with the Sultan: The Fine Art of Feasting,* organised by Linda
Komaroff, Department Head and Curator, Art of the Middle
East, at the Los Angeles County Museum of Art. Moving
beyond the elite social group of that previous show, *A Seat at
the Table* considers dining as a living practice at every level of
society throughout the Muslim world.

In essays amply accompanied by illustrations of artefacts in
the exhibition, from exquisite medieval manuscripts to a brass
lunchbox, the book explores topics such as traditions of bread

making, the migration of foods from region to region, the types of foods that are promised to us in Paradise, and the history and uses of glazed ceramics. Bringing the subject into the present day, the authors also consider innovation and food security in Qatar—issues of urgent relevance across the globe.

I congratulate the exhibition curators Dr Tara Desjardins of the Lusail Museum and Teslim Sanni of the Museum of Islamic Art, and Linda Komaroff, Daniel Newman, Reem Aboughazala, Nicoletta Fazio, Simone Struth and Mounia Chekhab Abudaya for their contributions to the book. I also thank the LACMA team for their support and our partners at Qatar Museums and the Qatar National Library for lending objects from their collections. My thanks go as well as to the Doha Film Institute, Heenat Salma farm, the Qatar Photography Centre, Abdulrahman Al-Mulla, and Aisha al Muhannadi.

Customs of dining offer us a way both to express our identity and to know one another better. *A Seat at the Table* invites you to share in the feast.

Shaika Nasser Al Nassr

Director, Museum of Islamic Art

Director's Foreword

More than any other activity, food brings people, cultures and communities together. Eating, whether sharing a meal or dining alone, goes well beyond the mere necessity of sustenance. It nurtures us physically, mentally and emotionally. Yet food has also helped to expand people's perspectives and encourage new experiences. Today, we travel to new destinations to experience food cultures. In some respects, food is the only ingredient that binds our differences, connecting our sensory pleasures and pallet to one another, beyond any prejudices we may have.

This exhibition—organised at the geographical heart of the Islamic world—speaks to and about the multitude of cultures represented in Qatar and beyond. The diversity of food practices and cuisines found here is astonishing, a true testament to the country's multi-national communities. *A Seat at the Table: Food and Feasting in the Islamic World* reflects the power of similar practices united under a common faith, highlighting similarities and differences whether found locally or across the globe.

We are grateful to the LACMA team, and especially to Linda Komaroff, Curator of Islamic Art and Head of the Art of the Middle East Department for her support in the exhibition. While both Qatar Museums and LACMA share an institutional partnership, the specific collaboration between the Museum of Islamic Art and LACMA, which started in 2012 with the exhibition *The Gift Tradition in Islamic Art*, has only further strengthened these bonds. I am particularly grateful to Linda for her openness in adapting their exhibition *Dining with the Sultan* to suit our local audience and permanent collection, as well as contributing an essay to our catalogue. I am also thankful to the curators, Tara Desjardins and Teslim Sanni, and the entire MIA team for helping to develop and realise this exhibition. I extend my gratitude to our local partners at both Qatar Museums and the Qatar National Library, as well as to the Doha Film Institute, Heenat Salma farm, the Qatar Photography Centre, Abdulrahman Al-Mulla, and Aisha Al Muhannadi, for their loans and support, which greatly enhanced the rich texture of the exhibition narrative and display. Lastly, I thank everyone who contributed to the catalogue, including Daniel Newman, whose expertise in the field of medieval Islamic gastronomy adds invaluable insights on the subject.

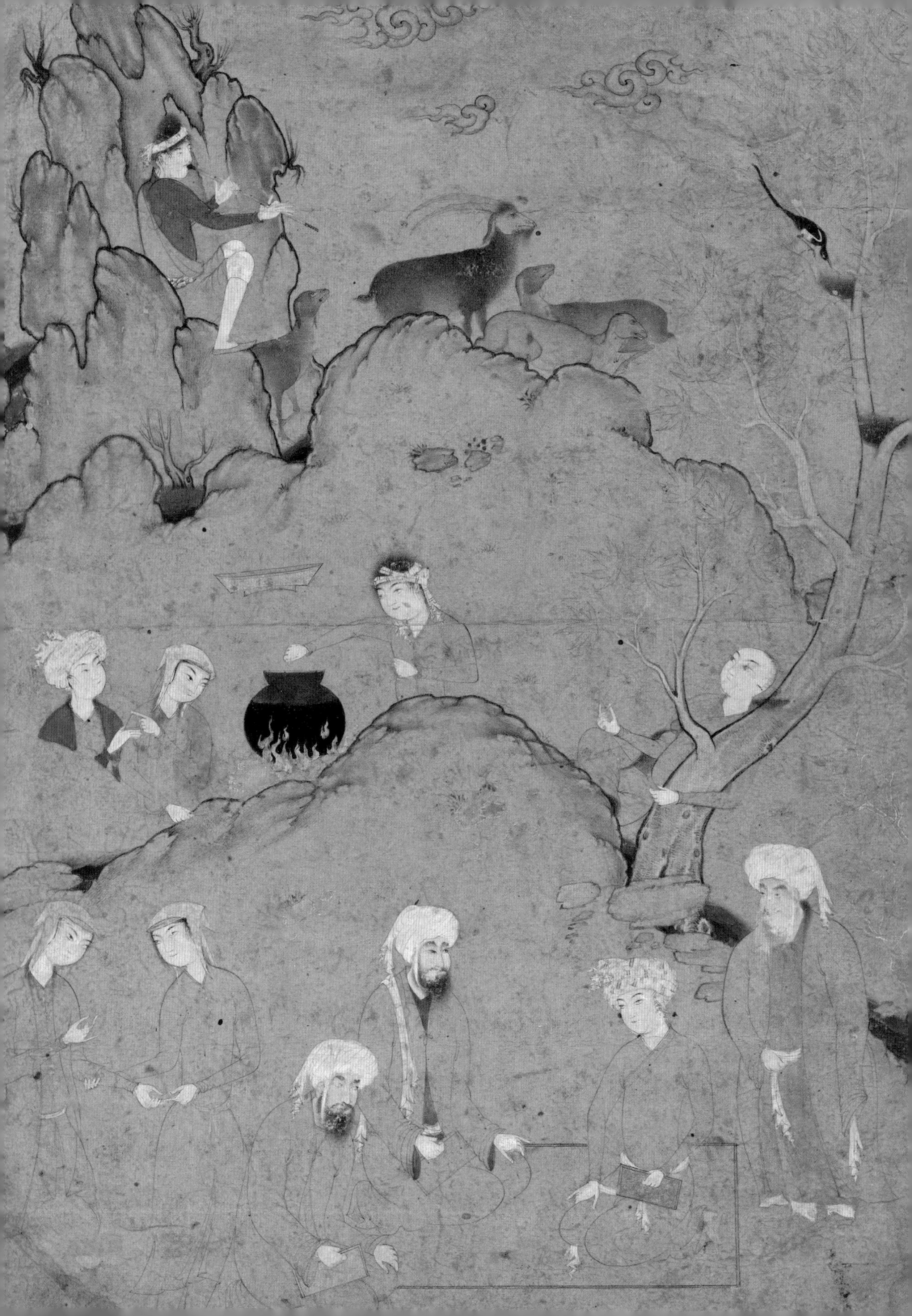

Tara Desjardins

Introduction

The history of food in the Islamic lands has recently been the focus of art historians and, in particular, museum professionals. While historic texts and treatises on food practices, dishes and food etiquette exist, these have been studied independently from the artefacts that museums typically display. Only recently have the two been studied together in a multidisciplinary approach, merging the two areas of research to construct a multi-layered picture of the objects on display. This has been demonstrated by the exhibition *Dining with the Sultan: The Fine Art of Feasting* (December 2023 – August 2024), curated by Linda Komaroff from the Los Angeles County Museum of Art (LACMA), which was accompanied by a catalogue of the same title. This exhibition was the first to explore Islamic art in the context of its associated culinary culture and food traditions, drawing from a large and impressive list of art works related to gastronomy and fine dining.

The exhibition presented at the Museum of Islamic Art, Doha (MIA) draws on the core concepts of LACMA's exhibition, while changing the storyline and object list to reflect local audiences and collections. Titled *A Seat at the Table: Food and Feasting in the Islamic World*, the storyline attempts to move beyond the role of dining and feasting within an elite context by presenting it as a living practice that unites different cultures and communities.

The MIA exhibition covers five broad themes, each addressed in essays written by the museum's curatorial

Cooking in a Landscape (detail), Afghanistan (Herat), Safavid period, *c.* 987 AH/1580 CE, opaque watercolour and ink on paper, 29 × 20 cm. Museum of Islamic Art, Doha, MIA.2013.151

team as well as two external authors: 'Breaking Bread', 'Food and Faith', 'Itinerant Ingredients', 'Dining with the Sultan', and 'Contemporary Cuisine: We Are What We Eat'. These themes reflect only a portion of the many plausible topics related to food and feasting in the Islamic world, but have been chosen to resonate with both local residents and visitors alike.

The first theme is explored in an emotionally charged essay by Nicoletta Fazio, which discusses different bread making traditions practised across the Islamic world. The message is simple yet powerful: we all share the same basic needs and breaking bread together can reinforce the bonds of a shared humanity.

The second theme, Food and Faith, is addressed in contributions by Daniel Newman and Teslim Sanni. Newman's essay discusses culinary practices in the early and medieval Islamic world, documenting shifts in cooking methods and food preferences between geographical regions, while Sanni's essay looks at the representation of food in Paradise as mentioned in the Qur'an and Hadiths.

In my essay for the third theme, I explore how ingredients travelled, often great distances, as part of a wider global transfer of commodities, luxury objects and foodstuffs at two moments in history: the early Abbasid period (3rd–5th centuries AH/9th–11th century CE) and at the time of the 'discovery' of the Americas (9th–10th centuries AH/15th–16th centuries CE).

For the fourth theme, in honour of LACMA's exhibition, Linda Komaroff has graciously contributed an essay on 'setting the table', a subject that examines how the rise of a courtly culinary culture in Abbasid Iraq prompted the production of an entirely new type of dining ware.

The last two essays deal with contemporary subjects, including the future of sustainable agricultural practices and the role of contemporary female chefs, both focusing on Qatar. The contributions in this section, by Teslim Sanni and

Tara Desjardins

Reem Aboughazala, remind us of the importance of food and culinary traditions today: we are what we eat, and if we fail to nurture the land from which we harvest our foods, we will face severe food shortages and indeed a threat to the future of humanity.

The publication is further supplemented by 30 catalogue entries of objects featured in the exhibition. The majority of these have never been published and therefore offer new and exciting research to the reader. The objects selected represent a diversity of types, periods and places of production, highlighting the variety of historical cooking and dining ware produced in the Islamic world and represented by MIA's collection.

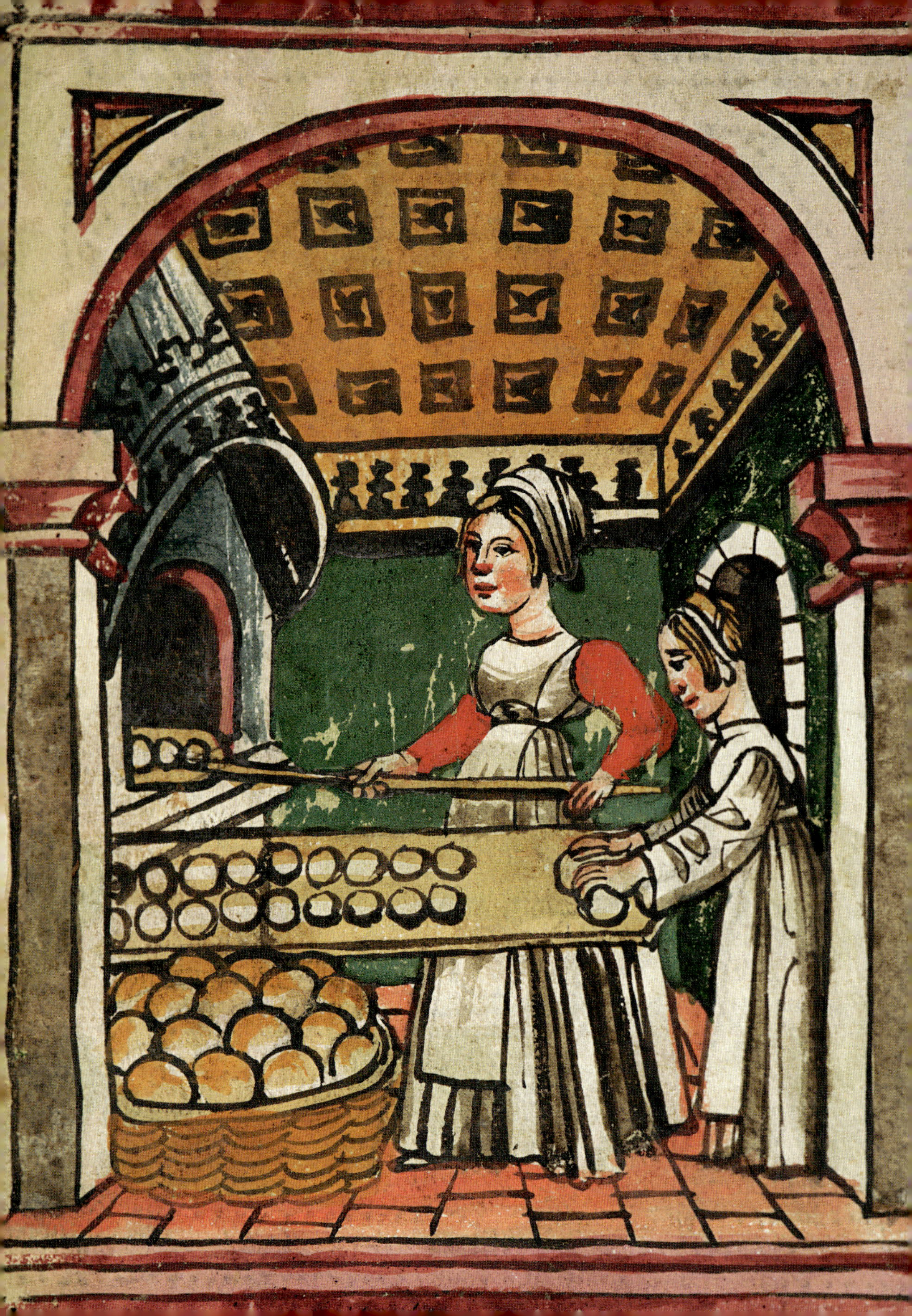

Nicoletta Fazio

Knead, Heat, Repeat:
The Dough of Life

[…] In my Divan I shall praise the cooked stuff; […]
Be it Rustam, or Bizhan, be it this or that,
they all are running about and roaming in search of bread…

Boshaq At'emeh Shirazi, *Dastan-e Moza'far u Boghra*[1]

On certain days, if you walk out of the Museum of Islamic Art at the right time, together with sand and salt, the wind carries the smell of freshly baked bread. Under the jaguar sun, this hearty smell never fails to bring me back to my hometown in Italy, to a time when I was trotting my way to school and waves of warm aromas would hit me as bakeries opened their doors. Dreams of soft bread and crispy focaccia—there are certainly worse ways to start a day, or to end one. There seems to be something primal in such a feeling, something ancestral that speaks of life and the heart of people.

The bread fragrance filling the air of Doha's Corniche comes from the imposing structures of Qatar's Flour Mills, a presence as much solid as they are alive and in motion, with parts of the buildings destined to become the creative grist for art and culture.[2] Standing as visual reminders of the transformation of a private activity into a fully industrialised process, the Flour Mills' silos embody the everchanging face of a nation firmly rooted in tradition while jumping into a wild future.[3] Bread indeed has this power. It elicits personal memories, as captured in the video installation *A Thread of Light Between My Mother's Fingers and*

Folio 76v (detail), *Tacuinum Sanitatis* ('Almanac of Health'), Italy, Sicily, c.1475 CE, ink and opaque watercolour on paper, 39.3 × 28.1 cm (closed). Museum of Islamic Art Library, Doha, RS79.L64.14[75]

Heaven (2023) by the Iraqi artist Sadik Kwaish Alfraji. This work, recently displayed in the exhibition *Dining with the Sultan*, was inspired by the artist's mother and the memories of her hands making bread. And as such, bread also holds a bittersweet promise: the taste of nostalgia.[4] It has however become so commodified today that we tend to forget its social function and cultural role in the past.

The ritual nature of bread making, a labour of patience repeated day after day, reflects not only its lasting presence in human history, from selecting seeds to baking dough, but also its centrality in religious practices since pre-Islamic times in the Fertile Crescent. It was here that wheat was first domesticated around ten thousand years ago, before spreading across Eurasia.[5] Bread is included, for instance, among the offerings to Zoroastrian fire temples mentioned in epigraphic and written sources from the Sasanian period onwards (3rd–4th centuries CE).[6] Its ritual and symbolic significance survived in popular and devotional practices among Turkic populations of Asia well after their conversion to Islam.[7] Although in Islamic cultures bread does not hold any particular sacred or ritual place—it is mentioned only once in the Qur'an (Q12:36) and in very literal terms[8]—it is nonetheless highly respected and handled with care, from table etiquette to disposal. Tradition requires bread to be broken by hand and not cut with a knife. If crumbs fall on the ground, they are picked up. Pieces of bread found on the road are traditionally placed on a raised, clean place and not thrown away.

The generic word for bread in Arabic is *khubz*, regardless of its shape, way of preparation or baking method. Yet the existence of several other words in both Classical Arabic and its dialects indicate many types of bread, and by extension the human ingenuity in creating such variety from three basic ingredients: water, flour and salt. Flatbread (*khubz faṭir*) is the most common, baked and sold across the Muslim world today, but leavened bread (*khubz khamir*) can also be found.[9] Because of the economics of pre-Islamic Arabia, wheat bread remained for centuries a commodity only the rich could afford to buy. This is reflected in the use of the expression *akil al-khubz* (bread-eater) to indicate a person of considerable means, as in the *Kitab al-Bukhala'* (Book of Misers) by the Abbasid author al-Jahiz (d. 254 AH/868 CE).[10]

Bread consumption increased in the region after the Arab conquest of West and Central Asia, where wheat was extensively

   Nicoletta Fazio

cultivated, to quickly become a staple of the Abbasid table. However, it was not eaten on its own, but rather shredded or crumbled into soups and meat stews, resulting in dishes equally nutritious and inexpensive, especially in rural contexts. This is how bread is still served in recipes such as *tharid* and *ab gusht* from the western Mediterranean to the Arabian Peninsula and the Iranian plateau.[11]

Across North Africa and Asia, for millennia—and in some cases up until today[12]—flatbreads of all kinds have been baked in domed clay ovens, both private or communal, known in Arabic as *tabun* or *tannur*.[13] This is the source of the term *tandoori*, a word that has entered common English vocabulary thanks to colonisation and globalisation. Because of its nature, unleavened flatbread has the undeniable advantage of lasting longer, and it can be consumed after being wet or baked a second time, hence its widespread presence among Eurasian nomadic populations. It is rather telling that the expression *nan khordan* in Persian (lit. to eat bread) also stands for 'to have a meal/ to eat', indicating the key place of such food in the daily diet of Persian-speaking populations.[14] While in modern-day Iran bread is a staple for most people,[15] it wrestles with rice for prominence on the table depending on the region. In drier areas of the country flatbread of different heights and textures are prevalent, while in humid regions rice or bread cakes made of rice flour are more common.[16]

Such geographical divides, and tasty 'rivalry', seems to even emerge in the satirical poem *Dastan-e Moza'far u Boghra* (The Story of Saffron Pilaf and Dumpling Soup) by the Shirazi poet Boshaq At'emeh (d. between 827 AH/1423 CE and 830 AH/1427 CE).[17] In his poem, a parodic culinary rendition of Firdausi's *Shahnama* (Book of Kings), Boshaq mentions that homemade flatbreads from Yazd join the ranks of King Moza'far's army as shields.[18] This humorous poetic image reflects the role of bread as the foundation of a meal and the perfect accompaniment to dips and dishes, as is still the case in the gastronomic traditions of West Asia in particular, from Turkish breakfast to *mezze*.

Food is a simple yet powerful means of bringing people together, a fitting metaphor of our world interconnected for centuries through trade, movements and exchanges (some violent). In this respect, the advent of European colonialism also impacted cuisines across the Islamic world. Along with armies and missionaries, Europeans brought with them their culinary heritage, including many new forms of bread. This is, for example, the case of *pav*, an iconic type of soft, fluffy bread common in western Indian states, whose roots are found in the baking tradition of the Portuguese *pão* (bread roll). Or the increasing popularity of European-style leavened bread among the urban upper middle classes of the eastern Mediterranean during the late Ottoman period, as is evidenced in periodicals of the period, such as the Arabic monthly *Al-Muqtataf* (The Digest).[19]

As we follow the peregrinations of this edible meeting point, bread serves us with an apt image: the expression 'breaking bread together' is often used to promote communal initiatives that foster dialogue within a shared, safe space. Hence, there is a strong social component in the many meanings that bread holds in human history. But as much as bread functions as a bridge for people to meet, connect and unite for a cause, it can also turn into an involuntary tool of social humiliation or, worse, systemic violence, and oppression. A well-documented episode in the modern history of the Arab world is the lack of white wheat bread caused by the famine that hit Greater Syria during World War I.[20] As bread darkened by the day, adulterated with a variety of substances, edible and inedible, social divides grew wider with mounting outrage, feeding grim emotions amongst a population already battered by the chronic lack of food. In the present day, spiking prices or shortages of bread have opened the doors to civil protest and revolution, most recently in 2010, shortly before the beginning of the Arab Spring, when it became a symbol of resistance and political uprising.[21]

A source of nourishment, bread can morph into a symbol of death in the blink of an eye. This is no more evident than in the Gaza Strip after 7 October 2023. A few weeks into the attack on Gaza, amidst large-scale massacres and a live-streamed humanitarian crisis, bakeries were bombed while people queued for hours to secure minimum rations of bread.[22] This was a deliberate attack by the occupying forces to provoke not only physical starvation, as hardly any food aid was allowed to enter the Strip, but also to cause what the sociologist Pitrim A. Sorokin calls 'psychosocial starvation', targeting a cornerstone of Palestinian diet and disrupting daily routine.[23] With the reopening of bakeries in Gaza in the spring of 2024, and the rise of Instagram accounts documenting Gazawis preparing meals for their communities,[24] it highlighted the fact that food stands as a coping tool, giving a sense of normalcy to a life that has, otherwise, lost it all.

          Nicoletta Fazio

Scrolling through images of bread and blood—words that should never come together in the same sentence—we should also be reminded that in various Arabic dialects the words for bread refer to life and sustenance, such as *'aysh, ma'isha, qut*. Bread is life, in its simplicity and warmth. And much like the small wheat seeds that travelled millennia and vast distances, bread holds that enduring quality of life, a striving force of resistance against all the odds, even in the run on. Even today.

But his children were spun of lilac and sunlight
They wanted milk and a loaf of bread
Inscrutable day. My face
A telegram made of wheat in a field of bullets
What is it wakes you now
Exactly five o'clock
And thirty people killed
Bread never had this taste before

Mahmoud Darwish, *Bread Poem*, 1975

Endnotes

1 Translated in Julia Rubanovich, 'Persian Narrative Poetry in the Eighth/Fourteenth to Early Ninth/Fifteenth Centuries and the Legacy of Ferdowsi's Shāhnāmeh', in *Iran after the Mongols*, ed. Sussan Babaie (London and New York: I.B. Tauris, 2019), pp. 235–269.

2 See 'The Introduction' volume, *Art Mill Museum 2030*, eds. Aurélien Lemonier and Maryam Al Thani (Milan: Silvana Editoriale and Qatar Museums, 2023).

3 See Shaima Al-Tamimi, *A Nation's Bread and a Morsel of Life (Logme al-'Aish)* /لقمة العيش, Lemonier and Al Thani, eds., *Art Mill Museum 2030*, no page number.

4 'When they told me about the concept, I immediately thought about my mother's fingers as she made bread. […] The touch of my mother's hand, the feeling when I'm watching her making bread; she takes it out of the oven and I just take it from her hand and eat it. That gives it a kind of taste that I haven't found anywhere', Sadik Kwaish Alfraji as told to Matt Stromberg in the exhibition review, 'New Show of Islamic Art Explores the Pleasure of Eating Together', *Hyperallergic*, published 19 December 2023; available online at https://hyperallergic.com/862806/new-show-of-islamic-art-at-lacma-explores-the-pleasure-of-eating-together/ (accessed 23 September 2024). Alfraji's video installation was on display in the exhibition *Dining with the Sultan: The Fine Art of Feasting*, Los Angeles County Museum of Art, 17 December 2023 – 04 August 2024.

5 While bread baking is mostly associated with wheat, other ground cereals such as corn, barley, sorghum, or rice, can be used to make bread. For the diffusion of wheat grains across Asia up to China, see Robert N. Spengler III, *Fruits from the Sands. The Silk Road Origins of the Food We Eat* (Oakland, CA: University of California Press, 2019), pp. 140–161.

6 Hélène Desmet-Grégoire, 'Bread', *Encyclopaedia Iranica*, 4/4, pp. 444–447; available online at https://www.iranicaonline.org/articles/bread-persian-nan (accessed 23 September 2024). See also Shervin Farridnejad, 'The Banquet for the Gods: Sacrificial Meat and Bread as the Main Ritual Foods in Zoroastrian Liturgies', in *Food for Gods, Food for Mortals: Culinary and Dining Practices in the Greater Iranian World*, eds. Shervin Farridnejad and Touraj Daryaee (Irvine, CA: University of Irvine, 2022), pp. 77–131.

7 Turkic populations of Central Asia were not completely converted to Islam until at least the 8th century AH/14th century CE. On the socio-cultural importance of wheat and bread in popular rituals and devotional practices among Turkic populations, see, for instance, Louise Bechtold, 'The Ritual Economy of Bread and Women's Identity in Southern Kyrgyzstan', in *Food and Identity in Central Asia*, ed. Aida Aaly Alymbaeva (Halle [Saale]: Max Planck Institute for Social Anthropology, 2017), pp. 103–116; and Jeanine Dağyeli, 'Wheat the Magnificent: Revisiting a Central Asian Agricultural Ritual', *Paideuma: Mitteilungen zur Kulturkunde* 64 (2018), pp. 203–226. See also the entry 'Food' for the *Silk Road Seattle* project by Elmira Köçümkulkïzï and Daniel C. Waugh (University of Washington); available at: https://depts.washington.edu/silkroad/culture/food/food.html (accessed 25 September 2024).

8 For an interpretation of this passage, see Mustansir Mir, 'Bread', *Encyclopaedia of the Qur'an*, vol. 1, pp. 255–256.

9 In 2016 the baking and sharing of different kinds of flatbread in culinary traditions of West and Central Asia was officially inscribed on the *Representative List of the Intangible Cultural Heritage of Humanity*; see the online announcement at https://web.archive.org/web/20161201212008/http://www.unesco.org/culture/ich/en/RL/flatbread-making-and-sharing-culture-lavash-katyrma-jupka-yufka-01181 (accessed 23 September 2024). Through migration flows and globalisation, flatbread has become extensively available and appreciated in Europe and the US.

10 See Charles Pellat, 'Khubz', *Encyclopaedia of Islam II*, vol. 5, pp. 41–43; M. Rodinson, 'Ghidha', *Encyclopaedia of Islam II*, vol. 2, pp. 1057–1072.

11 *Tharid* remains a very popular dish of the ancient culinary tradition of the Arabian Peninsula today. Its popularity during the pre-Islamic and the early Islamic period is even testified by one Hadith tradition transmitted by *Sahih al-Bukhari* in which the Prophet Muhammad (PBUH) equates the superiority of 'Aisha among women to the superiority of *tharid* over the rest of food (Muhammad Ibn Isma'il al-Bukhari, *Sahih al-Bukhari. The Translation of the Meanings of Sahiḥ al-Bukhari, Arabic-English*, trans. Muhammad Muhsin Khan (Riyadh: Darussalam, 1997), vol. 7, p. 211, no. 5427. For *ab gusht* see Elr and N. Ramazani, 'Āb-Gūšt', *Encyclopaedia Iranica*, 1/1, pp. 47–48; available online at

Nicoletta Fazio

https://www.iranicaonline.org/articles/ab-gust (accessed 25 September 2024).

12 As, for instance, the case of *kesra*, a flatbread made of semolina and flour, diffused in North Africa and known as *aghrom* among Amazigh communities.

13 See Antonella Pasqualone, 'Traditional Flat Breads Spread from the Fertile Crescent: Production Process and History of Baking Systems', *Journal of Ethnic Foods* 5/1 (March 2018), pp. 10–19. See also Sonia Gutiérrez Lloret, 'Panes, hogazas y fogones portátiles. Dos formas cerámicas destinadas a la cocción del pan en Al-Andalus: el hornillo (*tannūr*) y el plato (*tābaq*)', *Lucentum* 9–10 (1991), pp. 161–175. Another baking method utilises a *saj* or *tabaq*, a metal plate with curved profile whose concave surface is used to cook flatbread and pancakes.

14 See the entry نان خوردن on the online version of *Loghtanama Dehkhoda*; available online at https://dehkhoda.ut.ac.ir/fa/dictionary (accessed 25 September 2024).

15 For different kinds of breads available in Iran, see Vahid Mohammadpour Karizaki, 'Ethnic and Traditional Iranian Breads: Different Types, and Historical and Cultural Aspects', *Journal of Ethnic Foods* 4/1 (March 2017), pp. 8–14.

16 See Marcel Bazin, Christian Bromberger, Daniel Balland, and ṣoḡra Bazargan, 'Berenj', *Encyclopeadia Iranica*, vol. 4/2, pp. 147–163; available online at https://www.iranicaonline.org/articles/berenj-rice (accessed 25 September 2024).

17 See Heshmat Moayyad, 'Bosḥāq Aṭʿema', *Encyclopaedia Iranica*, vol. 4/4, pp. 382–383; available online at https://www.iranicaonline.org/articles/boshaq-atema (accessed 25 September 2024).

18 Rubanovich, 'Persian Narrative Poetry', p. 249.

19 See Christian Saßmannshausen, 'Food Consumption and Social Status in Late Ottoman Greater Syria', in *Insatiable Appetite: Food as Cultural Signifier in the Middle East and Beyond*, eds. Kirill Dmitriev, Julia Hauser and Bilal Orfali (Leiden: Brill, 2020), pp. 27–49, esp. pp. 40–43.

20 See Tylor Brand, 'Some Eat to Remember, Some to Forget: Starving, Eating, and Coping in the Syrian Famine of World War I', in Dmitriev et al., *Insatiable Appetite*, pp. 319–339, esp. pp. 333–336.

21 Tariq Basir and Soumya Datta, 'Bread, Freedom or Social Justice? An Empirical Investigation into the Determinants of the Arab Spring', *Democratization* 31/4 (2023), pp. 1–19.

22 See the Al-Jazeera photo gallery available online at https://www.aljazeera.com/gallery/2023/11/2/gaza-bakeries-destroyed-by-israeli-strikes (accessed 26 September 2024).

23 See Pitrim A. Sorokin, *Man and Society in Calamity: The Effects of War, Revolution, Famine, Pestilence upon Human Mind, Behavior, Social Organization and Cultural Life* (New York: E. P. Dutton & Company, 1943), pp. 14–21.

24 See, for instance, the news report by Mondoweiss, available online at https://mondoweiss.net/2024/04/bakeries-finally-reopen-in-northern-gaza-as-palestinians-continue-to-fight-famine/ (accessed 26 September 2024). On 9 October 2024, news media reported further destruction in northern Gaza, with military attacks targeting the only flour store remaining in the area; see the MEMO report available online at https://www.middleeastmonitor.com/20241009-israel-bombs-the-only-flour-store-in-northern-gaza/ (accessed 17 October 2024). Concomitantly, the UN has reported a new intensification of the starvation crisis since October 2024, see the CNN report available online at https://edition.cnn.com/2024/10/11/middleeast/food-northern-gaza-starvation-un-intl/index.html (accessed 17 October 2024).

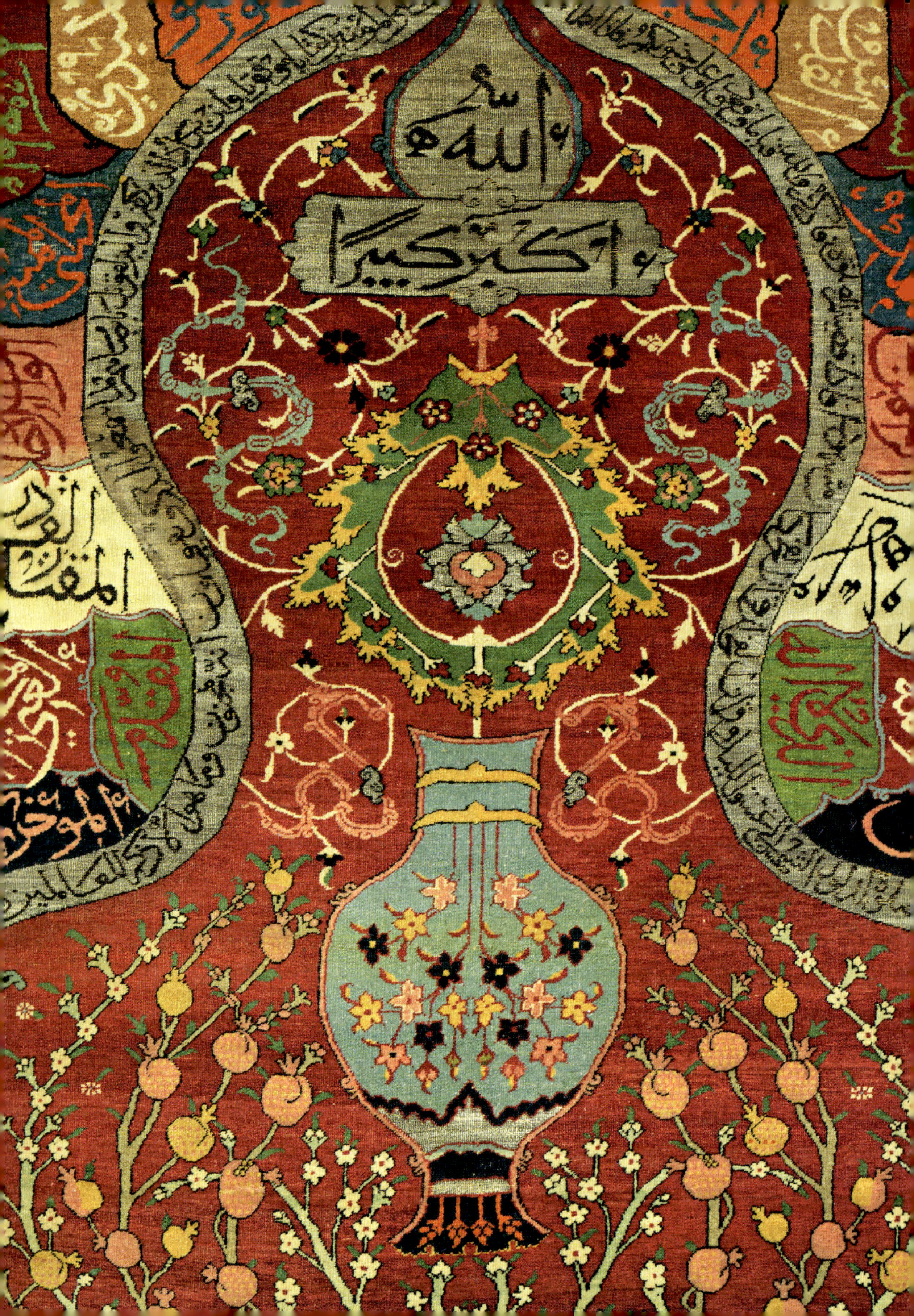

Teslim Sanni

Paradise's Menu: Understanding the Food and Drinks of *Jannah*

Prayer rug (detail), Central Iran, Safavid period, 10th century AH/16th century CE, wool, silk and metallic thread, 180 × 112 cm. Museum of Islamic Art, Doha, CA.85.2011

The term *Jannah* immediately evokes Qur'anic references to lush landscapes, flowing rivers and abundant sustenance. In Islam, the concept of *Jannah* is synonymous with Paradise and is central to understanding the afterlife, serving as the ultimate reward for a Muslim's *iman* (faith) and *'amal salih* (good deeds) in this life.[1] *Jannah* is described in the Qur'an as a place of unimaginable beauty and eternal bliss, contrasting starkly with the horrors of *Jahannam* (Hell; Q88:1–16). It is richly portrayed in the Qur'an and the Hadith (the sayings and traditions of Prophet Muhammad, PBUH) where it is described as a place of endless bounty of joy and comfort with exquisite drinks and foods.

The Qur'an frequently highlights a variety of fruits that will be enjoyed upon entering *Jannah*, mentioning dates, pomegranates and grapes the most often (for example, Q55:68–69). Not only do they symbolise prosperity and abundance, but these fruits were essential staples in early Arab societies of the Hijaz.[2] Among them, the date holds a special place of significance as it was a food easily cultivated in the harsh climate of the region, and therefore more commonly found in local cuisines of the early Muslim communities. The date palm, or *nakhl* in Arabic, is mentioned more often in the Qur'an than any other fruit-bearing plant, signifying its importance. This fruit is furthermore deeply connected to the life and practices of the Prophet Muhammad (PBUH), who regularly broke his fast with dates and encouraged his companions to do the same.[3] Additionally, early Muslims attributed spiritual importance to dates; the Prophet reportedly said that consuming seven *Ajwa* dates in the morning would protect against harm from magic and witchcraft.[4] Thus, dates in early Islamic life served multiple roles—providing nourishment, symbolising divine generosity and offering protection—making them a resonant symbol of both physical and spiritual sustenance in *Jannah*.

The Qur'an's depiction of *Jannah* also includes rivers of milk, honey and pure water that remain unspoiled and offer nourishment and sweetness beyond earthly experiences (Q47:15). These descriptions are not merely ornamental but carry deep cultural and spiritual symbolism. Milk, for example, is revered for its purity and nutritional value, symbolising sustenance that is fresh and unchanging. The Prophet Muhammad (PBUH) is known to have enjoyed milk and extolled its health benefits, citing its curative properties.[5] Honey, which has long been esteemed for its medicinal qualities is also described in the Qur'an as 'a healing for mankind' (Q16:69). The Prophet himself recommended honey for its therapeutic benefits, such as for treating stomach ailments.[6]

The inclusion of honey, milk and dates—essential sources of nourishment and healing in early Muslim life—in the description of *Jannah* emphasises not only their earthly relevance among Muslims but also their symbolic significance, representing divine wellness and the ultimate sweetness of Allah's grace. By drawing on elements deeply rooted in the lives of early Muslims, this depiction allows believers to envision Paradise in ways that are intimately relatable and comforting.

Folio 209v (detail), manuscript of the *En'am-i Sherif* ('The Noble En'am') (detail), copied by Haci Mehmed Resim and illuminated by Haci Ahmed Ayasofia, Istanbul, Ottoman period, dated 1294 AH/1877 CE, ink, opaque watercolour and gold on paper, 24.8 × 17 cm (closed). Museum of Islamic Art, Doha, MS.399.2007

Endnotes

1 See Sura al-Nisa (Q4:57).

2 The Hijaz is a region stretching along the Red Sea coast in western Saudi Arabia. It is Islam's birthplace and home to Mecca and Medina. Mecca is where Prophet Muhammad (PBUH) was born and received the first Qur'anic revelations, while Medina is the city where he lived the last ten years of his life.

3 Muhammad Ibn 'Isa al-Tirmidhi, *English Translation of Jami' At-Tirmidhi Compiled by: Imam Hafiz Abu 'Eisa Mohammad Ibn 'Eisa At-Tirmidhi*, trans. Abu Khaliyl (Riyadh: Darussalam, 2007), vol. 2, Hadith 694.

4 The *Ajwa* date is an oval-shaped, medium-sized date with black skin that is grown exclusively in the city of Medina.

5 Muhammad Ibn Isma'il al-Bukhari, *Sahih al-Bukhari: The Translation of the Meanings of Sahih al-Bukhari, Arabic-English*, trans. Muhammad Muhsin Khan (Riyadh: Darussalam, 1997), vol. 7, Book 71, Hadith 5686.

6 al-Tirmidhi, *Jami' At-Tirmidhi*, vol. 4, Book 2, Hadith 2082.

 Teslim Sanni

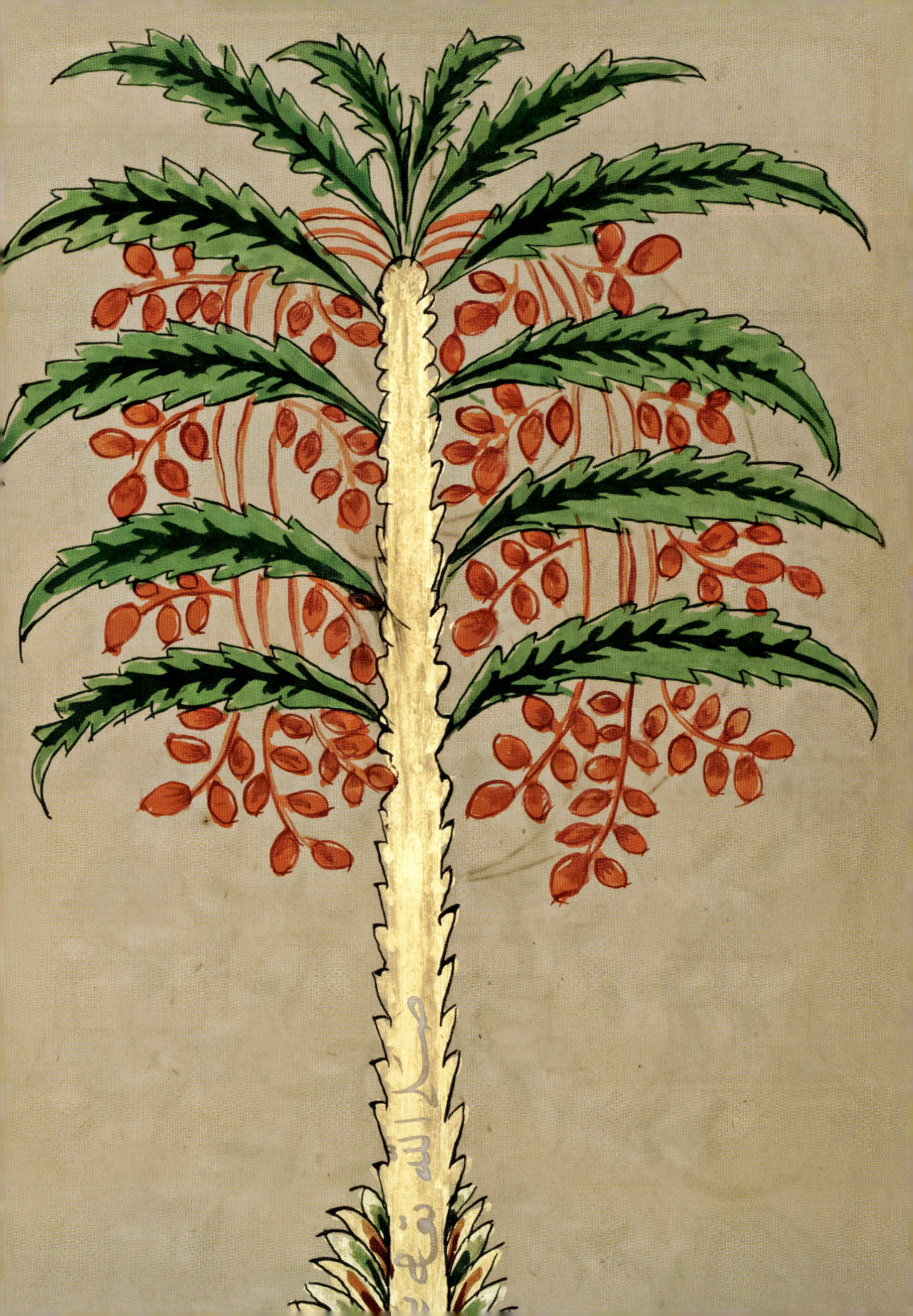
صورة النخل

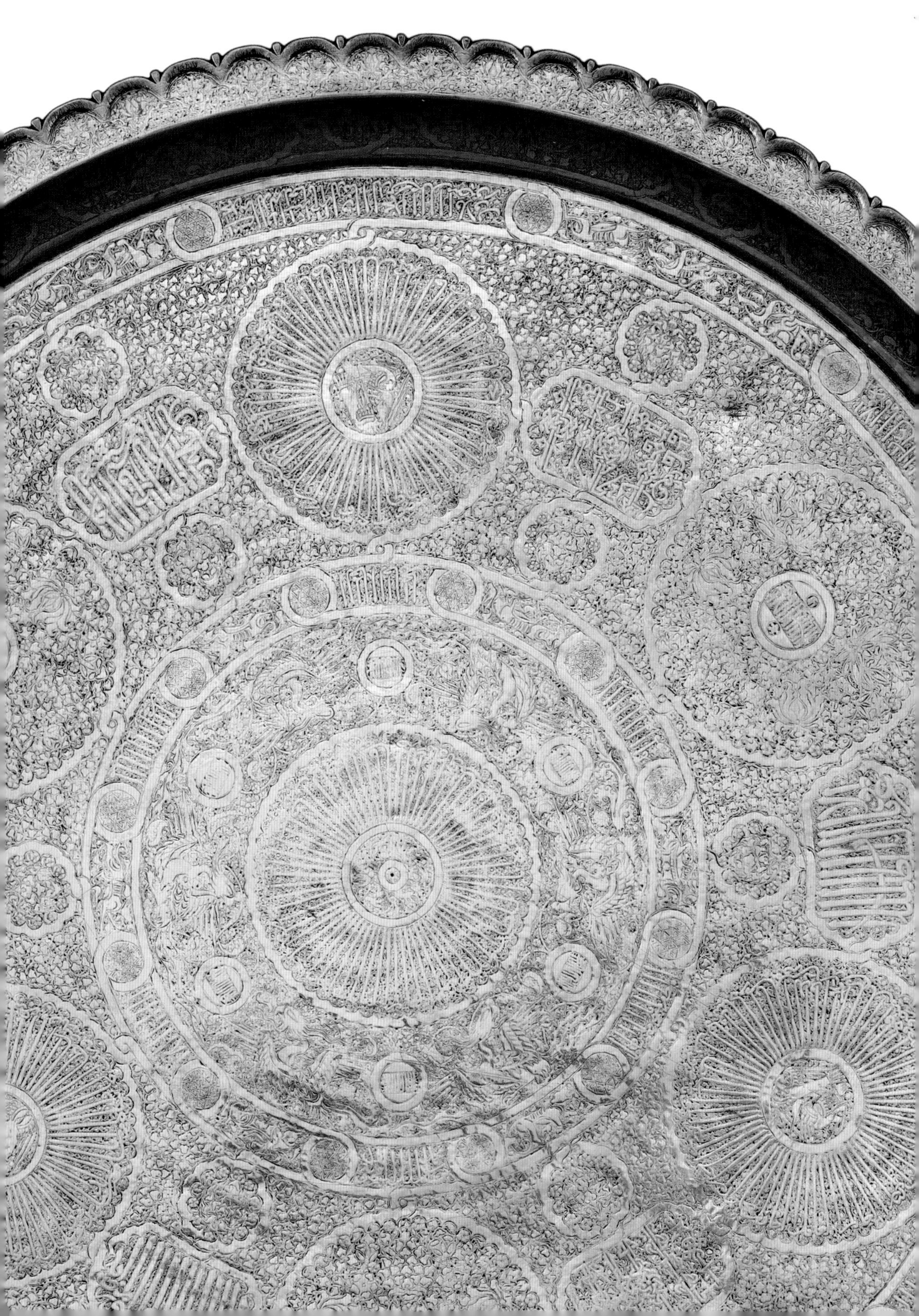

Daniel Newman

Cooking Across Empires:
The Culinary Traditions
of Medieval Islam

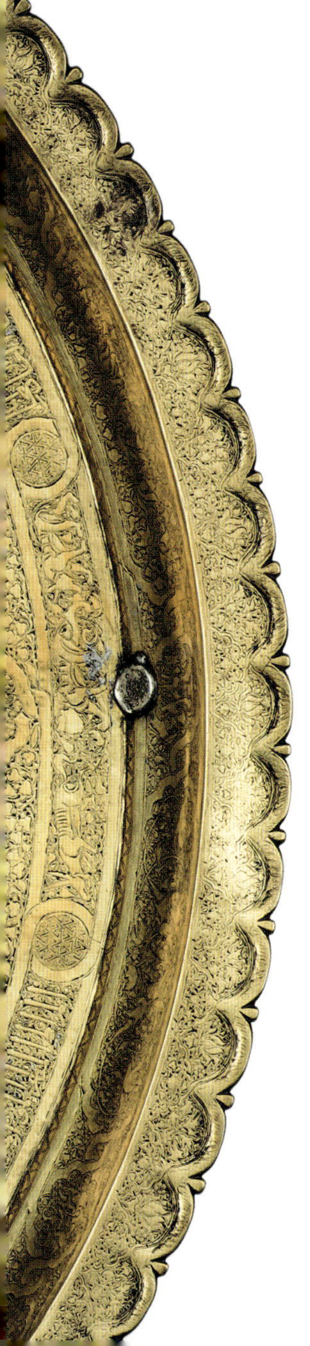

Sources for the culinary history in the Arabian Peninsula and the areas to the north—corresponding to what is today referred to as the Middle East—prior to the advent of Islam in the 1st century AH/ first quarter of the 7th century CE are few and far between. In the absence of cookbooks, our knowledge is limited to secondary sources, such as pre-Islamic poetry and early lexicography. The Peninsula was inhabited mostly by Bedouins, who were pastoral nomads, alongside sedentary populations in oases and towns, such as Makkah and Jeddah (known as Judda—meaning 'road'— to medieval Arabic geographers). The desert dwellers frequently faced scarcity of food, and except for areas along the coast, where fish was a staple, most of the region's inhabitants relied on what little their inhospitable environment provided: bread (usually made from millet), dates and milk, occasionally supplemented with the meat of the camel, sheep and desert animals. Other items, such as onions, garlic, grapes, figs, olives and gourds are mentioned in the Qur'an, alongside the more exotic pomegranate, ginger, mustard and basil, which came from outside the Peninsula and bear evidence to its role as an international trading hub. Hadiths, the sayings of the Prophet Muhammad (PBUH), make up another fertile source since they contain a number of references to food and dishes, as well as dietetic recommendations. For instance, the Prophet is reported to have warned against excess eating by pointing out that one-third of the stomach is for food, one-third for drink, and one-third for breath.

The diet was very simple and highly sustainable, with nothing going to waste. It mainly comprised gruels and porridges such as *harira*, which was made with flour and/or milk and grease, and thus bore little resemblance to the modern spicy North African soup by the same name. Clarified butter (*samn*) was the main fat. Most of the food had to be portable and so meat would be (sun-)dried and cured (as in *qadid*, 'jerky'), or cooked with spices and then preserved in an animal skin or a container with grease. The latter variety was known as *khaliʿ*, which has survived in almost identical form in the modern Moroccan *khlii*. Sweets were mainly simple puddings or porridges made with dates and/or honey.

Most of these preparations originated in the region, but there may also have been an influence from ancient Mesopotamia, home of the world's oldest culinary recipes (*c.* 1700 BCE).[1] Various dishes involve a broth with meat (lamb, venison, tripe) and vegetables (onion, leek, garlic) and spices (for instance, cumin, coriander) to which crushed grain cakes were added—not dissimilar to the later *tharid* (shredded bread topped with meat, vegetables and broth). This was a particularly popular dish among the Bedouin, and was allegedly highly prized by the Prophet Muhammad (PBUH), who is reported as saying that 'just as Aisha [his wife] is the most virtuous among women, the *tharid* is the finest of all dishes'.[2] Another recipe was for a wheat porridge, which in the Arabic tradition would become known as *harisa* (from a verb meaning 'to mash').

The conquest of the Persian Sasanian Empire in 30 AH/650 CE brought the Muslim armies into contact with a sophisticated courtly culture. This included an elaborate gastronomic tradition, first adopted during the Umayyad caliphate (41–132 AH/ 661–750 CE), which had Damascus as its centre and stretched from North Africa and Spain in the West to northern India in the East. However, it was during the Abbasid caliphate (132–656 AH/ 750–1258), with the emergence of Baghdad as the political, cultural and economic centre, that the *Kitab al-Ṭabikh* ('Cookery Book') appeared. Authored by a certain Ibn Sayyar al-Warraq, this represents a courtly cuisine from the 3rd–4th centuries AH/9th–10th centuries CE. It has been considered the second cookery book in history, after the 4th century CE Roman manual *De Re Coquinaria* ('On the Art of Cooking'), though a new Arabic text has recently been brought to light which may be contemporaneous to al-Warraq's, or even predate it.[3]

The *Kitab al-Ṭabikh* represents a highly advanced stage in culinary writing and presents food as an important subject of cultural discourse, as well as an integral marker of elite identity

     Daniel Newman

and refinement. In more ways than one, it is redolent of a manual for the educated person on how to act in civilised society and, besides recipes, contains a range of poetry, witticisms and rules of etiquette. The elite character of the text is further evidenced by the use of expensive ingredients—a multitude of meats and exotic spices—as well as sophisticated techniques and a wide array of dedicated equipment. The book is significant because of the large number of recipes it includes—over 600—as well as their variety, representing the full medieval banqueting experience from savoury dishes, breads, condiments, preserves, sweets and pastries, to perfumes, hand-washing powders and so on.

The Sasanian influence at this stage also becomes apparent from references to historical figures such as the ruler Khosrow (known in Arabic as *kisra*) I Anushirwan (reg. 531–579 CE). He is reported to have written a cookery book, and al-Warraq attributes to him a dish called *lakhsha*, which involves dough cooked in a meat broth, that may be the oldest pasta recipe in the world. Its name is related to a verb meaning 'to be slippery', presumably in reference to the texture of the cooked dough. Other examples of Persian influence include one of the most famous dishes of the Muslim Middle Ages, *sikbaj* (a vinegar stew which counts the Spanish *escabeche* and Latin American *ceviche* among its modern descendants), sweets like *lawzinaj* (an almond confection and ancestor of marzipan) and *shiraz* (a type of cottage cheese).

Other Arabic recipe collections were produced between the 7th and 9th centuries AH/13th and 15th centuries CE across the Muslim world: two in al-Andalus (Muslim Spain) and North Africa, three in Egypt, one in Iraq and two in Syria. All combined, they include well over 4000 recipes, making it the richest culinary literature of any language in history. Determining the authorship— or more precisely, the 'ownership'—of these recipes poses a significant challenge. To begin with, at least half of the culinary treatises lack clear or reliable attribution. In many, if not all, cases, it is unlikely that these works are entirely original compilations, and there are numerous instances of overlaps and/or borrowing, while one may speculate on the existence of a common pool, from which authors drew, either directly or indirectly.

It is worth pointing out the cultural and societal importance of gastronomy, as many grandees, scholars and rulers— most famously the Abbasid caliphs Ibrahim Ibn al-Mahdi (d. 224 AH/839 CE), al-Ma'mun (d. 218 AH/833 CE)—are known to have produced cookery books, which unfortunately have not survived. From the 7th century AH/13th century CE, the trend in cookery books was that of recipe collections intended for personal or household use. In some cases, the authors may well have been chefs but claims of recipe creations cannot always be taken at face value.

The cultural transformations within the Islamic world can be observed in the plethora of ingredients mentioned in the literature, often with preferred origins, such as Khorasani raisins, and Jurjani jujube, Syrian leeks and garlic, Sijistani pears, Greek (Byzantine) aniseed, Nabataean cabbage, leek and celery, Kermani cumin, or Isfahani quinces and apples. On one level, the culinary literature reveals a large number of common features, with often remarkably similar recipes and dishes being found in sources half a millennium apart and across a vast geographical area. This includes key ingredients such as pomegranates, rose water, honey, sugar, and spices and herbs such as pepper, cumin, coriander, cinnamon, saffron and mint. The fermented condiment known as *murri*, constitutes an interesting case, not least because it disappeared from history after the 9th century AH/15th century CE. Usually made with rotted barley, it was extremely popular and was used in many savoury dishes as an umami salting agent across the literature. According to some recipes, it could take more than two months or, in one extreme example, 133 days, though there were also 'express' versions.[4]

In terms of dishes, there was clearly a predilection for sweet-and-sour flavours, particularly in stews, which often included fresh fruit. Recipes for sweets are found across the literature and many of them are still familiar to contemporary readers, whether it be puddings such as *'asida*, fried dough (*zalabiyya, luqmat al-qadi, qatayif*), or biscuits (for instance, *cornes de gazelle* or *maqrud*). The cuisine was generally meat heavy (predominantly from sheep) as this was a prestige item. Vegetarian (even vegan) dishes are found in several works and are part of a subgenre of so-called 'counterfeit' dishes, known in Arabic as *muzawwarat*. These were aimed at fasting Christians, or people with illnesses, as the dishes in questions were considered lighter than those with meat or fish. The name derives from the fact that they copied similar dishes made with the missing ingredient in order to persuade the diner to eat them.

The literature reveals a clear influence from the medieval Islamic medical tradition, with dietary guidelines rooted in the works of Greek scholars like Hippocrates, Dioscorides and Galen, whose texts were translated into Arabic between the 2nd and

Daniel Newman

4th centuries AH/8th and 10th centuries CE, and commented and expanded upon. The medical framework was based on the theory of humours, within which food played a central role, and many of the culinary treatises include medicinal recipes or references to the humoral properties. The inextricable link between food and medicine is further evidenced by the inclusion of culinary recipes in several medieval Arabic pharmacological and medical works.

There was a great deal of mobility in the medieval Muslim world, mainly driven by trade or religion (the *hajj*), and thus it is no surprise that dishes, ingredients and techniques also moved freely, resulting in a highly porous medieval Arabic culinary culture. This often resulted in variations of existing dishes, such as the samosa (*sanbusaj, sanbusaq*), which in the Middle East had a savoury stuffing, but became a sweet in al-Andalus, Spain. In most cases, recipes moved discreetly, anonymously—one notable exception is that of the Abbasid exile Ziryab (d. 237 AH/852 CE), who settled in Córdoba, which was ruled by descendants of the Umayyad caliphate, and is said to have introduced both the asparagus and a dish called *tafaya*, which was the Berber name for what in the East was known by its Persian name *isfidhbaj* ('white stew').

At the same time, local culinary practices remained rooted in the region's ecological and cultural contexts, which could change over time. For instance, al-Warraq does not include any recipes for pickled foodstuffs (though he does discuss their medicinal properties), which indicates their absence from the culinary repertoire he chronicled. Conversely, a 7th century AH/13th century CE Syrian (Aleppine) collection contains nearly 60 recipes for pickled vegetables and fruit, which evidences their popularity in the region.

The surviving medieval Arabic culinary writings reveal a distinct geographical and cultural split between the Eastern and Western Islamic worlds, reflected in their culinary traditions. Their cuisines diverged over time due to local influences, such as Berber contributions in North Africa, as well as variations in available produce, cooking methods, utensils, and, of course, taste preferences. One of the differences between the two regions is the role of rice. In the Western Muslim Mediterranean, rice was rarely used, largely because it was not widely cultivated. On the other hand, the Western manuals feature significantly more fresh fish recipes than their Eastern counterparts. The use of spices also highlights regional distinctions, with sumac being far more prevalent in the East than in the West. Similarly, differences emerge in the use of fruits and vegetables; dates and raisins are less used in the West than in the East.

In the East, clarified butter (*samn*) was preferred, while fresh butter (*zubd*) was rarely used, appearing only once, for instance, in al-Warraq's treatise. Like today, olive oil was a cornerstone of Western Mediterranean cuisine, but it was used only sparingly in Eastern treatises. Eggs are another standout feature of Western texts, both in terms of the number of recipes in which they are used, but also in that stews were often topped with a layer of eggs (added with spices and breadcrumbs). Couscous occupies an interesting place; originally a Berber dish, it travelled eastward very early on, and a recipe is already found in 6th century AH/ 13th century CE Syria. Its popularity clearly grew throughout the ages as according to an 11th century AH/17th century CE Ottoman visitor to Cairo, couscous was one of the staple dishes of the Egyptians.[5]

The medieval Arab culinary tradition stands as a testament to the rich interplay of culture, geography and history. It reflects a sophisticated gastronomy shaped by trade, migration, and the intellectual currents of the Islamic Golden Age. From the vibrant kitchens of Abbasid Baghdad and Mamluk Cairo to the rustic hearths of al-Andalus, Arab cuisine not only catered to the palate but also carried cultural and medicinal significance. This tradition exemplifies a shared heritage that transcends boundaries, offering insight into the lives and values of its creators. As we study and preserve these culinary legacies, they continue to inspire and connect us across time and space.

Foio 17r (detail), manuscript of the *Dala'il al-Khayrat* ('Guide to Benevolent Deeds') (detail), written by Muhammad al-Jazuli, copied by Mehmed Emin and illuminated by Hafiz Mehmed Nuri, Istanbul, Ottoman period, dated 1216 AH/1801 CE, ink, opaque watercolour and gold on paper, 23.4 × 16.7 cm (closed). Museum of Islamic Art, Doha, MS.427.2007

Endnotes

1 Jean Bottéro, *Mesopotamian Culinary Texts*, trans. Jerrold Cooper (Winona Lake, IN: Eisenbrauns, 1995).

2 'Faḍl ʿĀʾisha ʿalā al-nisāʾ ka-fḍaḍl al-tharīd ʿalā sāʾir al-ṭaʿām', as recorded in Muhammad Ibn Ismaʿil al-Bukhari, *Sahih al-Bukhari. The Translation of the Meanings of Sahih al-Bukhari, Arabic-English*, trans. Muhammad Muhsin Khan (Riyadh: Darussalam, 1997), vol. 7, p. 211, no. 5427.

3 *Taṣanif al-atʿima*, in the collection of The Wellcome Library, London, WMS Arabic 57; see Ibn Mubārak Shāh, Daniel Newman, ed. and trans., *The Sultan's Feast: A Fifteenth-Century Egyptian Cookbook*, ed. and trans. Daniel Newman (London: Saqi Books, 2020), p. xvi. Daniel Newman is currently preparing a study, edition and translation of this work, *Taṣanif al-atʿima*.

4 Ibn Razīn Al-Tujībī, *The Exile's Cookbook: Medieval Gastronomic Treasures from al-Andalus and North Africa*, ed. and trans. Daniel Newman (London: Saqi Books, 2023), pp. 372–373.

5 Robert Dankoff and Sooyong Kim, *An Ottoman Traveller. Selections from the Book of Travels of Evliya Çelebi* (London: Eland Publishing, 2011), p. 398.

     Daniel Newman

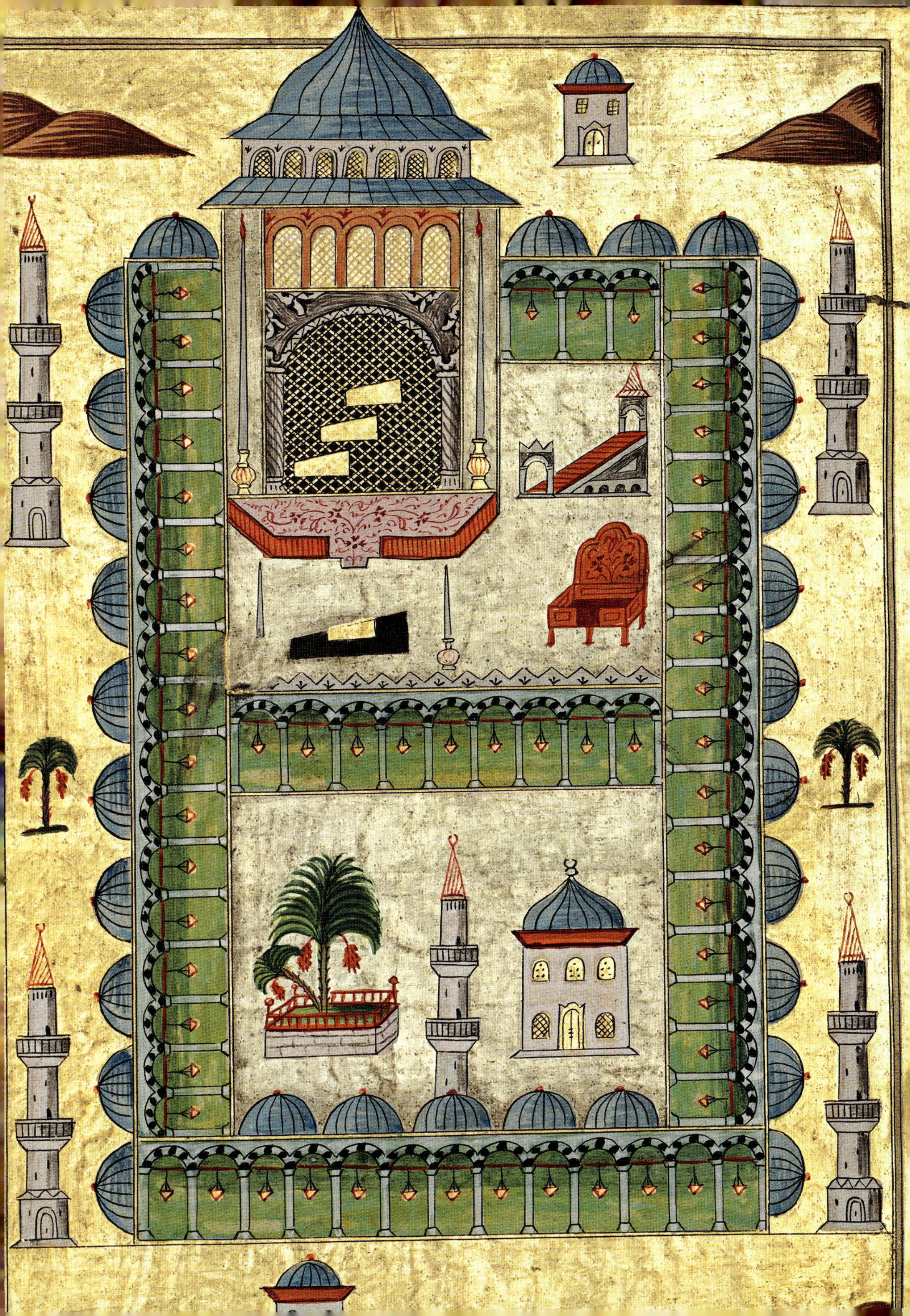

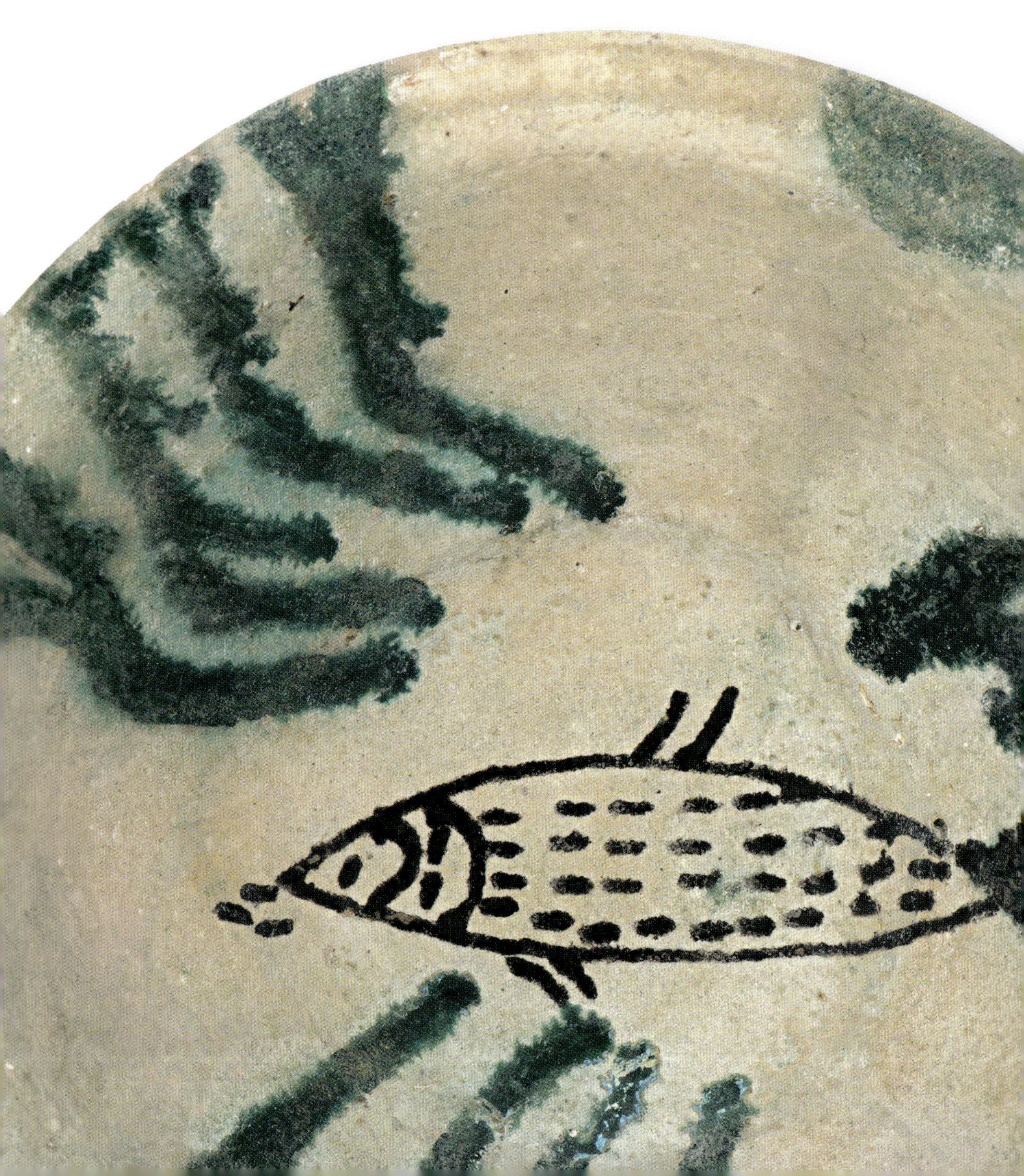

Linda Komaroff

Setting the Table: Deluxe Glazed Ceramics and the Art of Fine Dining

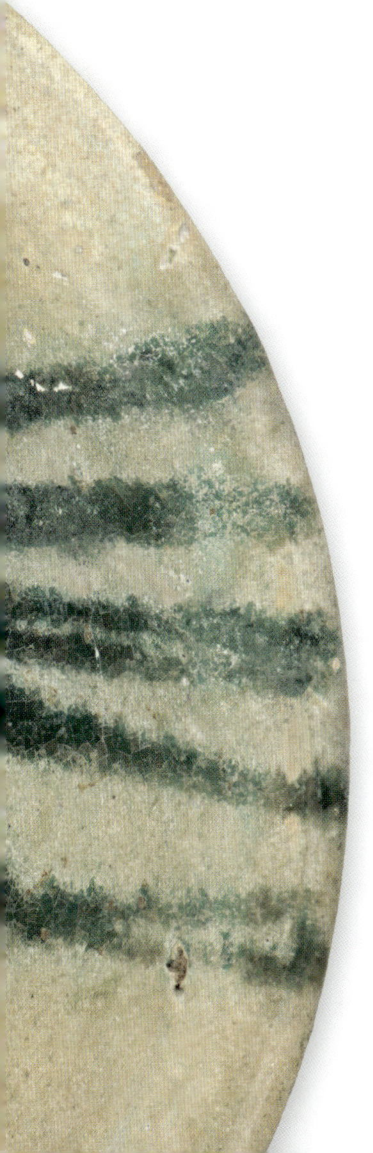

Glazed ceramics, predominantly for serving food and beverages, are one of the glories of Islamic art and also the most widespread in public and private collections. When showcased in museum installations, their original function as tableware is often obscured by the incentives of pure display as corroborated by their obvious visual appeal. Scholars have rarely considered how the dining-related purposes of these wares might have dictated their ultimate appearance. While a culinary-based approach to ceramic tableware was the subject of a larger study, this essay examines the origins of the proposed relationship between deluxe glazed ceramics and fine dining.[1]

Finely glazed pottery first became a significant art form around the first decades of the 3rd century AH/9th century CE. Although earlier glazed wares had been made under the Umayyad dynasty (41–132 AH/661–750 CE), particularly in Syria and Egypt, only in the early Abbasid era, c. 3rd–4th century AH/ 9th–10th century CE, did well-made wares with complex glazing techniques proliferate in Iraq, spreading rapidly throughout the empire. The sources for these new wares and their sophisticated and assured technology have been the frequent topic of scholarly research; however, what has not been considered so far is why these developments occurred in this place and time.[2] Often discussed in this context is the impact of imported Chinese wares, found in excavations on land and under the sea, as well as mentioned in textual accounts. Clearly there was a market to accommodate large numbers of Chinese wares alongside equivalent quantities of high quality domestic glazed ceramic tableware—but to what end? As this essay will propose, the driver for this market was the very recent and burgeoning interest in cuisine and fine dining as exemplified by the court in Baghdad (and briefly, Samarra). Changes in diet and dining habits generated the demand for new tableware alongside the proliferation in the variety and specificity of their shapes and sizes, demonstrating a direct relationship between the sourcing, preparation, serving and consumption of food and the evolution of a highly significant luxury ceramic ware industry in Iraq.

In the first centuries of the Islamic era, *c.* 80–500 AH/ 700–1100 CE, an agricultural revolution took place in the area between Iran and Spain. Propelled by the expanding Muslim polity, many new food crops were introduced, mainly from South Asia, in tandem with the development of novel methods of cultivation and land tenure.[3] The result was an enormous escalation in the quantity, quality, availability and variety of food essential for the creation of a true regional cuisine. These dietary changes both stimulated and were fuelled by ostentatious royal and courtly dining, as embodied by the early Abbasid caliphate in Baghdad. The siting of the city with its easy access to trade routes by land and water facilitated the importation of costly and exotic foods as well as the absorption of different culinary customs from throughout the empire. Often described as a Golden Age, the early Abbasid caliphate was also a new age for food culture in which elite cuisine was heavily influenced by the Persian court of the Sasanian dynasty (224–651 CE). The opulence and rituals of the Sasanian ruling class, including dining customs, as recorded in texts and preserved through palatial architecture and luxury objects, were deeply appreciated, serving as royal role models.

As at the Sasanian court, cooking contests took place under the Abbasids, sometimes with princely competitors, while many of the Sasanian dishes retained their Persian names, enhancing their prestige. Liquid and semi-liquid dipping sauces and condiments were also carried over from Iran into the new Arab gastronomy. Food and fine dining were sufficiently significant in Abbasid court circles that poets composed odes to the dishes served by their hosts.[4] Recipes from this era are preserved in the oldest of the surviving Arabic cookery books, written by Ibn Sayyar al-Warraq of Baghdad, which although dating to the 4th century AH/10th century CE is based on earlier sources that represent the beginning of Arab culinary writing.[5] Dining is depicted as a multisensory

 Linda Komaroff

experience of taste, aroma, texture and visual appeal. While the text does not describe tableware, it at times refers to plating and especially garnishes.

At the Abbasid court, food was more than sustenance. Fine dining was an act unto itself, a form of enjoyment and a means of entertainment; hosting a feast displayed wealth, power and erudition. Portrayals in poetry and literary narratives show that the fame of Abbasid gastronomy spread quickly, carried forward by those outside the court who were nonetheless fed in its kitchens.[6] Commensurate with the richness of their cuisine, notables dined on gold and silver plate, which have not survived, as well as Chinese porcelain of the type said to have been gifted to caliph Harun al–Rashid (r. 170–193 AH/786–809 CE).[7] These new habits of consumption were likely emulated in a downward diffusion to the freshly affluent urban elite, among others, creating consumer demand for luxury tableware available in different shapes and sizes appropriate to the recently adopted dining etiquette. For example, the various condiments and dipping sauces would have required multiple quantities of small bowls.

Indeed, the evidence suggests that around the same time a new cuisine emerged at the Abbasid court, a novel form of ceramic ware developed at Basra, in southern Iraq. Pottery of this type frequently copies the size and form of Chinese ceramics, especially bowls, and emulates the whiteness of the stoneware or porcelain fabric by covering the coarser earthenware body with an opaque white glaze. When considered from the vantage of fine dining, it is easy to appreciate the predilection for the clean, hard white surface of Chinese porcelain, perfected in its best-known form by the 2nd century AH/8th century CE. But the Basran wares should not be viewed as poor substitutes; they are original and technically advanced achievements in ceramic art. Rather than being content with mere imitations, Iraqi potters must have seen the white surface as a potential canvas on which to paint, in cobalt blue, bold abstract and floral designs and Arabic inscriptions that today are very difficult to decipher.

Alongside locally made deluxe tableware, great quantities of Chinese ceramics were imported by sea, as demonstrated by the Belitung Shipwreck discovered in 1998. This Arabian ship sank off the coast of Indonesia in the early 3rd century AH/9th century CE, likely on its return voyage, filled with Chinese goods including nearly 60,000 glazed bowls, jars and other ceramics.[8] Given the magnitude of ceramic wares from this one shipwreck, their importation was clearly based on market-driven demand. The large and diverse group of pottery included three white stoneware dishes painted with simple foliate designs around squares in cobalt blue. Decorated in a manner atypical of Chinese pottery, some scholars have suggested that these were possible prototypes commissioned by Arab merchants designed to appeal to the buyers of Basran blue on white wares.[9] Although there is no evidence to suggest such Chinese wares ever became competitive with the ones from Basra, they testify to the intense interchange of techniques and materials between Iraq and China.[10]

Among the Basran white glazed wares, vegetal designs of rosettes, palmettes, wreaths and palm trees predominate alongside medallions, rhombuses, triangles and six-pointed stars painted in blue. In addition, there are a rare few vessels decorated with a fish, suggesting a potential dining association (the same motif occurs on a related ware attributed to Iran).[11] Also characteristic are brief Arabic inscriptions rendered in Kufic script starkly isolated on the white ground or accompanied by vegetal or geometric designs. These difficult-to-decipher inscriptions are sometimes read as the name of the potter, or as short phrases such as 'Eat with enjoyment and fulfilment' (*Kul haniyan mariyan*) that refer to the function of the vessel.[12] Such decoration as found on the interior of bowls, dishes and plates would only be visible to diners as they consumed the food in them. Since dining was communal, two or more individuals would have partaken from the same bowl and shared the pleasure of finding a fish at the bottom of the vessel or appreciated the irony of reading a text beckoning them to enjoy their food, thereby enhancing the culinary experience. A contemporary text on manners and courtly etiquette written in 4th century AH/10th century CE Baghdad describes this type of visual and especially verbal punning and reflects the practices of an elite social group, whose ideas of wit and elegance were echoed beyond the Abbasid capital.[13] Decoration and inscriptions that allude or directly refer to the dining experience would become a mainstay of luxury tableware in Islamic lands.[14]

Abbasid potters also developed the complex and long-lived technique of lustreware. To make this type of ceramic ware, they first applied a paste of silver and copper compounds, ground with sulphur, onto the glazed vessels, and then fired them a second time in a reducing atmosphere, forcing the metals to give up their oxygen and creating a thin lustrous film fused to the glazed surface. The resulting wares are often spectacular show pieces. Diners must have relished seeing the gradually exposed glittering decoration as the serving vessel emptied. Such lustreware at times seems to relate to the consumption and enjoyment of the food contained in them. According to al-Warraq's Baghdad cookbook, the artfulness of a dish was not only in its flavour and aroma but also in its presentation and appearance, especially its colour. Dishes were sometimes decorated with green pistachios and almonds dyed red or yellow; in other instances, the dominant factor in the recipe was the colour.[15] As the colourful food diminished during a meal, revealing the vibrant, flickering interiors of the lustre bowls, the effect might have been to maintain a balance of colour. Some of the frequently occurring abstract motifs resemble dyed almonds and green pistachios, perhaps a clever allusion to what had just been eaten.[16] For an Abbasid audience, the reflective, semi-iridescent surface of lustreware is thought to have evoked a state of wonder (*ajab*),[17] and the revelation of the brilliant lustred surface and the 'reappearance' of the just eaten food would have enhanced that state.

The deluxe tableware of 3rd century AH/9th century CE Iraq, inspired by the novel cuisine and dining etiquette at the Abbasid court, introduced trends that were to continue in the following centuries. In the 4th century AH/10th century CE, new pottery centres arose in the eastern provinces, in major urban locales such as Nishapur and Samarqand, then under the control of the Samanid dynasty (204–395 CE/819–1005 CE). Samanid wares, though they were produced in various styles and colour schemes, share a common technique in which humble earthenware was disguised and beautified through the application of a white, black or coloured slip, a semifluid, coloured clay.

In subsequent centuries several techniques and technological advancements in ceramic production can be related back to early Abbasid tableware. For example, the complex practice of making lustreware spread outward from Iraq in the 4th century AH/10th century CE to new and discrete centres of production, most notably Kashan, in Iran. The interest in replicating the whiteness of Chinese porcelain led to the development in the 5th century AH/11th century CE of fritware, an artificial thin, white clay body combining ground quartz and glass frit. Fritware, which allowed for a greater variety of decorative techniques, became the mainstay for subsequent deluxe glazed tableware.

The extensive interchange between China and Iraq in the 3rd century AH/9th century CE, which incentivised Chinese potters to experiment with cobalt blue on a white glazed surface, culminated in the Yuan and Ming periods (7th–11th centuries AH/13th–17th centuries CE). These renowned blue-and-white porcelains were exported widely, becoming prized tableware at the Mamluk, Timurid, Safavid, Ottoman and Mughal courts. They also inspired local ceramic production and influenced designs in a variety of media.[18] The innovations of Abbasid tableware, as intertwined with the contemporaneous stimulus of fine dining, had a longstanding and extensive impact in Islamic lands and beyond.

Linda Komaroff

Endnotes

1 See Linda Komaroff, ed., *Dining with the Sultan: The Fine Art of Feasting* (Los Angeles: Los Angeles County Museum of Art and DelMonico Books, 2023), where this broader topic is considered regarding a variety of media.

2 Most notably Oliver Watson, *Ceramics from Islamic Lands* (London: Thames & Hudson, 2004) and 'Revisiting Samarra: The Rise of Islamic Glazed Pottery', *Beiträge zur Islamischen Kunst und Archäologie* 4 (2014), pp. 123–142.

3 See Andrew M. Watson, *Agricultural Innovation in the Early Islamic World: The Diffusion of Crops and Farming Techniques, 700–1100* (Cambridge: Cambridge University Press, 1983).

4 Geert Jan van Gelder, *Of Dishes and Discourse: Classical Arabic Literary Representations of Food* (New York: Routledge, 2011), p. 60.

5 Nawal Nasrallah, ed. and trans., *Annals of the Caliphs' Kitchens: Ibn Sayyār Al-Warrāq's Tenth-Century Baghdadi Cookbook* (Leiden: Brill, 2007).

6 On the theme of food and dining in Classical Arabic literature, see Van Gelder, *Of Dishes and Discourse*.

7 As related in the 5th century AH/ 11th century CE account of Persian historian Khawja Abulfazl Muhammad ibn Husein Bayhaqi, *Tarikh-i Bayhaqi*, ed. and annot. Manuchihr Danishpazhu (Tehran: Intisharat-i Hirmand, 1997), vol. 2, p. 632. The magnanimous gift from the governor of Khurasan included 'Two hundred pieces of *chini-yi faghfuri* (Imperial Chinese porcelain), from plates to bowls, etc., each of which was finer than anything that had ever been seen in any ruler's possession. Moreover, there were another two thousand pieces of *chini* (porcelain or possibly stoneware), chargers and large bowls, large and small Chinese goblets and other sorts'. I am grateful to Wheeler Thackston for this translation.

8 Regina Krahl, ed., *Shipwrecked: Tang Treasures and Monsoon Winds* (Washington, DC: Arthur M. Sackler Gallery, Smithsonian Institution, 2010).

9 See Krahl, *Shipwrecked*, pp. 209–211; and Watson, 'Revisiting Samarra', p. 125.

10 See Jessica Hallett, 'Iraq and China: Trade and Innovation in the Early Abbasid Period', *China-Mediterranean Sea: Routes and Exchange of Ceramics Prior to the 16th Century, Taoci: Revue Annuelle de la Société Française d'Étude de la Céramique Orientale* 4 (2005), pp. 21–29.

11 See Vera Tamari, 'Abbasid Blue-on-White Ware', in *Islamic Art in the Ashmolean Museum, Part Two*, ed. James Allan (Oxford: Oxford University Press, 1995), fig. 1.

12 See Vera Tamari, 'Ninth-Tenth Century White Mesopotamian Ceramic Ware with Blue Decoration' (Unpublished M. Phil thesis, University of Oxford, 1984), p. 44, pl. 64, where a slightly different reading of the inscription is given. Also, see Rebecca Wrightson, 'The Epigraphique Samarra Horizon: Blue-on-White Ceramics', in *Inscriptions in the Medieval Islamic World*, eds. Bernard O'Kane, A.C.S. Peacock and Mark Muehlhaeusler (Edinburgh: Edinburgh University Press, 2023), pp. 363–388.

13 See Abu Tayyib al-Washsha, *Le Livre de brocart ou La société raffinée de Bagdad au Xe siècle: (al-Kitâb al-Muwashshâ)*, trans. Siham Bouhlal (Paris: Éditions Gallimard, 2004), especially chapters 54-55, focusing on inscriptions on tableware. Also, see Yaron Klein, 'Abū Ṭayyib al-Washshā' and the Poetics of Inscribed Objects', *Journal of the American Oriental Society* 138/1 (January-March 2018), pp. 1–28.

14 See e.g. Komaroff, *Dining with the Sultan*, pp. 237–238, 256 and 262.

15 Nasrallah, *Annals of the Caliphs' Kitchens*, pp. 93, 391, 393, 425.

16 See Komaroff, *Dining with the Sultan*, p. 234.

17 Matthew D. Saba, 'Abbasid Lusterware and the Aesthetics of *'Ajab*', *Muqarnas* 29 (2012), pp. 187–212.

18 Even in the modern era, Chinese porcelain still retained its cachet so that the rulers of Qajar Iran such as Naser al-Din Shah (r. 1264–1313 AH/1848-96 CE) commissioned bespoke tableware from Canton. See MIA PO.666.2007.

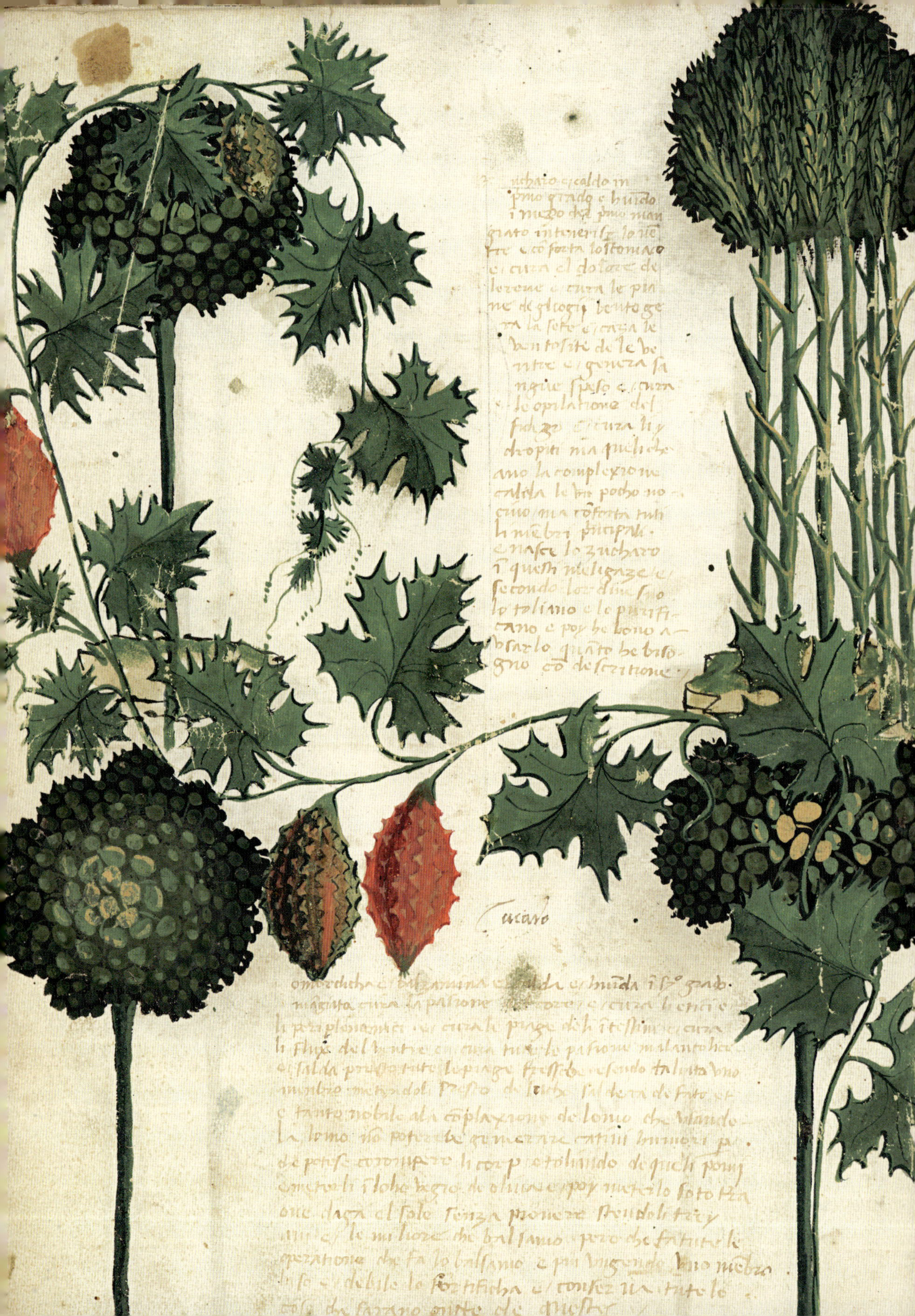

uchato e caldo in
pmo grado e huido
i nuzzo del pmo man
giato intenerise lo ue
tre e co foua to ftomaco
e cura el dolore de
lerene e cura le pri
me de gli cogni beuto ge
ra la fete e cuza le
bentosite de le be
ntre e genera sa
ngue spaso e cuza
le opilatione del
fedego e cura li
dropici nia quiliche
ano la complexione
calida le bru pocho no
cuo ma conforta tuti
li mebri principali
e nasce lo zucharo
i questi melegnaze e
secondo lo ordine suo
lo tolimo e lo purifi
cano e poy be bono a
brar lo quato be biso
gno co de fcrittone

Cucaro

omorcheta e balzamina e calda e humida i 3o grado.
magista cura la passione del core e cura le entio
li periplosiapuci na cura le piage dili itestini e cura
li flusi del uentre e cura tute le passione malancholie
e salda presto tute le piage frescha esendo tal usa uno
murbio menadoli presso de leche sal de ra de foco et
e tanto nobile ala complexione de lomo che usando
li lomo no potra gemerare altri humori pu
de pesse coromp re li corpi etoliando de quili pomi
e metroli i lolio uegro de oliua e poy meta lo soto ra
oue daga el sole senza promere stendoli fuy
ma e le migliore che balsamo pero che fa tute le
operatione che fa lo balsamo e piu vigendo uno mebro
se e debile lo fortificha e coufer ua tute le
cose che sarano uate de questo

Tara Desjardins

Itinerant Ingredients:
The Global Trade
in Foodstuffs

Throughout history, cuisines have evolved with the arrival of new ingredients, some introduced through trade and others through encounters between cultures and communities. Some of these ingredients took time to be integrated into popular dishes, while others were adopted immediately. Today, the origin of many ingredients commonly found in dishes widely considered to be national favourites are long forgotten, their journeys across time and place absorbed into the many dishes they flavour. However, it is through trade, especially in the Abbasid period in the 2nd century AH/8th century CE, and later with the European 'discovery' of maritime trade routes in the late 9th century AH/15th century CE, that many ingredients were introduced into Eastern cuisines. This essay explores this phenomenon through the examples of wheat, aubergine, chilli peppers, and the potato, documenting each one's culinary journey from Asia and the Americas to Europe and the Middle East.

It was not until the capital of the Abbasid Caliphate (132–656 AH/ 750–1258 CE) moved from Damascus to the newly built city of Baghdad in 144 AH/762 CE that a rich culinary culture began to emerge at the Abbasid court. This phenomenon was largely fuelled by innovations in irrigation, navigation and transport, which spurred a revolution in both agriculture and gastronomy. The agricultural revolution was, at first, a result of Baghdad's strategic location, nestled in the fertile lands of the Jazira between the Tigris and Euphrates rivers, an area naturally suited to the cultivation of crops. The early Abbasids exploited this by building a complex system of canals and waterways that could

Folio 62v (detail), *Tacuinum Sanitatis* ('Almanac of Health') Italy, Sicily, *c.* 1475 CE, ink and opaque watercolour on paper, 39.3 × 28.1 cm (closed). Museum of Islamic Art Library, Doha, RS79.L64.14[75]

easily connect Baghdad with the Islamic heartland and the southern port town of Basra, easily exporting foods across the empire and beyond in exchange for luxury goods. Within a few decades, Baghdad emerged as a great economic capital at the heart of the vast Abbasid empire stretching from the Indus west to the Atlantic.[1]

Baghdad's prosperity stemmed largely from commerce and trade. The many crops and spices sold in the city's famous markets arrived both overland from the Islamic kingdoms of North Africa, Sicily and the Iberian Peninsula, and via sea routes from West Africa, China and Southeast Asia. Due to advancements in seafaring technologies, especially navigation, Arab sailors were now able to travel further eastwards across the Indian Ocean to the famous 'Spice Islands' of Indonesia. Archaeological discoveries and accounts written by Abbasid geographers and historians, such as Ibn Khurradadhbih (d. 299 AH/912 CE) and al-Mas'udi (d. 345 AH/956 CE), describe Arab merchants returning from China with silk, cinnamon, sandalwood, cloves and nutmeg; from Kilah (identified as *Kra*, in the Malay Peninsula) with pepper; and from present-day Vietnam with cardamom and cubeb. While these imports enriched Baghdad's markets and flavoured Abbasid dishes, locally grown crops were as important in creating a distinct culinary culture.

Along with dates, wheat was the most lucrative commodity traded in the Abbasid period, consumed both locally and exported abroad. The Abbasids cultivated several varieties of grain: according to Ibn Hawqal's late 4th century AH/10th century CE manuscript, the *Kitab Surat Al-Ard* (translated literally as 'Book of the Image of the Earth'), these crops grew in abundance around the middle Euphrates River.[2] Wheat was transported on a large scale from the surrounding countryside to the great market of western Baghdad, *al-Karkh*, where it was consumed in huge quantities to make bread, known as *khubz*.[3] The flour was typically bought from the market already prepared, and was then kneaded at home before being taken to a local bakehouse (*farran*).[4] In some regions, so much wheat was grown that the excess was exported, shipped from Baghdad to Basra and then Siraf (in present-day Iran) and then transported great distances by ship.[5] Because of this, Baghdad became known as the 'breadbasket' of the Abbasid empire.[6]

Unlike wheat, which was cultivated domestically, the aubergine was first introduced from India, having travelled to China and later Central Asia, where it was discovered by Arabs

 Tara Desjardins

during their campaigns in Iran.[7] By the 4th century AH/10th century CE, the aubergine was firmly established as a favourite food throughout the Arab world, appearing not only in treatises on farming but also in works of fiction, collections of poetry and cookbooks.[8] Although today found in dishes across the Middle East, the aubergine's initial reputation and reception into early Abbasid cuisine was far from positive: physicians believed it to be unhealthy, while people generally found it too bitter, claiming that its 'colour is that of a scorpion's abdomen, and [its] taste is like its sting'.[9] This all changed in the 3rd century AH/9th century CE when a new dish, known as *badhinjan buran* (Buran's aubergine), was invented for the marriage of Caliph al-Ma'mun to Khadija, the daughter of the former vizier, who was commonly called Buran. To mark the occasion on 5 Ramadan 210 AH/23 December 825 CE, a new method for cooking aubergines was presented: they were sliced, salted, and fried. The salting drew out the bitterness, while the frying concentrated it, reducing the acidity. Shortly thereafter, fried aubergines were used to enhance the flavour of many dishes.

Buran's recipe was a turning point in food history: Hamadani's 3rd century AH/9th century CE collection of stories, titled *Maqamat*, mentions friend aubergine (*badhinjan muqla*) as one of the most important courses at a feast, while the caliph Wathiq (r. 227–232 AH/842–847 CE) was so fond of aubergines that he ate 40 at a time.[10] Its popularity and abundance were so great that, by the turn of the century, 100 aubergines could be purchased at Baghdad's market for only 1 *danaq*.[11] The aubergine quickly travelled beyond Baghdad, reportedly reaching Qatar by the 4th century AH/10th century CE.[12] It was later recorded in agricultural texts in Spain, and by the 8th century AH/14th century CE was cultivated in the Muslim state of Kanem, in northern Nigeria.[13]

The end of the Abbasid caliphate was marked by a period of immense change and upheaval across the Muslim world: in 655 AH/1258 CE Baghdad was sacked by the Mongols; in 747 AH/1347 CE the plague killed an estimated 40 per cent of the global population; and in 922 AH/1517 CE the Mamluks succumbed to the might of the Ottomans.[14] During this time, European powers began to grow considerably, causing political, social and economic consequences for the Muslim countries that lay between the Atlas Mountains in the West and the River Indus in the East. With a shift in maritime domination came the introduction of new ingredients into Europe, the Middle East and Asia.

The catalyst for this far-reaching change was when Vasco da Gama's fleet of four ships and roughly 170 crewmen landed in Calicut, India (modern-day Kozhikode) on 20 Ramadan 903 AH/20 May 1498 CE, marking the first successful all-sea voyage from Europe to Southeast Asia. Da Gama's passage opened a new chapter for the Spice Route, connecting Europe to Asia and leading to the distribution of new flavours, notably black pepper and cinnamon, around the globe.[15] As a result, Arab merchants were deprived of their monopoly in this trade, which had for centuries created highly lucrative profits. The other, equally significant revolution in global trade was the 'discovery' of the Americas in 897–898 AH/1492 CE by a flotilla of Spanish ships commanded by adventurer Christopher Columbus. Alongside the huge quantities of precious metal, a wide range of plants were sent from the New World to Europe, including maize, tobacco and tomatoes. Many of these plants from the Americas were initially regarded as nothing more than curiosities and were cultivated in the botanical gardens of the European aristocracy. It took several generations for them to find their way into the kitchens and cooking pots of both Europe and the Middle East. Amongst these 'new' plants was the red chilli pepper and potato, both of which today feature heavily in the cuisines of South Asia and the Ottoman world.

Red chilli peppers did not exist anywhere in the Middle East or Asia prior to the 10th century AH/16th century CE. They are believed to have been domesticated some six thousand years ago in Mexico[16] and were first brought back to western Europe by Columbus during his second voyage across the Atlantic in 898–902/1493–1496 CE. In contrast to other crops from the Americas, the chilli pepper gained a very quick acceptance in Europe because of the initial belief that it was a variation of the precious black pepper plant from the East, for which it became a substitute, deemed to be hotter, tastier and far less expensive.[17] A printed illustration of the 'Indian red pepper' (Indian referring to 'native American') first appears in Europe in Leonhart Fuchs's comprehensive catalogue of over 500 plants from the New World, published in German in 949–995 AH/1543 CE with the title *New Kreüterbuch* ('New Herbal').[18] By the late 9th century AH/16th century CE, the chilli pepper was widely known throughout Europe (although climatic conditions meant they could not be grown everywhere). It was also successfully used as a remedy

 Tara Desjardins

for scurvy, despite the fact its high vitamin C content was only discovered much later.[19]

In the Ottoman world, sailors in the navy were familiar with the pepper as early as 918 AH/1513 CE, and they helped it spread throughout the sultan's dominions of the Middle East and North Africa. Some research suggests that the Ottoman Turks may even have been instrumental in introducing the pepper into central Europe, first to Hungary, which they conquered in 932 AH/1526 CE, followed by Austria, with the siege of Vienna.[20] In India the plant arrived around 915 AH/1510 CE, shortly after the western port town of Goa, located on the spice-rich Malabar Coast, fell to the Portuguese. According to a Portuguese official in India from 905–921 AH AH/1500–1516 CE, the spice of chilli peppers was welcomed by Indian cooks who, accustomed to pungent black pepper and biting ginger, already produced spicy foods.[21] It was also easily cultivated and, by the 12th century AH/18th century CE, the chilli pepper was widely known and regularly used in the Ottoman court and in South Asian dishes.

Unlike the pepper, the potato arrived much later into Middle Eastern cuisine. Although already seen in the High Andes in South America by the Spanish conquistador Francisco Pizarro in around 938–939 AH/1532 CE, it did not arrive in Europe for another 40 years.[22] In 980 AH/1573 CE potatoes figured amongst the purchases of the Sangre hospital in Seville, Spain.[23] In the 11th century AH/17th century CE, they began to be cultivated as a food crop in Ireland and Lower Austria and, over the course of the 12th and 13th centuries AH/18th and 19th centuries CE, gradually spread to other parts of Europe. In 1250 AH/1835 CE, potatoes began to appear in Istanbul but were only grown more widely across the Ottoman Empire following a succession of poor wheat harvests in the 1290s–1300s AH/1880s CE and the great famine of 1304 AH/1887 CE.[24] In Qajar Iran, potatoes were first brought to Fath Ali Shah (r. 1211–1150 AH/1797–1834 CE) by Sir John Malcolm, the British consul to Iran, who ordered for their immediate cultivation in the village of Pashand, near Tehran.[25] According to Charles Willis, an English physician employed by the Indo-European Telegraph Department in Iran (1282–1299 AH/ 1866–1881 CE), potatoes were only cultivated in abundance in the late 13th century AH/19th century CE, at which point they became a common food item in dishes.[26]

It is curious to reflect upon the long and often perilous journey ingredients once travelled before becoming staples in dishes deemed national favourites today. The four ingredients highlighted here—wheat, aubergine, peppers, and potatoes—reflect periods in history often defined by new 'discoveries' spurred by innovations in navigation and travel. However, they also reflect people's curiosity and interest in the unknown. What may have once been strange or exotic can, over time, become common. The potato, for example, now equated with the ubiquitous French fry, is found around the world in cultures and countries where, for centuries, rice and bread were predominantly used. Ingredients, much like recipes, can reflect people and cultures that, when mixed together, represent changes in societies. Ingredients will remain itinerant, continuing to transform dishes as people travel and cultures evolve.

 Tara Desjardins

Endnotes

1 See Hugh Kennedy, 'Baghdad and the Markets', in *Baghdad: Eye's Delight*, ed. Julia Gonnella, et. al. (Milan: Silvana Editoriale, 2022), pp. 201–207.

2 Muḥammad Ibn Ḥawqal, *Configuration de la terre (Kitab Surat Al-Ard)*, trans. J.H. Kramers and Gaston Wiet (Paris: G.P. Maisonneuve & Larose, 1964).

3 Muhammad Manazir Ahsan, *Social Life Under the Abbasids* (London and New York: Longman, 1979), p. 150.

4 Ahsan, *Social Life Under the Abbasids*, p. 88.

5 Adam Mez, *The Renaissance of Islam*, trans. S. Khuda Bakhsh and D.S. Magoliouth, (Patna: Jubilee Printing and Publishing House, 1937), p. 430; Eliyahu Ashtor, *A Social and Economic History of the Near East in the Middle Ages* (Los Angeles: University of California Press, 1976), pp. 41–42.

6 Kennedy, 'Baghdad and the Markets', pp. 201–207.

7 Charles Perry, 'A Canvas of Cuisines', in Linda Komaroff, ed., *Dining with the Sultan: The Fine Art of Feasting*, (Los Angeles: Los Angeles County Museum of Art, DelMonico Books, 2023), p. 38.

8 See Nawal Nasrallah, ed. and trans., *Annals of the Caliphs' Kitchens: Ibn Sayyār Al-Warrāq's Tenth-Century Baghdadi Cookbook* (Leiden: Brill, 2007).

9 Peter Heine, *The Culinary Crescent: A History of Middle Eastern Cuisine* (London: Gingko, 2018), p. 51.

10 See Ahsan, *Social Life Under the Abbasids*, p. 94, n. 134 and 135.

11 Al-Khatib Al-Baghdadi, *Al-Tatfil wa Hikayat al-Tufayliyyin* (Damascus 1346 AH/1927 CE), p. 79 as referenced in Ahsan, *Social Life Under the Abbasids*, p. 94, n. 137.

12 Aubergine seeds were amongst the archeological finds excavated from the Abbasid period site of Ain Mohammed North B, in northern Qatar, dated to the 2nd century AH/8th–early 9th century CE. The author is grateful to the Qatar Museums archaeological team for bringing this to her attention, as well as Hannah Russ and Robert Carter for identifying the seeds.

13 8th century AH/14th century CE historical accounts testify to its presence in both Ethiopia and Nigeria. See Heine, *The Culinary Crescent*, p. 126.

14 See Ibn Mubārak Shāh, *The Sultan's Feast: A Fifteenth-Century Egyptian Cookbook*, ed. and trans. Daniel Newman (London: Saqi Books, 2020), the introduction and in particular p. 23.

15 Bailey Diffie and George Winius, *Foundations of the Portuguese Empire, 1415–1850: Europe and the World in the Age of Expansion* (Minneapolis: University of Minnesota Press, 1977).

16 Robert N. Spengler III, *Fruit from the Sands: The Silk Road Origins of the Foods We Eat* (Oakland, CA: University of California Press, 2019), p. 272.

17 Jean-Louis Flandrin and Massimo Montanari, eds., *Food: A Culinary History from Antiquity to the Present* (New York: Columbia University Press, 1999), p. 358.

18 A copy of this manuscript, printed in Basel, Switzerland, is in the Qatar Museums collection and appeared in the exhibition, with this page displayed (STM.NH.BO.0034, pp. 145–146).

19 Heine, *The Culinary Crescent*, p. 143.

20 Jean Andrews, 'Diffusion of Mesoamerican Food Complex to Southeastern Europe', *Geographical Review* 83/ 2 (1993), p. 201.

21 Andrews, 'Diffusion of Mesoamerican Food Complex', p. 199.

22 Heine, *The Culinary Crescent*, p. 133.

23 Flandrin and Montanari, eds., *Food: A Culinary History*, p. 357.

24 Heine, *The Culinary Crescent*, p. 133.

25 Known as the Pashandi potato, this is the largest variety of potato consumed in Iran today. This type of potato had a high adaptability to its environment and naturally high resistance to pests and disease, especially fungal disease, making it ideally suited for local farmers to cultivate, and the most readily available potato in Iran.

26 Khodadad Rezakhani, 'From Street Food to National Cuisine: Cooking and Modernity in Twentieth Century Iran', in Komaroff, ed., *Dining with the Sultan*, p. 121.

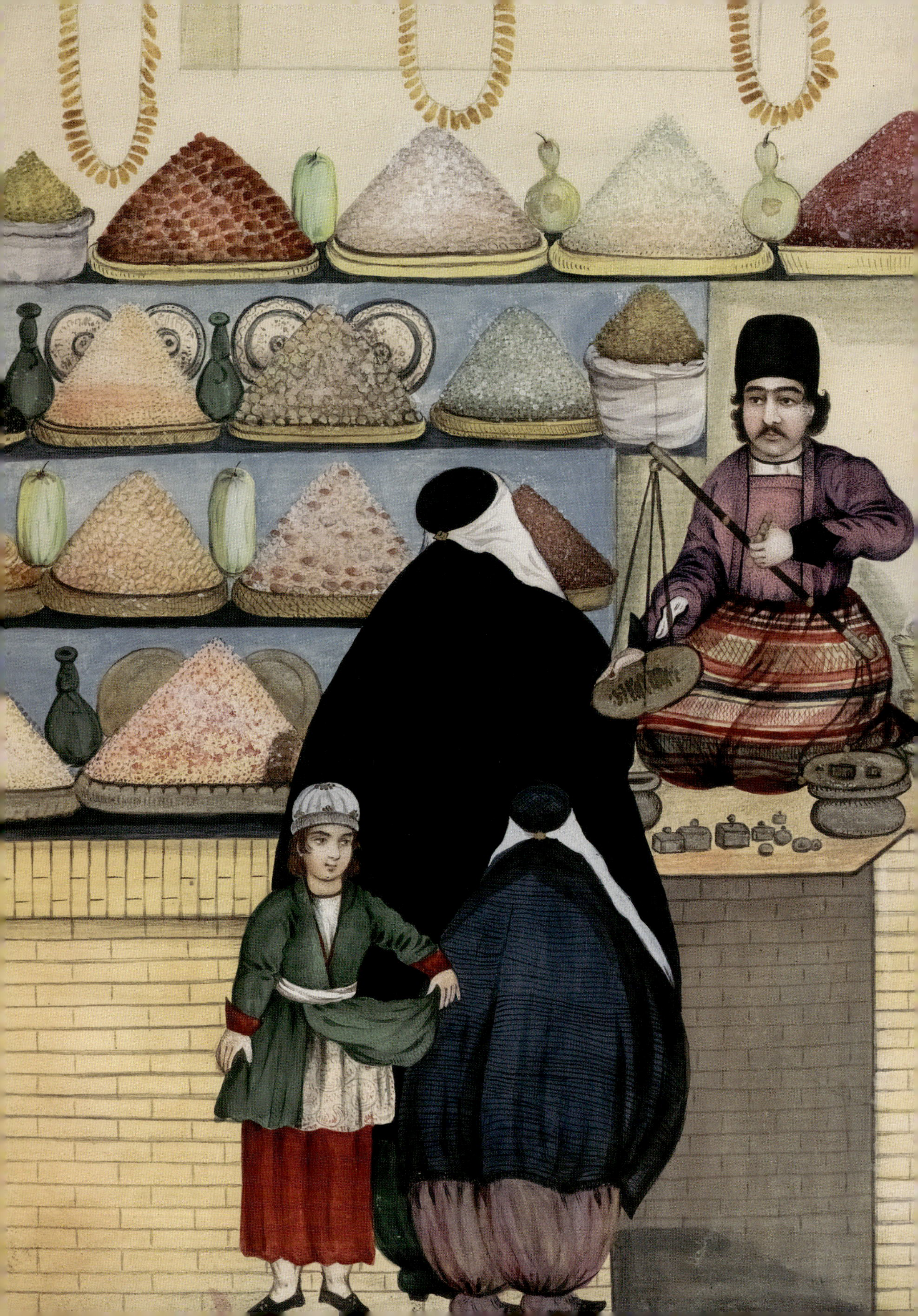

Reem Aboughazala

Maryam Mohammed Abdulla: Crafting a Culinary Legacy in Qatar

Over the last decades, various chefs have risen to wide-spread fame, with their platforms expanding thanks to the popularity of cookbooks and cooking shows. This is especially true in Qatar, where one of the earliest chefs Maryam Mohammed Abdulla (b. 1952) became the first female to appear on Qatar TV, despite societal views against women appearing on television at the time. Between 1991 and 1992, Mrs Maryam, or 'Umm Mohammed' as she was known by close friends, presented 60 episodes featuring over 120 recipes on the art of home cooking. She hosted two television shows, the first titled *Daily Dish*, followed by *Khafayif* ('Light Recipes'), on which she based the title of her Arabic recipe books *Khafayif* (1993), *Khafayif: Tastier and More Delicious* (1996), and *Khafayif: Home Cooking* (1998). She also published an English version for the wider audience, titled *Taste of Home: The Best Light and Traditional Recipes of the Gulf* (2000). Mrs Maryam was very passionate about cooking and always wanted to share her recipes to benefit her community.

For Mrs Maryam, cooking was a way of nurturing her family and children. She worked hard to ensure that her children had the best quality, home-cooked foods, to the extent that she would wake up early to prepare freshly baked bread every morning for their breakfast. She was self-taught, without formal or professional training. Instead, she grew up watching her elder sister cook for the family, a practice she continued even when her sister married. Shortly thereafter, she took a job as a school teacher of Home Economics, teaching girls how to perfect their skills in cooking, sewing and handicrafts. She continued working

Spice Market (detail), Iran, Qajar period, 13th century AH/late 19th century CE, gouache on paper, 38.2 × 31.1 cm (each page). Museum of Islamic Art, Doha, MS.772.2011.2

in education at various schools and teaching different age groups while also sharing with her local community her love of cooking.[1]

Much later on, in 1991, Mrs Maryam received a call from a producer at Qatar TV asking if she could host a cooking show during the holy month of Ramadan. Mrs Maryam agreed. The show was so popular that it subsequently evolved into a permanent programme dedicated to cooking. This was transformative for Mrs Maryam and the many women who tuned in to watch her programme, as they forged new friendships and recipes along the way. To expand her knowledge on both regional and international dishes, Mrs Maryam would test diverse recipes shared by her friends from all around the region and tweak them with her own touch. She would even meet diplomatic figures such as ambassadors' wives in Doha in order to learn some of their traditional recipes. This helped her reach an even wider audience and learn more about various cuisines. In turn, women from all across Doha, and later the Gulf, would call her, asking about recipes, spices or cooking tools. Through TV, Mrs Maryam was able to connect with thousands of women who, in their own right, served as inspiration for her cooking. This connection continues today, with women calling and thanking her for being the source of inspiration for improving their skills and approaches to cooking. Today, these friendships are the most cherished memories of her TV programme.

Mrs Maryam's success spurred the growth of Qatar's culinary arts, inspiring other chefs to pursue their ambitions on an international stage. One example is Mrs Maryam's sister, Aisha Mohammad Al-Tamimi, an award-winning culinary artist celebrated for her traditional dishes. It is interesting to observe that in Mrs Maryam and Chef Aisha's cookbooks, recipes of dishes from the early Abbasid period (2nd–4th centuries AH/8th–10th century CE) can be found, with a few alterations and more detailed descriptions of the ingredients. In *Taste of Home* by Mrs Maryam, there is a recipe for *kunafa*, one of the most celebrated Middle Eastern desserts, which can also be found in the earliest known example of a cookbook from the Islamic world, the 4th century AH/10th century CE Abbasid text *Kitab al-Tabikh* (Book of Dishes) compiled by Ibn Sayyar al-Warraq (d. 350 AH/ 961 CE).[2] There are other common recipes including another famous dessert from the region known as *muhalabia*, a type of Middle Eastern milk pudding. These recipes are often served at social gatherings and during important celebrations, such as engagements, weddings, and other festive occasions.[3]

 Reem Aboughazala

The tradition of using these old recipes that were passed down through generations is especially seen during the month of Ramadan, a time of year that focuses on generosity. During Ramadan, families exchange meals, and food is donated for distribution amongst the less fortunate. Both Mrs Maryam and Chef Aisha emphasised the importance of this tradition. For example, during Ramadan the most beloved dish of Prophet Muhammad (PBUH) was *tharid* (a bread soup or stew),[4] which today is one of the most commonly shared dishes amongst families and neighbours. Chef Aisha recently published a book in 2023 titled *Mawaed Shaabia Qataria* ('Popular Qatari Dining Tables') in which she discusses how these same traditions are passed down through generations, and in which a recipe of the *tharid* can still be found.[5] It is important to also note that these inherited recipes have often evolved across cultures based on the availability of ingredients.

A mother's cooking holds a special place in every family, symbolising love, care and nourishment. For Mrs Maryam, her passion for cooking was deeply rooted in her devotion to her family, and this was the reason behind her success. Her love of cooking for the family has inspired future generations to pursue a career in culinary arts and appreciate the creativity in preparing food.

Endnotes

1 Maryam Mohammed Abdulla, interview by Reem Aboughazala, 18 September 2024.

2 Compare Maryam Mohammed Abdulla, *Taste of Home: The Best Light and Traditional Recipes of the Gulf* (Doha: Self-pubished, 2000), p. 206 and Nawal Nasrallah, ed. and trans., *Annals of the Caliph's Kitchens: Ibn Sayyār al-Warrāq's Tenth-Century Baghdadi Cookbook* (Leiden: Brill, 2010), p. 29.

3 Charles Perry, ed. and trans., *Scents and Flavors: A Syrian Cookbook* (New York: NYU Press, 2017).

4 Sevim Demir Akgün and Levent Öztürk, 'Cuisine and Dishes in Use During the Prophet Muhammed Era (A.D. 569-632)', *European Journal of Islamic Studies* 9/4 (2018), p. 82.

5 Aisha Mohammad Al-Tamimi, *Mawaed Shaabia Qataria* (Doha: Roza Publishing House, 2023).

Peonia è cal da in[primo] e secha i[n] secõdo grado
magiore p[ro]uocha la orina e mõ[n]difica le
rene, la radice apichata al colo a li puri p[r]inzip
[cura] la epilensia e la radice beuta i[n] quã[n]tita
de una amandola mõ[n]difica le done per le mes-
[t]rue che nõ sono bone mõdificate nel pasto e beuta cõ[n] uino cura la ystortiõ[n] e lo dolore del uentre
e de la rasicha e de li p[r]eni e cota cõ[n] uino
strinze lo uentre e le mestrue e dece grani
beuta col uino stiptico nõ[n] lassa generare la p[r]e-
ta e quindexe grani cura la suffucatione
de la matrice con mele rosto e lo dolore
de la matrice.

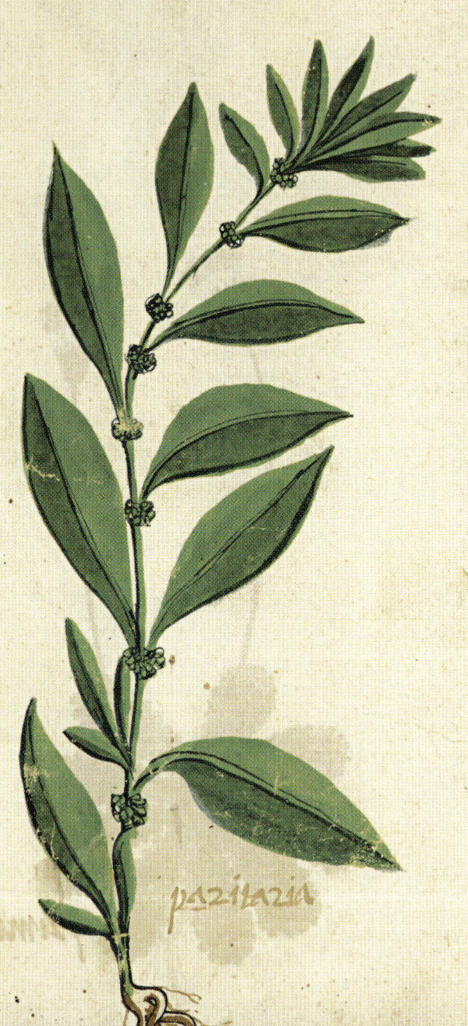

Paritaria è [c]ristola e calda e secha nel ter[z]o
grado e enplastrata suso la podagra la
[cura] e la squeta [d]iezza del focho e [o]ngiuto
le amigdale postene le ura il succho beuto cura
[fisto]se e cura li e moroyn[e] e cura el dolore del sto-
macho e de li i[n] testini che p[r]o crede de fegi-
ta e uale anche a rompere la p[r]eta me[no]-
ne apulpita suso lo petenegio e fa orinare ben
e leua li dolori de flanchi.

Teslim Sanni

Cultivating Resilience: Qatar's Agricultural Innovations and the Future of Food Security

Folio 41r (detail), *Tacuinum Sanitatis* ('Almanac of Health') Italy, Sicily, *c.* 1475 CE, ink and opaque watercolour on paper, 39.3 × 28.1 cm (closed). Museum of Islamic Art Library, Doha, RS79.L64.14[75]

The agricultural sector across the Arab world has long grappled with significant challenges, including arid climates, water scarcity and the growing impacts of global warming. Qatar, a noteworthy example in this context, has taken proactive steps to address these issues by enacting sustainable agricultural practices. Before the sudden 2017–2021 blockade imposed by neighbouring Gulf countries—Bahrain, the UAE and Saudi Arabia—these nations provided over 80% of Qatar's food imports.[1] The blockade, which involved severing diplomatic ties, closing borders and restricting food exports to Qatar, intensified the nation's focus on food security and self-sufficiency. It also accelerated Qatar's commitment to sustainable agriculture, an effort that began nearly a decade earlier. By investing in modern farming technologies and adapting to both environmental and geopolitical challenges, Qatar has made substantial strides toward food self-sufficiency while reinforcing its resilience and resourcefulness.

One of the primary environmental issues facing Qatar—and the Arab world at large—is its desert climate and limited access to fresh water, making food production a significant challenge. Prior to 2008, Qatar relied on imports for over 90% of its food supply. However, in response to the 2008 global food crisis and concerns about potential future disruptions, the Qatari government launched its first Qatar National Food Security Programme (QNFSP), adopting advanced agricultural technologies in order to achieve national food security, which aligned with the Qatar National Vision 2030.[2] This included the use of hydroponic and vertical farming, both of which were well-suited solutions to Qatar's environmental restrictions. Hydroponic farming involves growing plants in a water-based nutrient solution rather than soil, an effective method given Qatar's limited arable land. Vertical farming, on the other hand, allows crops to be cultivated in stacked layers, maximising crop yield per square foot—a valuable approach for a country with limited land area.

In 2012, the QNFSP underwent revisions to refine its approach to food security. As part of these efforts, Qatar's state-owned agricultural investment company, Hassad Food, initiated a national hydroponics project. This project aimed to ensure a reliable supply of fresh produce to the community while reducing the environmental impact of traditional farming methods.[3] In addition to hydroponics and vertical farming, Qatar also invested in smart greenhouse technology, which continues to play a crucial role in optimising agricultural production in extreme weather conditions. Greenhouses equipped with automated systems that regulate temperature, humidity and light, create controlled microclimates allowing for year-round cultivation while conserving resources. Implemented across nearly 400 local farms, smart greenhouses have contributed to an approximately 70% reduction in water usage, compared to traditional methods, proving instrumental in enhancing Qatar's food security.[4] By combining smart greenhouses with drip irrigation systems, which deliver water directly to the roots of plants, Qatar has further maximised its water efficiency.

While water scarcity had initially inspired Qatar's agricultural ambitions, its surrounding geopolitical landscape, in particular the 2017 blockade, served as the critical turning point. In response to the blockade, which completely restricted food imports arriving from neighbouring countries, Qatar's government immediately launched a new National Food Security Programme, which set out ambitious targets to reduce import dependency and boost local food production by 70%. By 2018, local vegetable production in Qatar had risen by nearly 30%, with targets set for the years ahead.[5] Progress accelerated as Agrico, a leader in Qatar's organic farming sector, implemented more efficient hydroponic systems that further reduced water usage and supported year-round crop production. By 2020, Qatar expanded its greenhouse capacity by 85%, enabling the annual production of up to 6000 tonnes of vegetables, including tomatoes, eggplants and zucchinis.[6] As of 2021, Qatar's vertical and hydroponic farms supplied approximately 41% of the country's vegetable demand, with an aim to achieve 60% self-sufficiency in vegetables by 2025.[7] A prominent achievement under this food security strategy was the rise of Baladna, a Qatari dairy company. Baladna invested millions to import over 4000 Holstein dairy cows—a breed renowned for high milk production—from Europe, the United States and Australia.[8] This swift expansion enabled Baladna to meet local demands, helping Qatar to respond to the crisis of 2017 and achieve 100% self-sufficiency in fresh milk by 2019.[9] Another important milestone was achieved in 2019 through a collaborative initiative by the Qatar Ministry of Municipality and the Environment (MME) and the Qatar Development Bank (QDB), which established eight egg production projects on selected local farms. With a goal of producing over 200 million eggs annually, Qatar reached this target by 2022, achieving nearly 80% self-sufficiency in table eggs.[10]

Today, Qatar's agricultural landscape includes over 1400 farms of various scales, many of which supply products to major supermarket chains and restaurants across the country.[11] These farms collectively produce a wide array of crops, including tomatoes, okra, cucumbers, onions and chillies.[12] Looking ahead, Qatar continues to invest in infrastructure and technology to support further expansion of local agriculture. Local farms like Heenat Salma are developing agricultural systems rooted in permaculture and regenerative agriculture principles.[13] Permaculture focuses on creating self-sustaining, ecologically harmonious systems by mimicking natural ecosystems, while regenerative agriculture emphasises restoring soil health, enhancing biodiversity, and increasing resilience through sustainable practices. The ongoing advancement of sustainable farming systems has been essential to Qatar's food security efforts, expanding the range of locally grown produce, and reducing reliance on imports while also ensuring the safety of the environment. With this chain of developments, Qatar has not only increased its self-sufficiency but also contributed to the sustainability of its agricultural practices, serving as an inspiring model of sustainable and resilient food production in the Arab world.

Endnotes

1 'Qatar Food Imports Hit After Arab Nations Cut Ties: Trade Sources', *Reuters*, published 5 June 2017, available online at https://www.reuters.com/article/markets/us/qatar-food-imports-hit-after-arab-nations-cut-ties-trade-sources-idUSL8N1J23IC/ (accessed 11 November 2024).

2 Qatar's National Vision seeks to build an advanced, self-sustaining society by 2030, providing a high quality of life for its citizens. It outlines long-term goals and serves as a framework for developing national strategies and implementation plans. 'National Vision 2030', *Government Communications Office Qatar*, available online at https://www.gco.gov.qa/en/about-qatar/national-vision2030/ (accessed 11 November 2024).

3 'Soil-Free Greenhouses to Help Qatar Grow Up to 70% of Its Veg by 2023', *Doha News*, published 25 August 2015, available online at https://dohanews.co/soil-free-greenhouses-to-help-qatar-grow-up-to-70-of-its-veg-by-2023/ (accessed 11 November 2024).

4 'Fruits & Vegetables Report', *Qatar Development Bank*, n.d., available online at https://ossform.qdb.qa/Documents/Fruits%20_%20Vegetable%20Report%20Final%20ENG.pdf (accessed 11 November 2024).

5 'Qatar Achieves Huge Leaps in Food Self-Sufficiency', *The Peninsula Qatar*, published 16 October 2021, available online at https://thepeninsulaqatar.com/article/16/10/2021/Qatar-achieves-huge-leaps-in-food-self-sufficiency (accessed 11 November 2024).

6 'Hydroponic Technology', *Agrico Qatar*, n.d., available online at https://agrico.qa/technology/hydroponic (accessed 11 November 2024).

7 'Qatar Achieves Self-Sufficiency in Vegetables in 2021', *The Peninsula Qatar*, published 30 December 2021, available online at https://thepeninsulaqatar.com/article/30/12/2021/qatar-achieves-41-self-sufficiency-in-vegetables-in-2021 (accessed 11 November 2024).

8 'Qatar Airways Cargo Flies in 230 Holstein Cows for Baladna Farm to Support Local Dairy Demand', *The Peninsula Qatar*, published on 18 July 2017, available online at https://thepeninsulaqatar.com/article/18/07/2017/Qatar-Airways-Cargo-flies-in-230-Holstein-cows-for-Baladna-farm-to-support-local-dairy-demand (accessed 11 November 2024).

9 'Bovine Heroes: The Quest for Food Security in Qatar', *Baladna*, published 3 July 2021, available online at https://baladna.com/en/bovine-heroes-the-quest-for-food-security-in-qatar#:~:text=As%20part%20of%20the%20event,story%20worthy%20of%20retelling%20here (accessed 11 November 2024).

10 'Expo 2023 Doha: Qatar Makes Noticeable Progress in Self-Sufficiency from Agricultural Products – Report', *Qatar News Agency*, published 28 September 2023, available online at https://www.qna.org.qa/en/News-Area/Special-News/2023-09/28/0050-expo-2023-doha-qatar-makes-noticeable-progress-in-self-sufficiency-from-agricultural-products---report (accessed 11 November 2024).

11 'Qatar's Next Big Purchase: A Farming Sector', *Reuters*, published 6 January 2012, available online at https://www.reuters.com/article/business/environment/qatars-next-big-purchase-a-farming-sector-idUSTRE8051V4/#:~:text=%22Today%2C%20there%20are%201%2C400%20farms,percent%20of%20our%20market%20needs (accessed 11 November 2024).

12 'Qatar Achieves Substantial Growth in Vegetable Self-Sufficiency', *Gulf Times*, published 19 December 2023, available online at https://www.gulf-times.com/article/673898/qatar/qatar-achieves-substantial-growth-in-vegetable-self-sufficiency (accessed 11 November 2024).

13 'Agriculture', *Heenat Salma*, n.d., available online at https://heenatsalma.earth/agriculture/ (accessed 11 November 2024).

Folio 3v (detail), *Tacuinum Sanitatis* ('Almanac of Health') Italy, Sicily, *c.* 1475 CE, ink and opaque watercolour on paper, 39.3 × 28.1 cm (closed). Museum of Islamic Art Library, Doha, RS79.L64.14[75]

Teslim Sanni

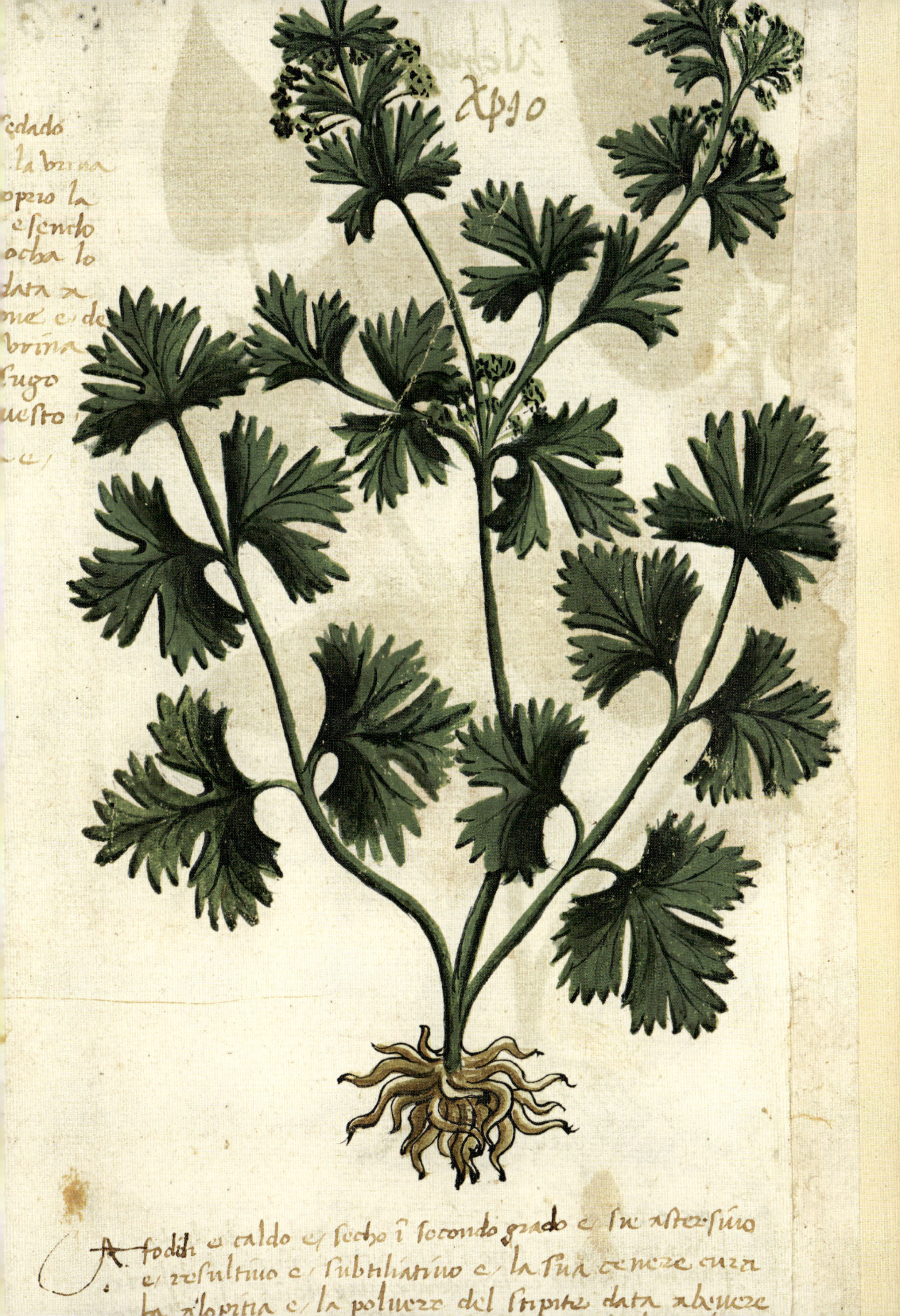

çdadó
la brina
opero la
e sendo
ocha lo
data a
me e de
brina
sugo
uesto
e
apio
A. fodih e caldo e secho i secondo grado e su astersiuo
e resultiuo e subtiliatiuo e la sua cenere cura
la ... e la poluere del stipite data abeuere

Exhibition Album

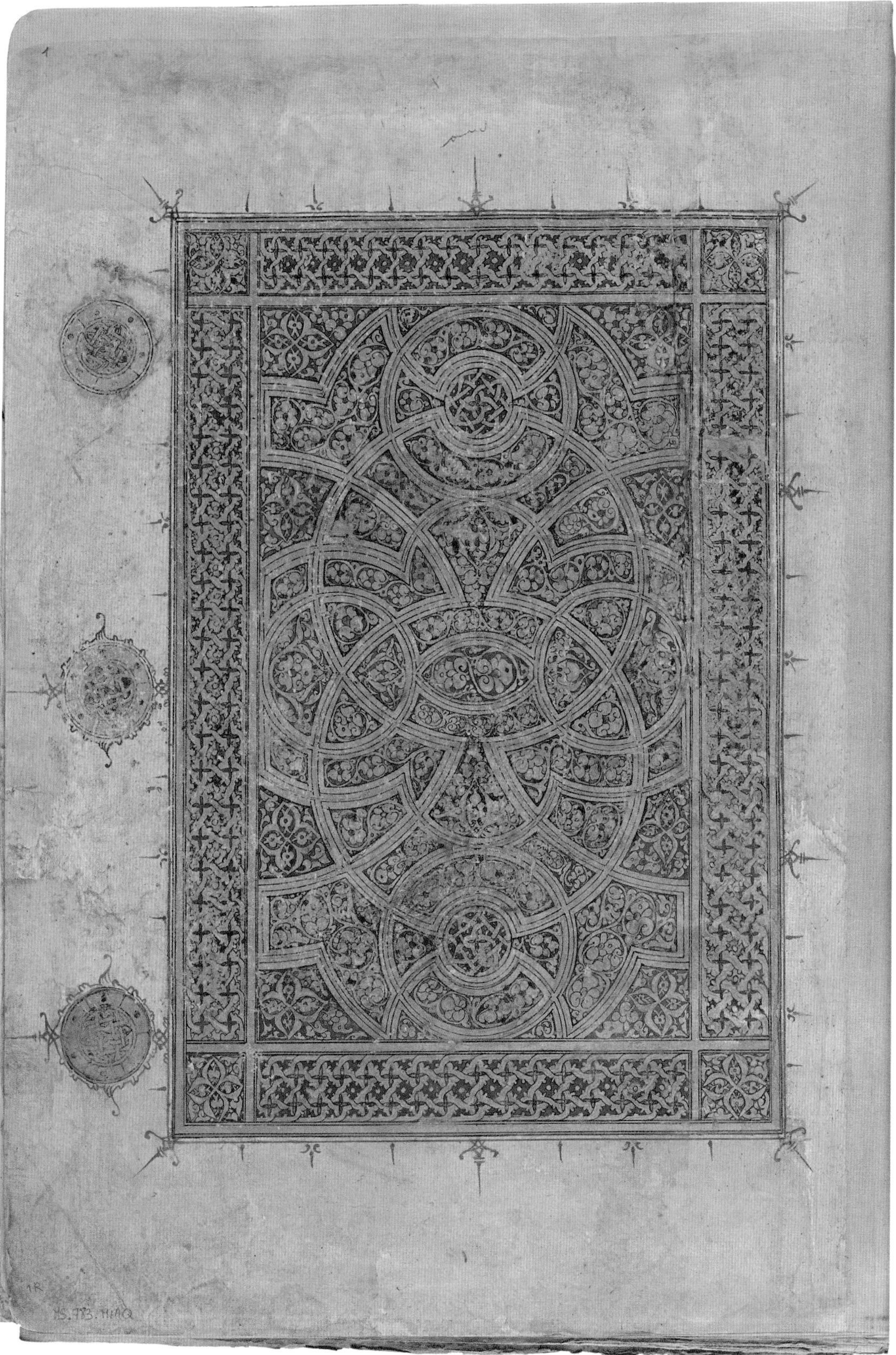

Manuscript copy of the *Qur'an*
Iran, Abbasid period, 7th century AH/13th century CE
Ink, opaque watercolour and gold on paper with leather binding
47 × 34.5 cm (closed); 66 × 85.5 cm (open)
Museum of Islamic Art, MS.783.2011

Apart from its impressive size, the exquisite illumination of this manuscript makes it a remarkable example of Qur'anic art of the Abbasid period. Especially notable are its frontispiece (of which the left side survives, as shown here), and the illuminated frames of the following folios (containing the first chapter of the Qur'an and the start of the second). The main text throughout the manuscript is written in *naskh* script, while the *sura* (chapter) headings and finispiece are written in *thuluth* script inscribed in white ink against a shimmering gold ground.

The Qur'an includes several verses on food and eating that define Islamic principles of purity, health and ethics. For Muslims, the Qur'an's dietary laws address both individual and communal responsibilities. On an individual level, the Qur'an states that it is a book without doubt, serving as guidance for those who believe in Allah (Q2:2). On a communal level, the Qur'an commands Muslims to 'enjoin what is right and forbid evil' (Q3:104). The page shown overleaf features a verse from *Sura Al-Baqarah* (Q2:172), which reads:

'O you who have believed, eat from the good things which We have provided for you, and be grateful to Allah if it is [indeed] Him that you worship.'

This verse is pivotal in understanding the relationship between food, faith and gratitude in Islam. Here, the Qur'an encourages believers to partake in the sustenance provided by Allah, but with a significant caveat, that they must do so with a sense of gratitude and consciousness of their faith.

For Muslims, gratitude is in fact a central component of consuming food. This reflects a broader Qur'anic teaching that views food not simply as a physical necessity, but as a divine blessing that requires acknowledgment and thankfulness. The act of eating, therefore, is seen as an opportunity to engage in spiritual reflection, to recognise the mercy of Allah in providing sustenance, and to maintain a sense of humility. This verse and others like it remind Muslims that their actions, including what they eat, impact not only their personal relationship with God but also their role in fostering an ethical and righteous community.[1]

The verse also provides guidance on specific restrictions. The phrase 'good things' refers to *halal* (permissible) foods, which are those that conform to Islamic dietary laws. In contrast, foods considered *haram* (forbidden), such as pork or intoxicants like alcohol, are prohibited and seen as spiritually harmful.[2] TS

1 For more examples of similar verses, see Q5:3 and Q20:81.

2 Detailed explanations can be found in medieval commentaries on the Qur'an, such as the 4th century AH/10th century CE *Jāmi' al-bayān 'an ta'wīl āy al-Qur'ān*, vol. 2 by al-Tabari, and the 9th century AH/14th century CE *Tafsir al-Qur'an al-Azim* vol. 2 by Ibn Kathir. For further discussion, see Idris, 'Prohibition in Qur'an', p. 66.

مِمَّا تَرَكَ وَإِن كَانُوٓا۟ إِخْوَةً رِّجَالًا وَنِسَآءً فَلِلذَّكَرِ مِثْلُ حَظِّ ٱلْأُنثَيَيْنِ

يُبَيِّنُ ٱللَّهُ لَكُمْ أَن تَضِلُّوا۟ وَٱللَّهُ بِكُلِّ شَىْءٍ عَلِيمٌ

سُورَةُ ٱلْمَائِدَةِ وَهِيَ مِائَةٌ وَعِشْرُونَ آيَةً

بِسْمِ ٱللَّهِ ٱلرَّحْمَٰنِ ٱلرَّحِيمِ

يَٰٓأَيُّهَا ٱلَّذِينَ آمَنُوٓا۟ أَوْفُوا۟ بِٱلْعُقُودِ أُحِلَّتْ لَكُم بَهِيمَةُ ٱلْأَنْعَٰمِ إِلَّا مَا

يُتْلَىٰ عَلَيْكُمْ غَيْرَ مُحِلِّى ٱلصَّيْدِ وَأَنتُمْ حُرُمٌ إِنَّ ٱللَّهَ يَحْكُمُ مَا يُرِيدُ يَٰٓأَيُّهَا

ٱلَّذِينَ آمَنُوا۟ لَا تُحِلُّوا۟ شَعَائِرَ ٱللَّهِ وَلَا ٱلشَّهْرَ ٱلْحَرَامَ وَلَا ٱلْهَدْىَ وَلَا ٱلْقَلَائِدَ

وَلَآ آمِّينَ ٱلْبَيْتَ ٱلْحَرَامَ يَبْتَغُونَ فَضْلًا مِّن رَّبِّهِمْ وَرِضْوَانًا وَإِذَا حَلَلْتُمْ

فَٱصْطَادُوا۟ وَلَا يَجْرِمَنَّكُمْ شَنَآنُ قَوْمٍ أَن صَدُّوكُمْ عَنِ ٱلْمَسْجِدِ

ٱلْحَرَامِ أَن تَعْتَدُوا۟ وَتَعَاوَنُوا۟ عَلَى ٱلْبِرِّ وَٱلتَّقْوَىٰ وَلَا تَعَاوَنُوا۟ عَلَى ٱلْإِثْمِ

وَٱلْعُدْوَانِ وَٱتَّقُوا۟ ٱللَّهَ إِنَّ ٱللَّهَ شَدِيدُ ٱلْعِقَابِ حُرِّمَتْ عَلَيْكُمُ ٱلْمَيْتَةُ

وَٱلدَّمُ وَلَحْمُ ٱلْخِنزِيرِ وَمَآ أُهِلَّ لِغَيْرِ ٱللَّهِ بِهِ وَٱلْمُنْخَنِقَةُ وَٱلْمَوْقُوذَةُ

وَٱلْمُتَرَدِّيَةُ وَٱلنَّطِيحَةُ وَمَآ أَكَلَ ٱلسَّبُعُ إِلَّا مَا ذَكَّيْتُمْ وَمَا ذُبِحَ عَلَى ٱلنُّصُبِ

وَأَن تَسْتَقْسِمُوا۟ بِٱلْأَزْلَامِ ذَٰلِكُمْ فِسْقٌ ٱلْيَوْمَ يَئِسَ ٱلَّذِينَ كَفَرُوا۟

مِن دِينِكُمْ فَلَا تَخْشَوْهُمْ وَٱخْشَوْنِ ٱلْيَوْمَ أَكْمَلْتُ لَكُمْ دِينَكُمْ وَأَتْمَمْتُ

2a
Manuscript of the *En'am-i Sherif* ('The Noble En'am')
Copied by Haci Mehmed Resim and illuminated
by Haci Ahmed Ayasofia
Istanbul, Ottoman period, dated 1294 AH/1877 CE
Ink, opaque watercolour and gold on paper
24.8 × 17 cm (closed)
Museum of Islamic Art, MS.399.2007

The devotional prayer book commonly known as *En'am-i Sherif*
contains a selection of Qur'anic *suras*, prayers, religious poems
and paintings. This copy was commissioned by Princess Refia
Sultan (d. 1297 AH/1880 CE) as a gift for the Prophet's Mosque in
Medina, in memory of her father, Sultan Abdülmecid I
(r. 1255–1277 AH/1839–1861 CE). Among the key visual elements
of the manuscript is the depiction of Mecca and Medina (folios
211v and 212r). The Prophet's Mosque in Medina is portrayed with
the three tombs of Prophet Muhammad (PBUH), Abu Bakr and
'Umar under a green dome radiating light, alongside a palm tree
in the courtyard'. Another page features the 'miraculous palm
tree of the Prophet' (*khorme-i muʿcize-i Resul Allah*, as denoted
in Turkish in the manuscript) as a date-bearing palm with a
golden trunk (folio 209v).

These illustrations highlight the cultural and religious
significance of the date palm in the Islamic world. Beyond its
spiritual symbolism, the palm tree was valued in pre-Islamic
times for its practical uses, providing food, shelter and materials
in the desert environment. Numerous Hadiths underscore its
importance, such as the story of the palm tree that wept when
the Prophet no longer stood by it to deliver sermons.[1] This
connection between the palm tree and the Prophet emphasises
its role as a symbol of life, sustenance and divine blessings,
resonating deeply in Islamic art, literature and daily life.

1 *Sahih al-Bukhari*, vol. 4, book 61, Hadith
no. 3584.

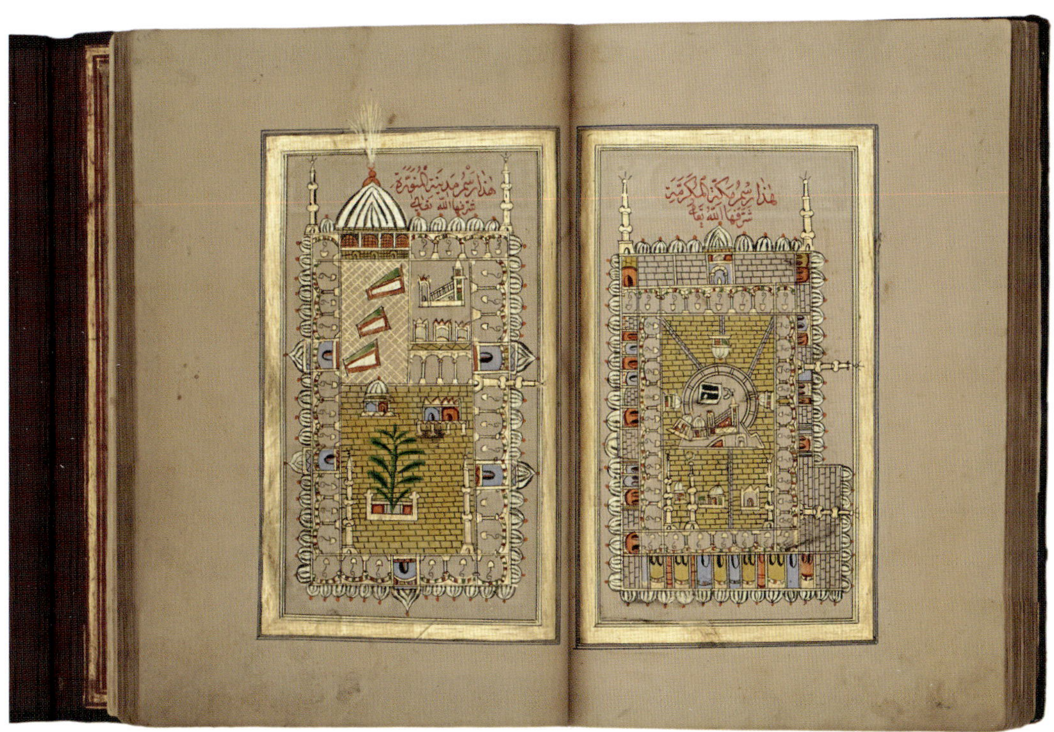

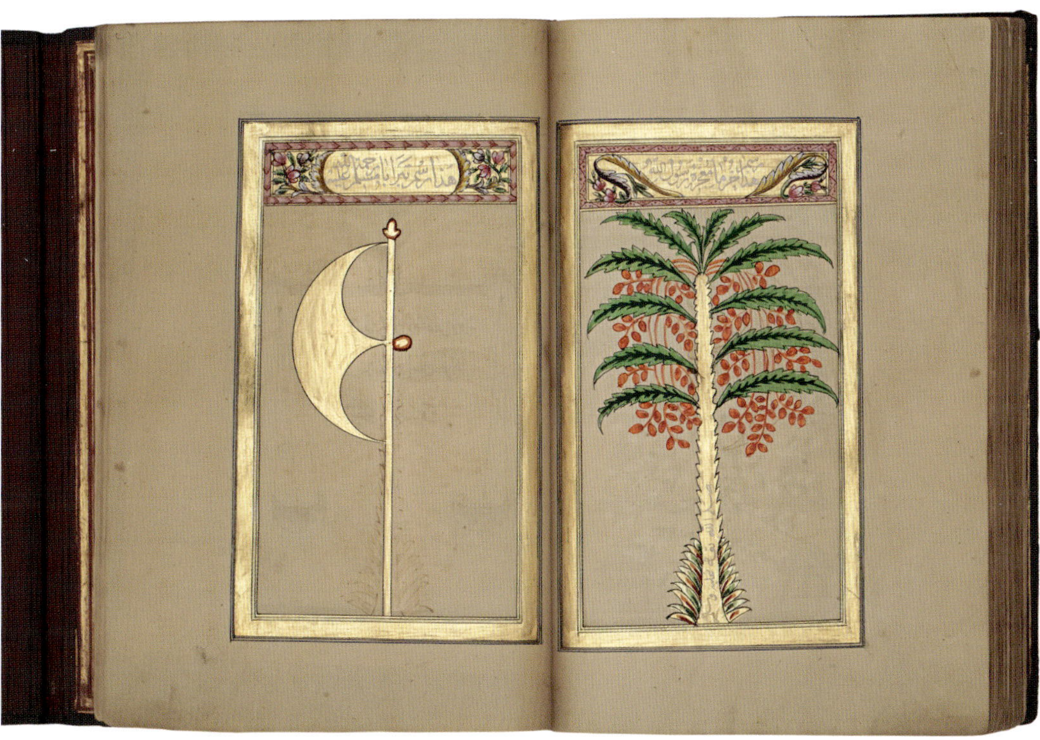

2b

Manuscript of the *Dala'il al-Khayrat* ('Guide to Benevolent Deeds')
Written by Muhammad al-Jazuli
Copied by Mehmed Emin and illuminated by Hafiz Mehmed Nuri
Istanbul, Ottoman period, dated 1216 AH/1801 CE
Ink, opaque watercolour and gold on paper
23.4 × 16.7 cm (closed)
Museum of Islamic Art, MS.427.2007

Dala'il al-Khayrat is a renowned 9th-century AH/15th-century CE Moroccan prayer book, traditionally used during visits to the Prophet's Mosque in Medina. This manuscript was copied in Istanbul by Mehmed Emin, the head clerk of the Imperial Chancery (*divan-i hümayun*), and contains several illuminated pages, including depictions of Mecca and Medina (folios 16v and 17r). The Prophet's Mosque in Medina is shown with the *mihrab*, *minbar*, the three tombs under the green dome and a courtyard featuring a domed structure among palm trees.[2]

The sacred symbols in these manuscripts are central to Ottoman devotional art, with the palm tree holding particular significance. Associated with the Prophet and his family, it is linked to the garden planted in Medina by his daughter Fatima. The 'blessed palm tree' (*khorme sherif*) symbolises the Prophet's miracles and the paradisiacal realm, serving as a bridge between the earthly and divine. It is often depicted alongside the Tuba tree, which may reference the *sidrat al-muntaha* mentioned in the Qur'an (Q53:16–19). The Qur'an frequently describes trees in the gardens of paradise, symbolising eternal abundance (Q69:23 and 76:14). MCA

2 Chekhab Abudaya and Nur Sobers-Khan, 'Acts of Devotion in Late Ottoman Prayer Books: Examination of an Illustrated Manuscript in the Collection of The Museum of Islamic Art, Doha', *Muqarnas* 41 (in press).

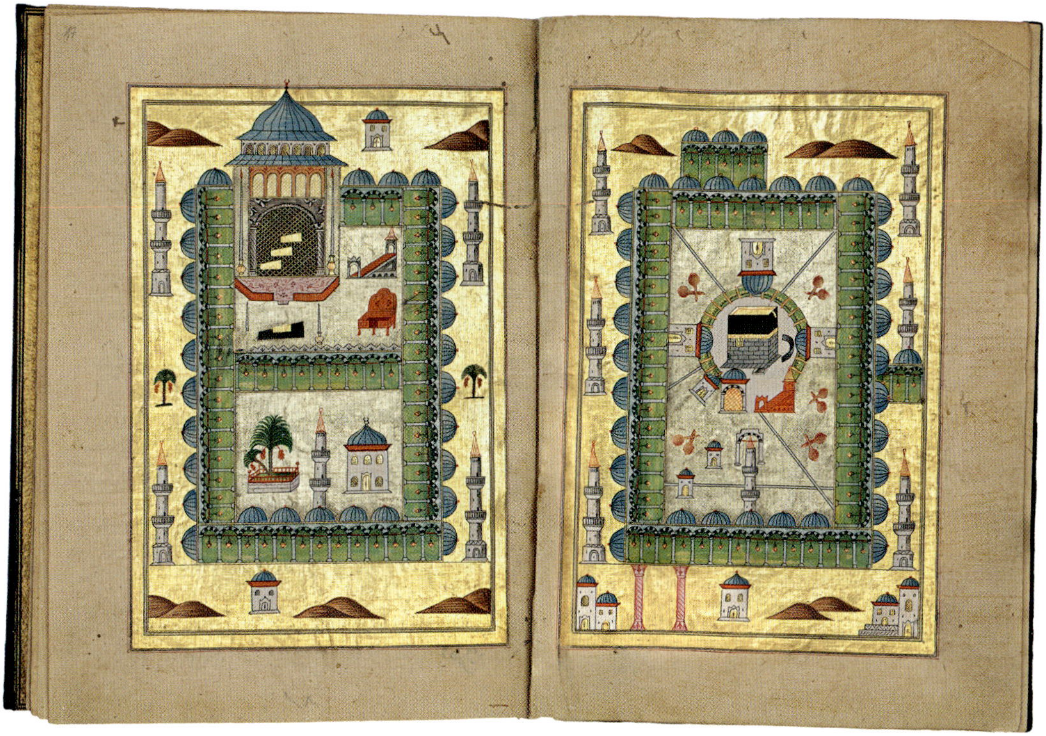

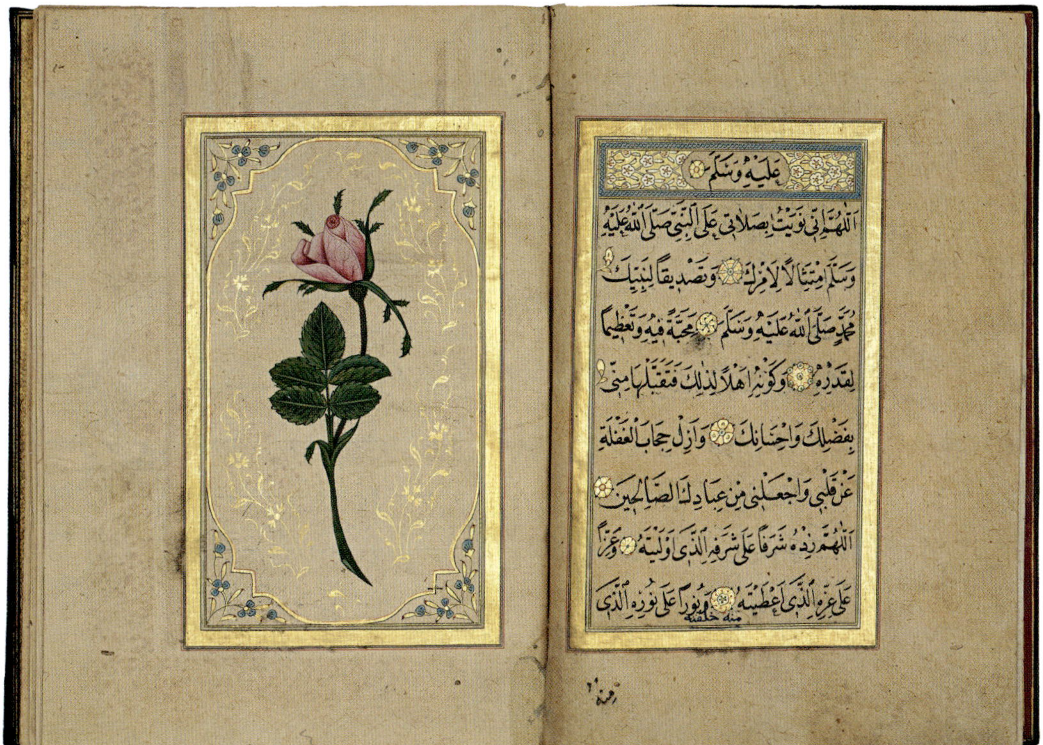

عليه وسلم

اللهم اني نويت بصلاتي على النبي صلى الله عليه
وسلم امتثالا لامرك وتصديقا لنبيك
محمد صلى الله عليه وسلم ومحبة فيه وتعظيما
لقدره وكونه اهلا لذلك فتقبلها مني
بفضلك واحسانك وازل حجاب الغفلة
عن قلبي واجعلني من عبادك الصالحين
اللهم زده شرفا على شرفه الذي اوليته وعزا
على عزه الذي اعطيته ونورا على نوره الذي
منه خلقته

3
Zebu cow and calf figurine
Syria (Raqqa), Ayyubid period,
7th century AH/13th century CE
Turquoise-glazed fritware
29.5 × 38 × 16.9 cm
Museum of Islamic Art, PO.788.2008

Medieval cookbooks mention milk as an ingredient for drinking, as well as for making butter and yoghurt, while several religious texts speak of it in both a medical and spiritual context. The Qur'an claims it is a beneficence of Allah and 'pleasant to drink' (Q16:66). It is also one of the four types of drink mentioned in the Qur'an, promised to the inhabitants of Paradise as 'rivers of milk unchanging in taste' (Q47:15). Yoghurt was considered an important part of the diet of Arab Muslims from the time of the Prophet Muhammed (PBUH), with flocks of sheep, goats or camels providing milk; however, it was yoghurt made from cow's milk and butter that was believed to be 'medicine' (*dawa*').[1]

This figurine depicts a zebu cow and her calf. The mother is shown standing while her calf suckles. The hanging dewlap, small hump, swept-back horns and large cloven hooves characteristic of the breed are accurately modelled. This breed of cow is indigenous to Syria and would have been seen in the fields of the Euphrates Valley. Animal figurines, especially depicting cows and bulls, were a short-lived phenomenon of the late 6th to 7th centuries AH/12th to 13th centuries CE in both Syria and Iran. In Iran, most functioned as vessels, with a filler spout in the back and an open mouth through which to pour liquid in the front. In Syria, however, the trend was for figurines with a purely decorative function. The fact that the basic form of the cow would have been moulded suggests that a cast was used to create multiple versions of the same figure. Other examples of contemporaneous figurines, such as a water buffalo being milked, are typically decorated with a turquoise-green glaze. This colour is commonly associated with Raqqa, Syria, a city with a long tradition of manufacturing ceramics and glass.[2] TD

1 Ibn Razīn Al-Tujībī, *The Exile's Cookbook*, ed. and trans. Daniel Newman, p. 38.

2 See the example in the Department of Islamic Art, Musée du Louvre, Paris (MAO 2031), which was excavated in Raqqa.

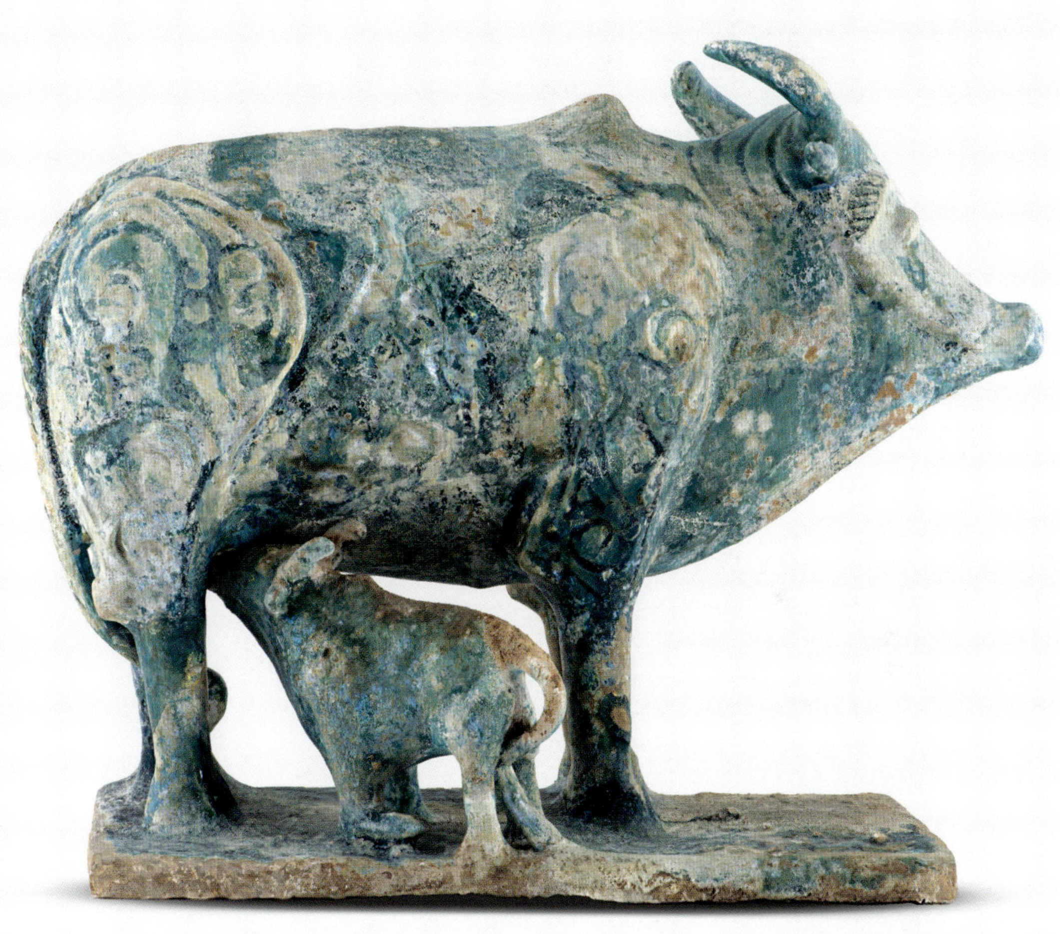

4
Bowl
Iraq (probably Basra), Abbasid period,
3rd century AH/9th century CE
Earthenware, with opaque white and cobalt blue glazes
ø 20.1 cm
Museum of Islamic Art, PO.566.2007

Ceramics such as this bowl were likely intended for serving food. Produced in a variety of sizes and shapes, and with many different decorative patterns, these dishes were either made for export or for use as tableware by the ruling Abbasid elite. The Abbasids, who governed primarily from Baghdad and Samarra between 132 AH/750 CE and 656 AH/1258 CE, were renowned for their sophisticated culinary culture. Their caliphal seats acted not only as the political, economic and intellectual capitals but also evolved into culinary hubs. The Abbasid caliphs brought in expert chefs from across their caliphate and perfected the art of cooking. The introduction of new crops and spices further fuelled their bustling markets, leading to the opening of new and vibrant shops and restaurants, which transformed these cities into what we would call today 'Foodie Hotspots'. This luxury was evident in their extravagant festivities and events, where food and drink served in high quality ceramic dishes were essential elements.[1]

Made of yellowish buff earthenware, covered with an opaque white tin glaze and painted with cobalt pigments, this bowl features a stylised palm tree design. It was most likely produced in Old Basra (near Zubayr, southwest of modern-day Basra), reflecting the Iraqi potters' response to the expensive porcelain imported from China during the Tang and Song dynasties (618–907 CE and 960–1279 CE). Among these Chinese ceramics were exquisite tea sets, including ewers, small boxes and bowls, which were particularly esteemed imports. The Abbasids held these vessels in such high regard that they applied the term *sini* ('Chinese') to describe the Chinese products as well as any other items from this period considered to be of the finest quality.[2]

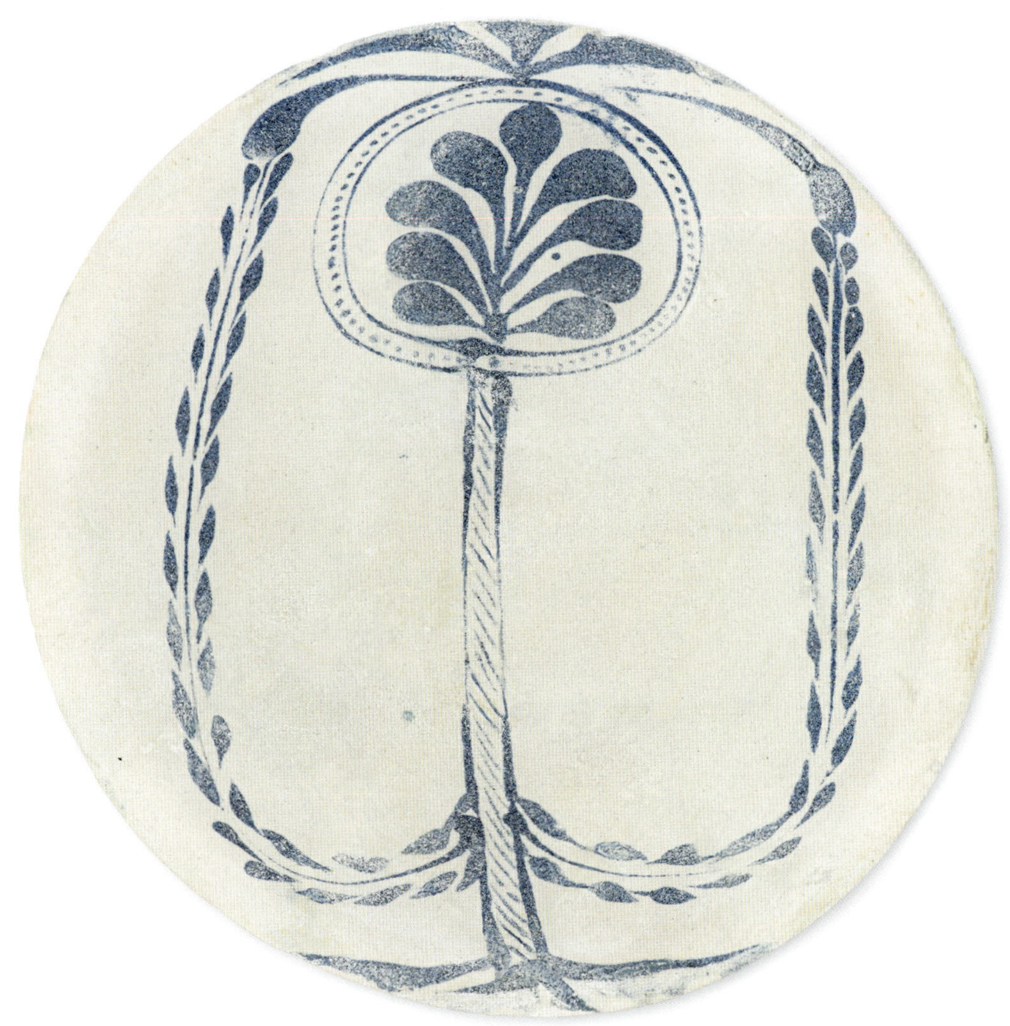

1 See Jessica Hallett, 'Abbasid Tableware and Changing Food Culture', in Komaroff, ed., *Dining with the Sultan*, p. 41.

2 See Ahsan, *Social Life Under the Abbasids*, p. 122.

3 See Jessica Hallett, 'Basra as a Center of Mobility and Innovation in Ceramics in the Abbasid Period', in Dalal et al., eds, *The Seas and the Mobility of Islamic Art*, p. 137.

4 Comparable bowls featuring a stylised palm tree design are at the Museé du Louvre in Paris (MAO 359) and the Museum für Islamische Kunst – Staatliche Museen zu Berlin (I. 74/62 and I.5311).

During the mid-2nd and 3rd centuries AH/mid-8th and 9th centuries CE, *sini* ceramics were exported in significant quantities across the Indian Ocean to Western Asia, South and Southeast Asia and as far as the east coast of Africa. In exchange for goods from China, Iraq primarily traded agricultural products such as date molasses, a rich, syrup-like, natural sweetener made from pressed dates, known as *dibs*. This ingredient was highly praised in Chinese pharmacopoeia for its healing properties.[3] Given that dates and date products were among Iraq's main exports, this may explain the stylised date palm depicted on the bowl.[4] SST

5
Jar
Syria, Mamluk period,
8th century AH/14th century CE
Underglaze painted fritware
34.9 × Ø 27.8 cm
Museum of Islamic Art, PO.738.2007

Of a broad, baluster form painted with blue and black underglaze on a white fritware body, this jar is typical of 8th century AH/ 14th century CE Syrian ceramic production. While some similarly shaped jars feature legible Arabic inscriptions in bold *thuluth* script, generally offering glory, prosperity and good fortune to the owner, the calligraphy on this example cannot be deciphered. Its fine pseudo-script is arranged into vertical panels alternating with blue stylised leaves and black floral scrolls. Glazed earthenware jars such as this were used as storage containers. Most were not made with lids but had thick, everted rims that allowed for a protective cover, probably of paper, parchment or cloth, to be more easily secured with string or, if travelling great distances, wax.

Arabic cookbooks provide a considerable amount of information on how to store condiments such as citrus fruits, grapes and various vinegars, the latter a staple in both the Eastern and Western Mediterranean, where it was commonly eaten as a dip with bread.[1] A 9th century AH/15th century CE Egyptian cookbook written by Ibn Mubarak Shah, for instance, lists no fewer than 16 different vinegars, including those made with lime, lemon and sour grapes. He mentions that a 'large earthenware vessel or cask, which tapers into a rounded bottom' and a 'wide-mouthed clay jar' were used for storing grapes and pickles, respectively.[2]

As out-of-season fruits were commonly preserved in storage jars, often with strong, corrosive vinegars, it was imperative that these ceramics were properly glazed to protect and preserve the vessels from their contents. Thus, market inspectors in medieval Cairo enforced strict rules about the thickness of the glaze on pottery offered for sale.[3] These vessels were most certainly made in abundance as they reflect both the type and popularity of preserved foods in medieval Egypt and Syria. TD

1 Ibn Razīn Al-Tujībī, *The Exile's Cookbook*, ed. and trans. Daniel Newman, p. 57.

2 Ibn Mubārak Shāh, *The Sultan's Feast*, ed. and trans. Daniel Newman, Recipe 205, p. 89 and Recipe 232, p. 99.

3 Nasrallah, *Treasure Trove of Benefits*, p. 594.

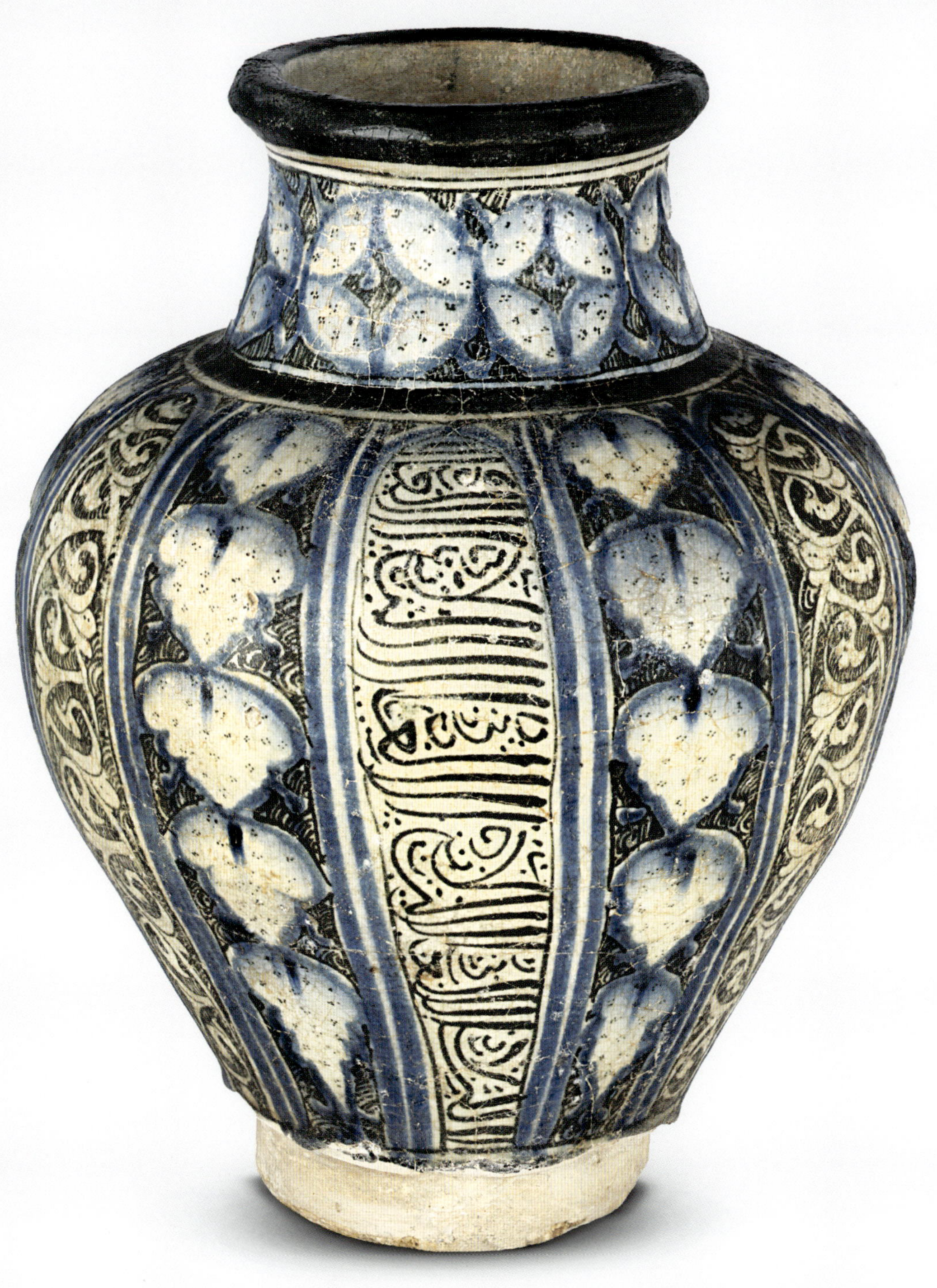

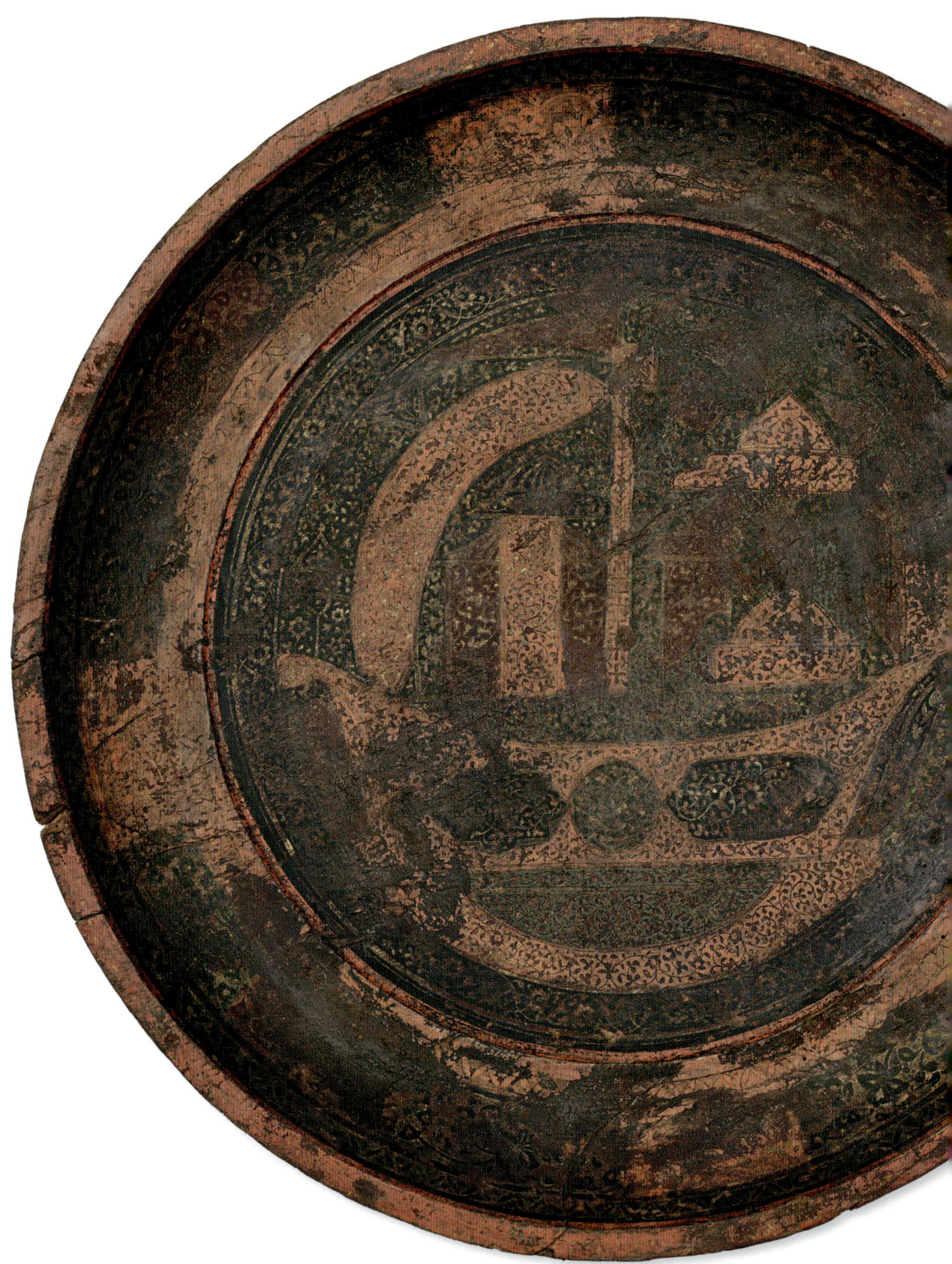

6
Tray with ship ('junk')
India (Surat or Cambay), Mughal period,
10th–11th century AH/late 16th–early 17th century CE
Lacquered and gilded turned wood
ø 75 cm
Museum of Islamic Art, WW.110.2007

Lacquered wooden objects from the early medieval Islamic period are generally attributed to Iran or Afghanistan.[1] This tray, however, finds closer parallels with 10th–11th century AH/16th–17th century CE lacquer and mother-of-pearl caskets, cabinets and dishes made in Gujarat—a region on the western coast of India known for its fine woodworking. The Mughal emperor Akbar conquered Gujarat in 979 AH/1572 CE, gaining direct access to the Red Sea and the wealth of imports (and ingredients) arriving into the ports of Surat and Cambay in exchange for spices and silks.

This impressively large, lacquered tray was once gilded, suggesting it was only used as a commemorative dish to serve or present items. It depicts a ship carrying one mainsail. Known in Mughal sources as a 'junk', these ships could swiftly harness the favourable monsoon winds needed to travel by sea. Emperor Akbar's 10th century AH/16th century CE court history, the *Akbarnama* (Book of Akbar), mentions a 'caravan of junk-voyagers' (*qafila-yi jank*) when speaking of a group of family members voyaging from Gujarat to Mecca on *hajj*.[2] In 983 AH/1576 CE, Akbar's aunt, Gulbadan Begum, and other women of the imperial family made their first perilous pilgrimage to Mecca on a single-mast ship similar to the one illustrated on this tray. The two-tiered, domed structures seen on the tray represent curtained quarters where women would have been concealed, as seen in the late 16th century painting depicting a voyage from Delhi to Agra by river.[3] On this tray, the orange panels hanging vertically on the front of the structure likely depict the type of velvet curtains seen in the painting. TD

1 See, for example, a small box in the David Collection, Copenhagen (49/1998), as well as the article by Folsach, 'A Number of Pigmented Wooden Objects', particularly figs 22 and 23, pp. 88–89.

2 See Anjum, 'Ship Construction in Mughal India', p. 298.

3 See the painting currently in the Victoria & Albert Museum, London (IS.2:4-1896).

7
Albarello with portrait of Ibn Sina
Italy (Palermo), 10th century AH/16th century CE
Tin-glazed earthenware (*maiolica*)
30.5 × Ø 14.2 cm
Museum of Islamic Art, PO.1086.2011

In the medieval Islamic world, food and medicine were deeply interconnected. Ingredients such as ginger and milk, for example, were consumed for both their nutritional and medicinal properties. This reflects the broader belief, which is also mainstream today, that food and medicine are inseparable—what nourishes the body can also heal it.

This holistic approach to health and wellbeing shaped the tools and vessels associated with medical practices. Among these is the albarello (plural: albarelli), a waisted cylindrical earthenware jar used to store medicinal substances such as ointments and herbs. Originating in 5th century AH/11th century CE Syria, these jars were used in apothecaries. The form later spread to Italy and Spain, where albarelli were manufactured in large quantities in several renowned ceramic centres.[1] This particular albarello was made in Palermo, Sicily, and is adorned with an intricate design painted in underglaze cobalt blue, yellow, green, brown and black. It bears a Latin inscription, *Sy de isapo* ('syrup of hyssopus'), indicating its contents: hyssopus, a plant traditionally used as an antiseptic or to treat coughs. At its centre is a portrait of a bearded, turbaned figure identified as the renowned Arab physician Ibn Sina. Known in Europe by his Latinised name, Avicenna, Ibn Sina was a 5th century AH/11th century CE philosopher, physician and polymath from Bukhara (in present-day Uzbekistan). He is regarded as the father of modern medicine and is most famous for his medical encyclopaedia, *The Canon of Medicine*. This influential work, later translated into Latin, remained a foundational text in European universities until the 11th century AH/17th century CE. The depiction of Ibn Sina on this albarello is particularly significant, not only paying tribute to his lasting influence on medicine in Italy and Europe at large, but also emphasising the medicinal function of the jar itself. This example, with its distinct decorative style known in Italian as *quartieri* (segmented decoration), exemplifies one of the earliest known ceramics produced in Sicily under the stylistic influence of Faenza,[2] a town renowned for its durable, smooth semi-matte tin-glazes. TS

1 Zidan, 'Cross-Cultural Exchange Between the Islamic World and Europe', p. 9.

2 Comparable examples are held at The Metropolitan Museum of Art, New York (02.5.21), the Science Museum Group, UK (A240205), and the British Museum, London (1885,0508.25).

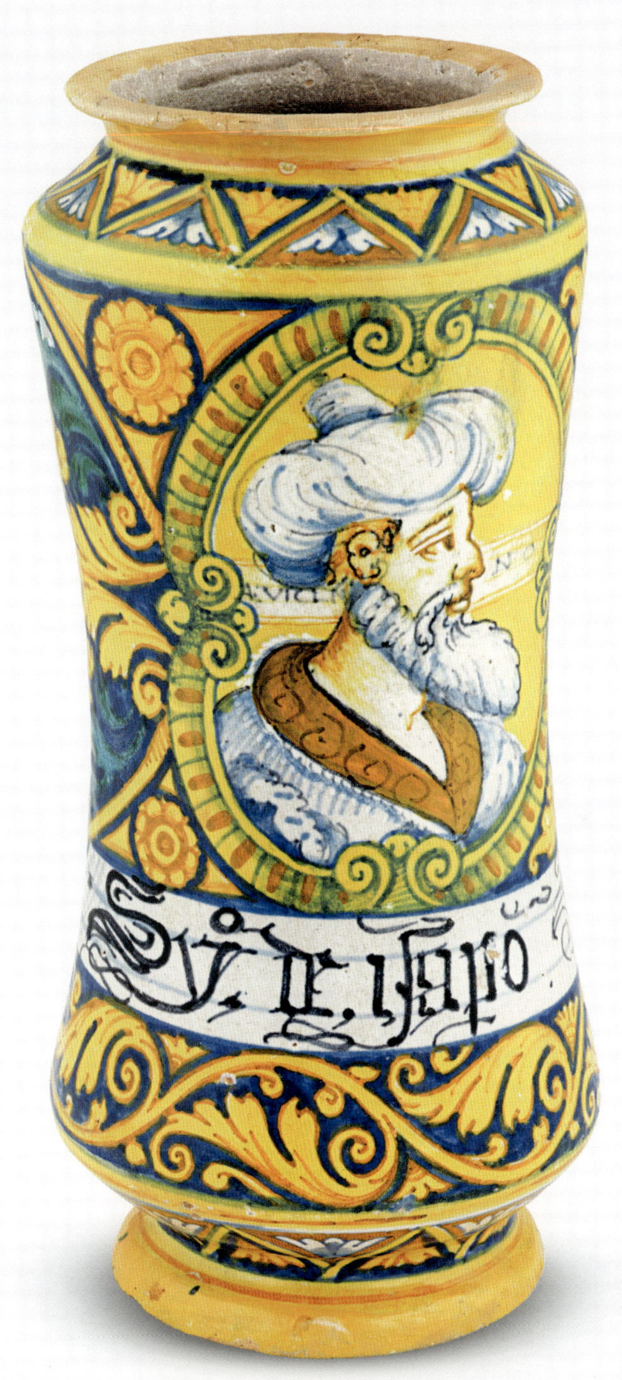Sÿ. d. fapo

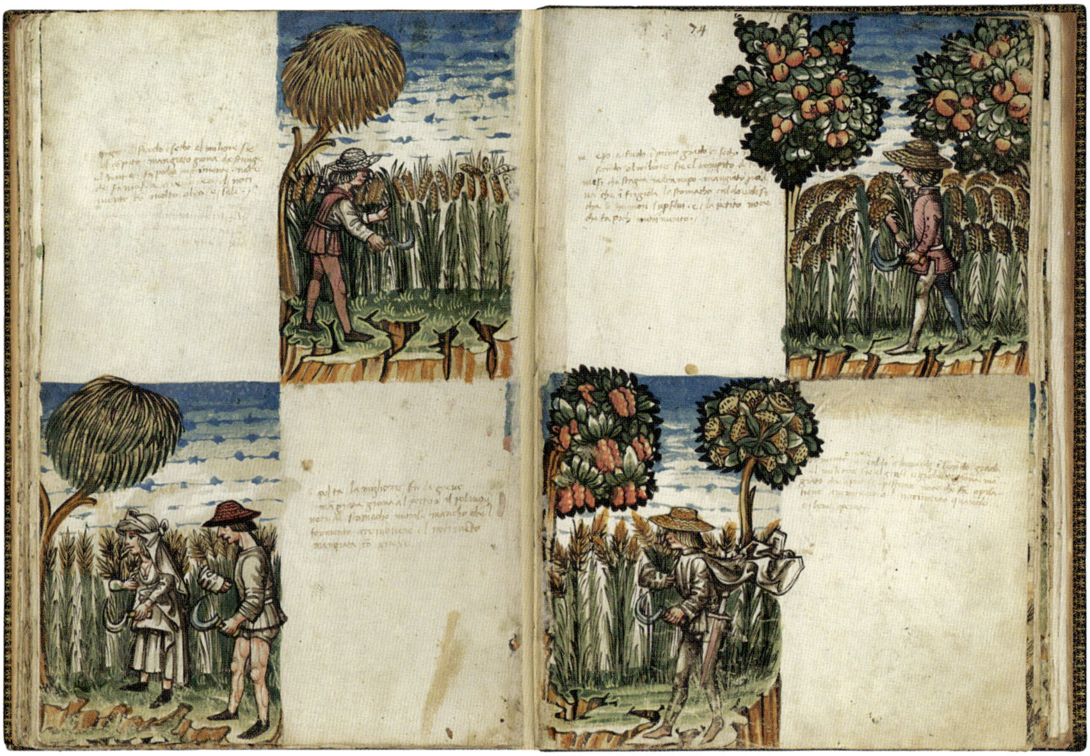

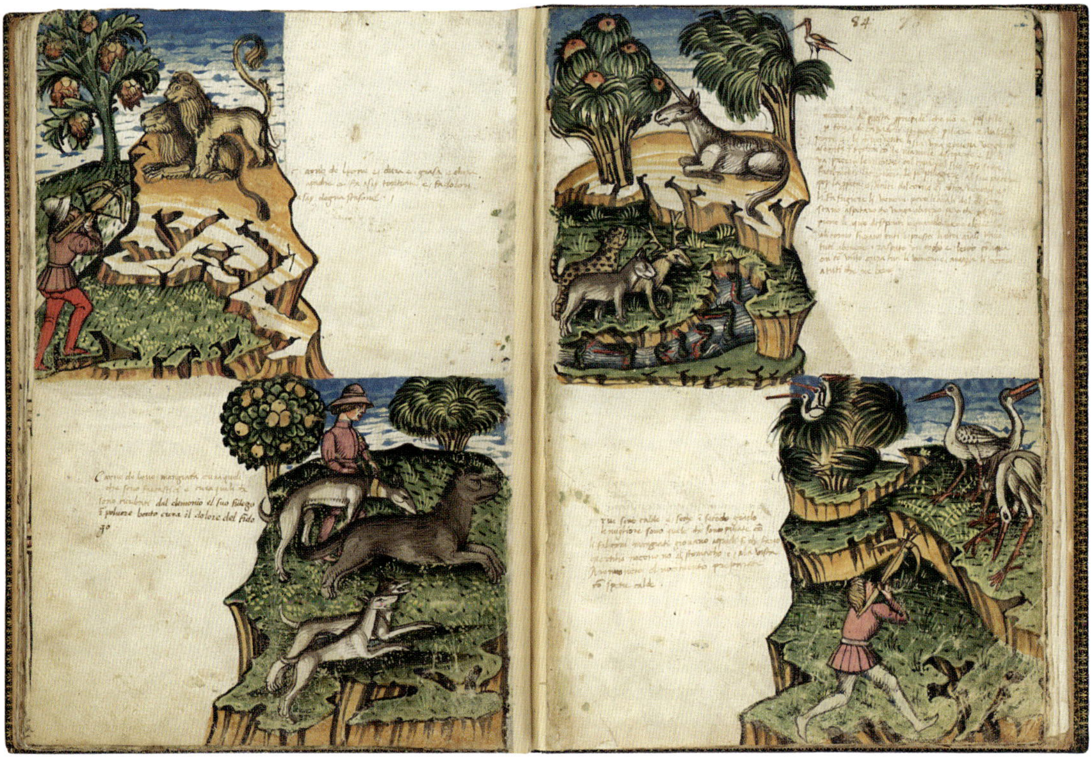

8
Tacuinum Sanitatis ('Almanac of Health')
Italy, Sicily, *c.* 1475 CE
Ink and opaque watercolour on paper
39.3 × 28.1 cm (closed)
Museum of Islamic Art Library, Qatar Museums, Doha,
RS79.L64.14[75]

These double-page spreads are from a late 9th century AH/ 15th century CE Italian manuscript of the *Tacuinum Sanitatis*. The text of *Tacuinum Sanitatis* derives from the 5th century AH/11th century CE medical treatise *Taqwim aṣ-Ṣiḥḥa* (Almanac of Health) by the Arab-Christian physician and philosopher Ibn Butlan of Baghdad (d. 455 AH/1063 CE), underscoring the cross-cultural exchanges that influenced dietary practices across medieval Europe and the Islamic world. Its contents serve as a guide to healthy living, integrating dietary recommendations, seasonal advice and agricultural practices based on humoural theory.[1] The images depict seasonal agricultural activities critical to medieval food systems and their perceived role in maintaining health. On the upper left folio, workers harvest grain and tend to orchards, while on the upper right, fruits and vegetables are being collected. The bottom double page shows various hunting scenes. These illustrations emphasise the importance of fresh, seasonal produce in sustaining the balance of the four humours, a key tenet of medieval medicine. The visual pairing of agricultural labour with handwritten annotations underscores the manuscript's function as both a practical guide and a didactic text. The accompanying text elaborates on the health benefits of the depicted produce and the alignment of agricultural practices with seasonal rhythms. The manuscript highlights the need for balance, both in diet and agricultural labour, and the belief that natural produce, when consumed in its proper season, could prevent illness and maintain bodily harmony. TS

1 For more on this see Mendelsohn,
'The *Tacuinum Sanitatis*: A Medieval Health
Manual', p. 70.

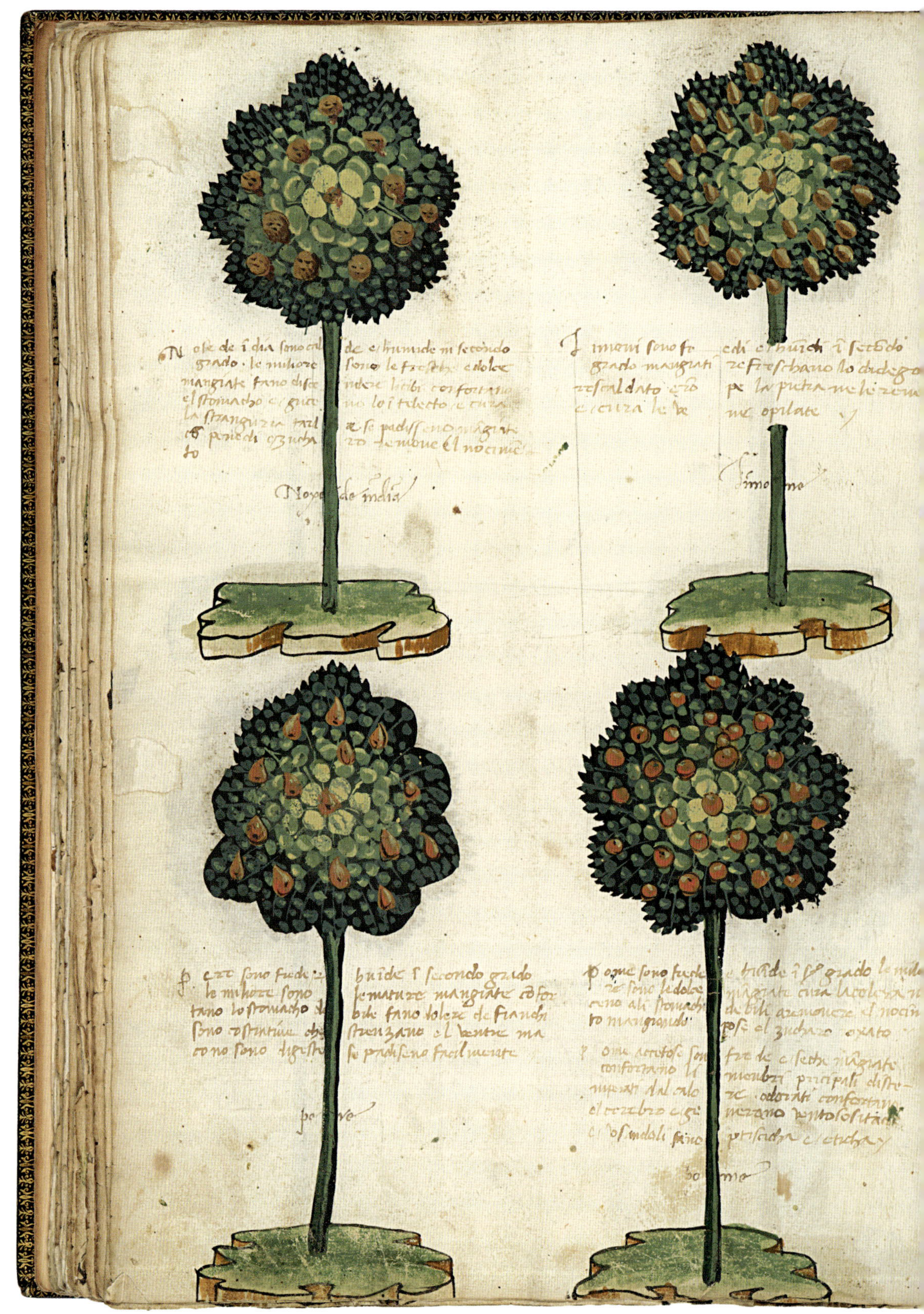
Noce de india
Limonzelo
pero
pomo

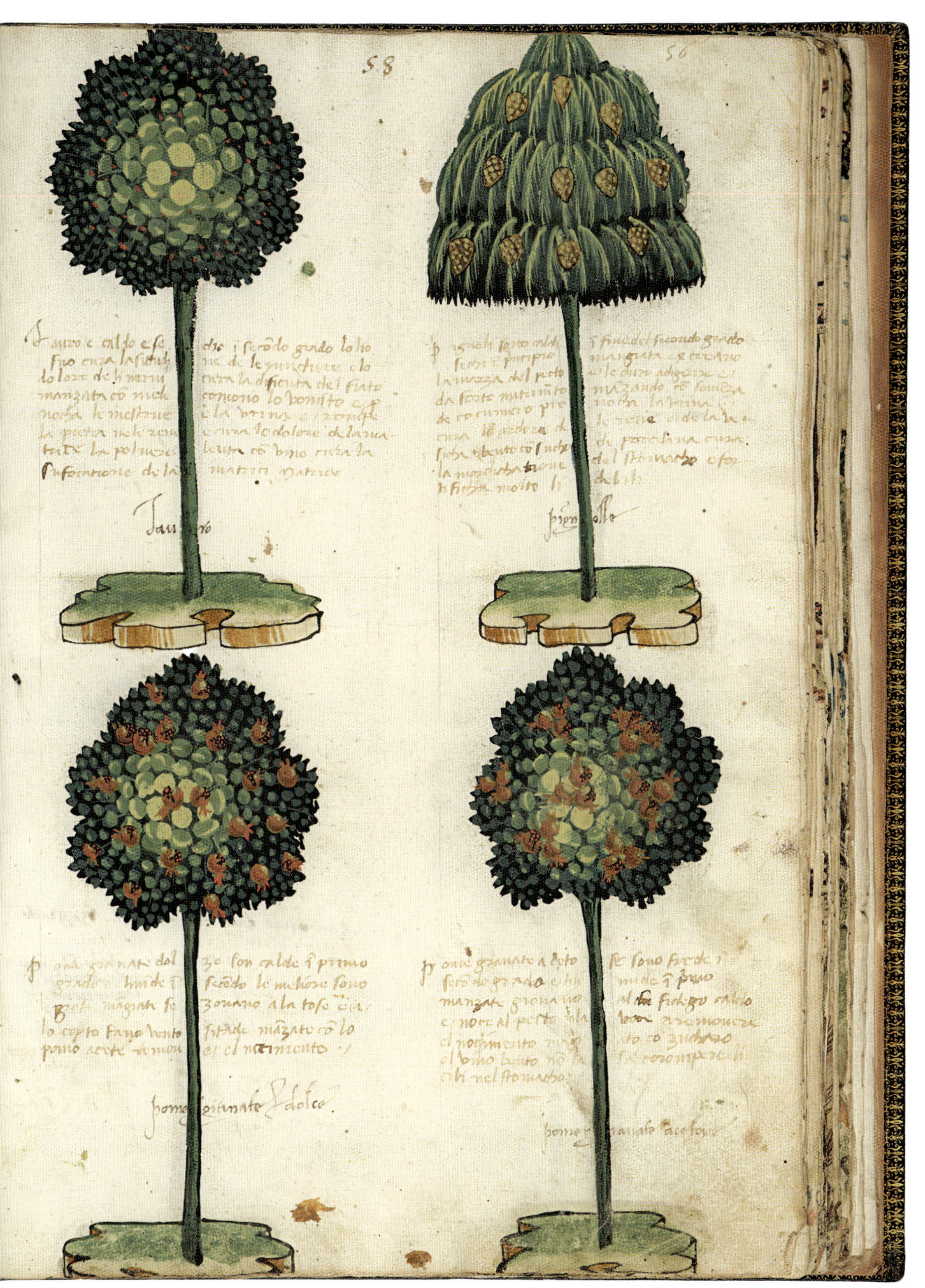
58
56
Tamarro
pignotto
pome granate dolce
pome granato acetose

Mortar (*havan*)
Western Iran, late Seljuk or early Ilkhanid period,
late 6th–early 7th century AH/12th–early 13th century CE
Cast copper, tin, zinc and lead alloy
14.9 cm × ø 20.2 cm
Museum of Islamic Art, MIA.2014.74

Mortars exist in varying sizes, some more suited to being held while others, such as this larger and heavier example, are designed to be used on a flat surface. This bronze mortar (*havan*) is octagonal in shape (its edges considerably worn), concealing a cylindrical container with an everted rim and slanting base. Loops moulded with bull's heads appear on either side, fitted with ring-handles to facilitate the transport of this heavy vessel. The mortar's body is divided into three horizontal registers incised with a combination of running animals, calligraphic inscriptions, and foliate scrolls. The upper band features the same decorative programme, yet the calligraphy is written in *naskh* script, with the word *al-'izz* (glory) faintly visible. The middle panel features a series of single or triple prunts in high relief, framed by polylobed arches, which were no doubt designed to help hold the vessel more securely in place when grinding with a pestle. A band of eight panels of *kufic* calligraphy alternating with foliate roundels runs around the top rim, forming a continuous blessing to an unknown patron. The combination of both scripts (*kufic* and *naskh*) appears less frequently and suggests that this mortar is a transitional one between the late Seljuk and Ilkhanid periods. The lower band is engraved with running animals (a dog or feline) chasing its prey, a motif commonly seen across metalwork and lustre-painted ceramics from the period.

Mortars were an essential utensil used for grinding substances such as spices and herbs (for food and curatives alike) and appear in medieval illustrated manuscripts. In the folio 'Physician Preparing an Elixir' a seated figure—the physician, pharmacist, or perhaps his assistant—is working a large pestle and mortar to prepare a therapeutic syrup.[1] Historically, most mortars were made of wood or stone (these are no longer extant),

1 This folio is in The Metropolitan Museum of Art, New York (13.152.6).

2 Ibn Razīn Al-Tujībī, *The Exile's Cookbook*, ed. and trans. Daniel Newman, p. 69.

but a great number of cast-metal examples from medieval Spain and Iran survive.[2] Later, mortars were also made in porcelain and marble. The worn nature of this example, which would have been accompanied by a pestle of similar decoration, suggests its excessive use by a cook, alchemist or pharmacist. TD

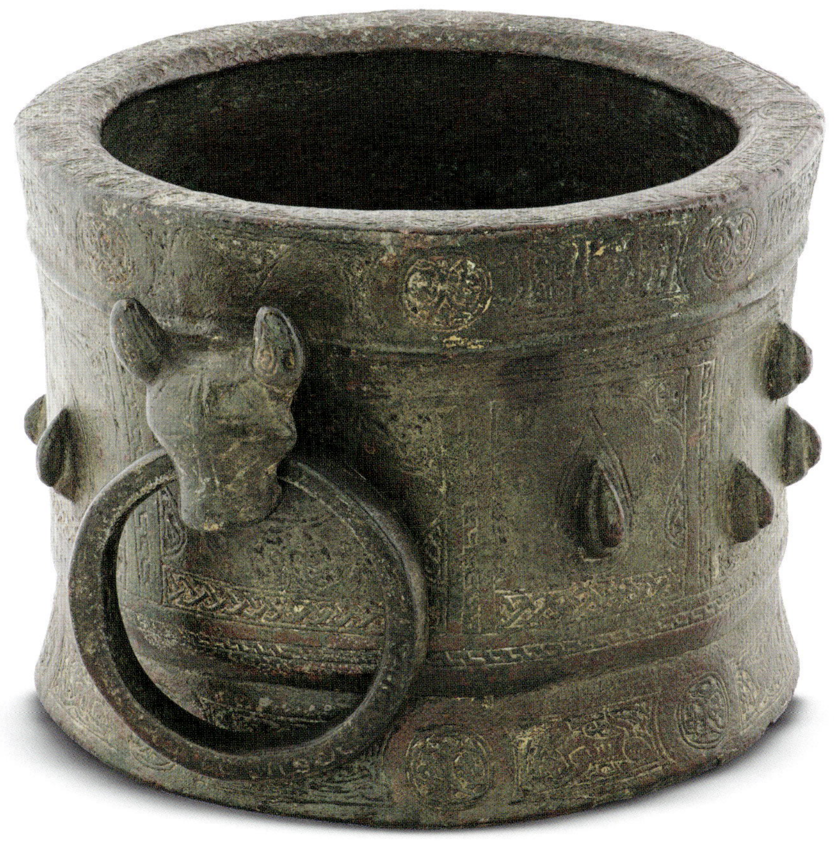

10
Brazier
Iran or Central Asia, Mongol or Ilkhanid period,
7th–8th century AH/13th–14th century CE
Hammered and chiselled cast iron with velvet
25.2 × 53.2 cm
Museum of Islamic Art, MIA.2014.81

Braziers have been used for heating and cooking while travelling since ancient times; in Arabic these vessels are referred to as *manqal*, meaning portable. They often take the form of a metal box or bowl with feet that help circulate air below the box and feed the fire with oxygen. When used for cooking, an open metal grill could be placed inside the brazier, balancing on small metal slabs protruding from each side. Alternatively, skewers could be balanced along the edges or inside the hooks and openwork decoration, allowing the spits to be easily turned while keeping the food a reasonable distance from the coals.

This cast-bronze brazier is octagonal in shape with openwork panels secured behind by thin metal sheets. Each panel is decorated with a lion and dragon in combat flanked by palmettes. The upper edge of the brazier features 14 foliate finials terminating in incised heads, and the bottom is supported on eight triangular feet. Two handles on the sides allow the brazier to be easily carried. It would have originally had a metal sheet fixed across its interior, with a concave centre to hold coals and keep heat concentrated in the middle. Braziers attributed to 9th century AH/15th century CE India and Iran include this feature.[1]

Polygonal braziers with openwork sides, finials, and short legs date to the Seljuk period (432–552 AH/1040–1157 CE).[2] This example is attributed to Ilkhanid Iran (653–651 AH/1256–1353 CE) based on the openwork technique, crenelation around the upper and lower borders, and the dragons in combat motif which arrived into Central Asia and Iran with the Mongols in the 7th century AH/13th century CE. Rather curiously, this example retains fragments of red velvet between the openwork and metal sheets, a feature not typically found in an object used for heating or cooking. Nonetheless, the inclusion of this costly material suggests that this brazier was made for a wealthy or high-status patron. TD

1 See, for example, Sotheby's London, Arts of the Islamic World & India Including Fine Rugs and Carpets, 30 March 2022, lot 105, and The Metropolitan Museum of Art, New York (1988.293).

2 See Pope and Ackermann, *A Survey of Persian Art*, vol. 6, fig. 1379B; and Folsach, *Art from the World of Islam*, p. 313, no. 500.

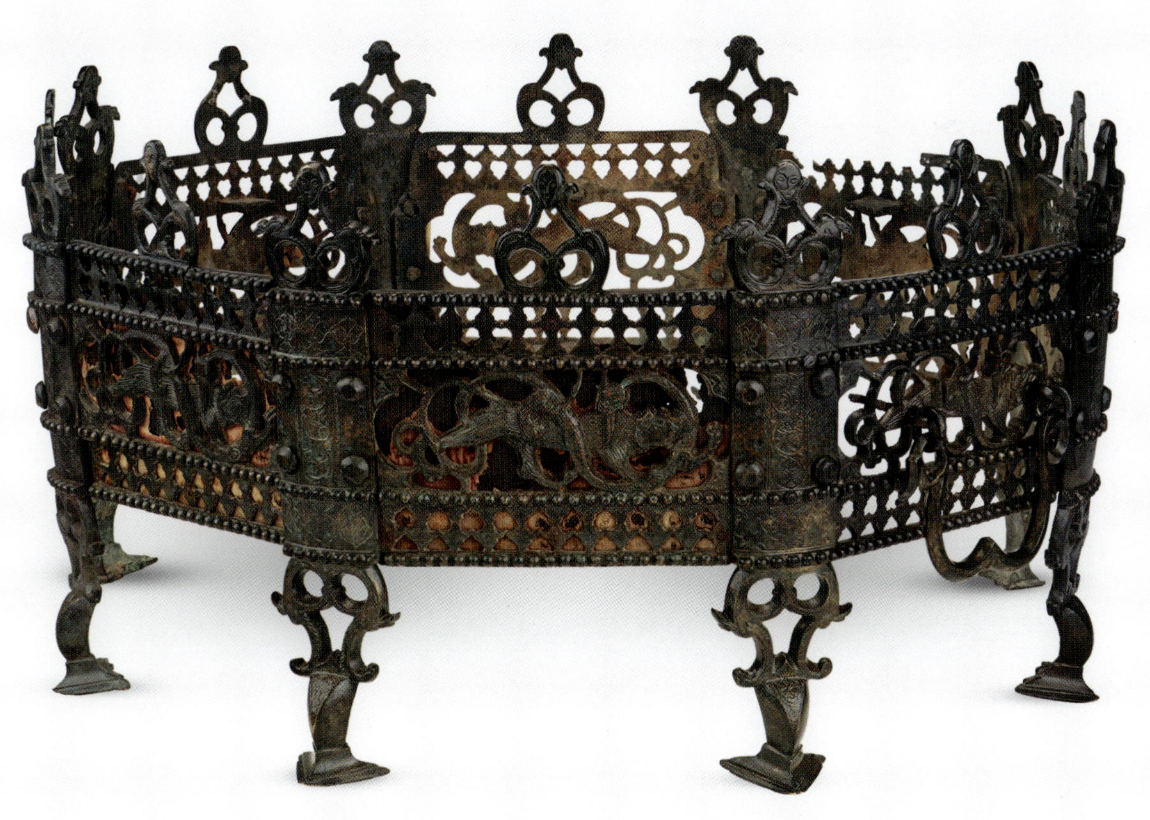

11

Lunchbox
Egypt or Yemen, Mamluk period,
9th century AH/15th century CE
Hammered brass inlaid with silver
17.8 × 28 × 27.6 cm
MW.157.2000

This brass box, inlaid with silver, was used as a portable food container. Receptacles of this shape have generally been referred to as 'lunchboxes'.[1] Those attributed to the Mamluk period (647–923 AH/1250–1517 CE, with interruptions) seem to have existed in several forms, including a type comprising vertically-stacked containers attached by slender metal shafts similar to the *tiffin*, still used across the Indian subcontinent today. Other examples of similarly shaped lunchboxes attributed to Syria in the late 9th century AH/late 15th century CE also exist. These typically have removable lids which, rather cleverly, could have been used as plates.[2] This example is oval in shape and has a coffered lid that is secured to the body by a central clasp terminating in a teardrop finial. On the body is a band bearing an Arabic inscription written in bold *thuluth* script interrupted by four, eight-petalled swirling rosettes. Like many other Mamluk-period metal objects, it offers benedictory blessings to an unnamed ruler. A patron and place of production are suggested, however, by the similarity of the inscription to that on a lunchbox in the Museum of Islamic Art, Cairo. That box states that it was made in Sana'a, Yemen for an *imam* who was the commander of Sharaf al-din b. Shams al-din (877–962 AH/ 1473–1555 CE).[3] Like many rulers, the Mamluk sultans served extravagant quantities of food at formal banquets, as quantity was an indicator of status and wealth. During the feast to celebrate the marriage of the daughter of Sultan al-Nasir Muhammed (r. 683–742 AH/1285–1341 CE), for example, 5000 sheep, 1000 cows, 50 horses, and a great number of fowl and geese were served together with sweets and beverages made from 11,000 cones of sugar.[4] For such an occasion, containers of similar shape and size were used to store and transport the abundance of prepared foods. Sources also speak of a Mamluk vizier who, every night, sent an official to the main street of Cairo to buy small fried birds, such as chickens, pigeons and sparrows, which were transported back to the vizier in a container such as this, the equivalent of today's 'takeaway box'.[5] TD

Inscription:
عمل برسم الجناب العالى، المولوى، الامامى، الثاغرى، المجاهدى، مولانا عز الدنيا والدين، بن مولانا امير المومنين، شرف الدين نصرة الله

'Made at the order of his high excellency, the lord, the Imam, the guardian of the frontier, the warrior of the holy wars, our master, glory of the world and religion, son of our master, commander of the faithful, the dignity of religion, who may Allah help him.'

1 Allan, 'Later Mamluk Metalwork-II: A Series of Lunch-Boxes', pp. 156–164.

2 See Komaroff, ed., *Dining with the Sultan*, cats. 94a and 94b, p. 279.

3 See Wiet, *Catalogue Genéral du Musée Arabe du Caire*, no. 3259, pl. 64.

4 Levanoni, 'Food and Cooking during the Mamluk Era', p. 216.

5 Lewicka, *Food and Foodways of Medieval Cairenes*, p. 126.

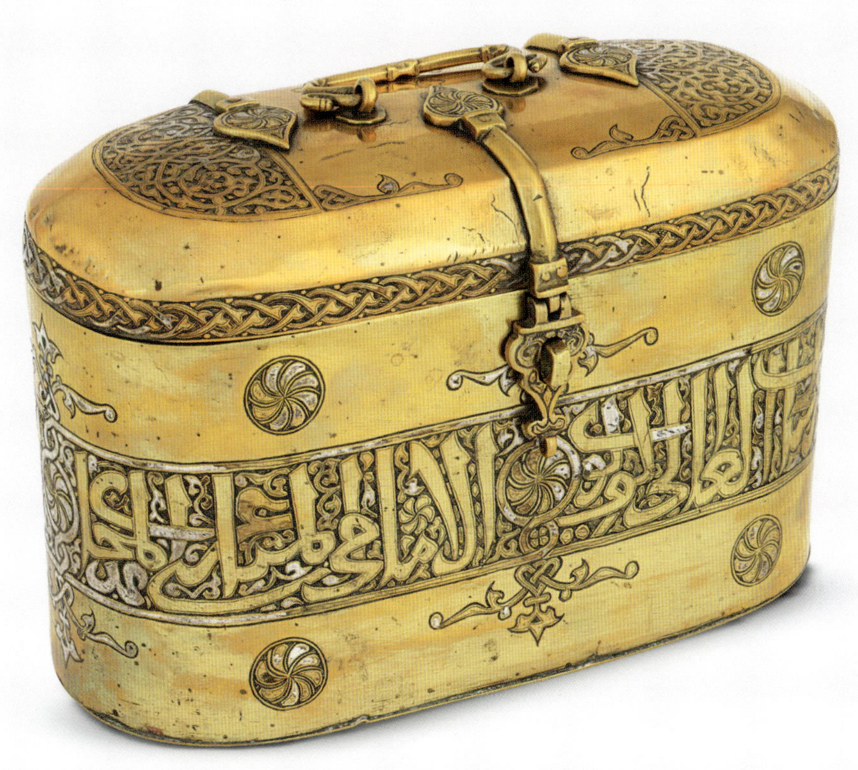

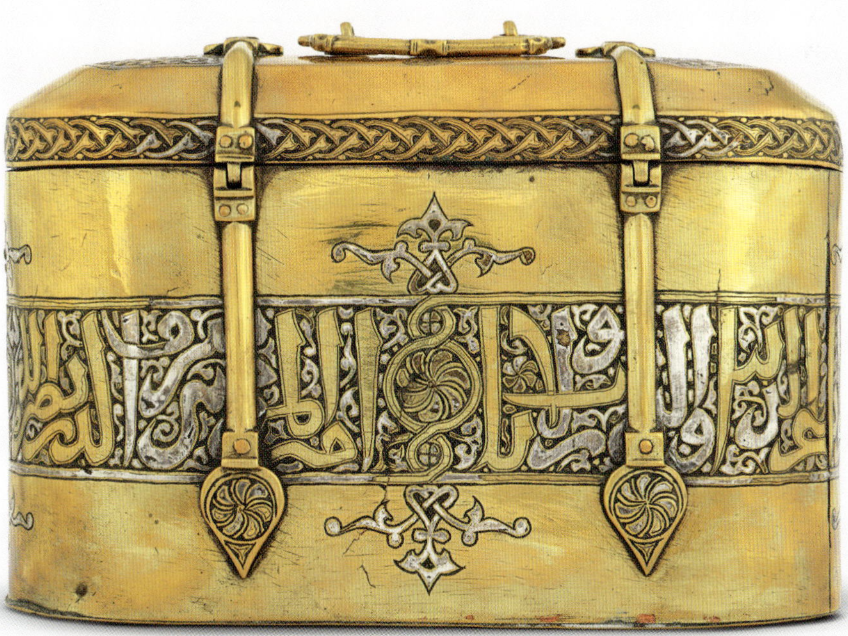

12
Spoon
Possibly Iran or Iraq, Saminid or Abbasid period,
3rd–4th century AH/9th–10th century CE
Blown glass with wheel-cut decoration
3.8 × 20.3 × 4.6 cm
Museum of Islamic Art, GL.527.2011

Spoons from the early Islamic period, whether made of metal, wood or glass, are extremely rare and seldom survived. This glass spoon, likely produced in Iran or Iraq during the 3rd or 4th century AH/9th or 10th century CE, stands as an exceptional example. It is made of greenish-blue glass, with high-relief discs and almond-shaped bosses on the back. The design resembles the omphalos motifs seen on glass vessels unearthed at sites dated to the 3rd or 4th century AH/9th and 10th century CE such as Samarra, Iraq and Nishapur, Iran. The back of the handle features an elegantly curled finial shaped like a stylised ram's head.

Glass spoons of translucent blue-green colour and with wheel-cut decoration are known from Roman times (1st to 3rd century CE), particularly in the Mediterranean region. They remained in use through the early Islamic period, and like their Roman prototypes, the spoons from this era often featured finials of human or animal heads.

Spoons like this one may have been used to serve sugar, originally a product of India, as well as white honey from Isfahan. Both sweeteners were in high demand during the Abbasid caliphate.[1] According to Hadiths, honey was gifted to the Prophet Muhammad (PBUH), and was shared one spoonful at a time.[2]

At the Abbasid court, spoons may also have been used to serve desserts like *khabis*, a pudding made with starch and nuts, carrots or fruits such as dates and apples. This dish is mentioned in the 4th century AH/10th century CE Baghdadi cookbook *Kitab al-Tabikh wa Iṣlaḥ al-aghdhiyat al-maʾkuulat* by Ibn Sayyar al-Warraq (d. early 4th century AH/ 10th century CE), and remains a popular traditional dessert in the Gulf region today.[3] SST

1 See Ahsan, *Social Life Under the Abbasids*, pp. 100–101.

2 See Sunan Ibn Mājah, No. 3451, Book 31, Hadith 16.

3 See Nasrallah, *Annals of the Caliphs' Kitchens*, pp. 388–403.

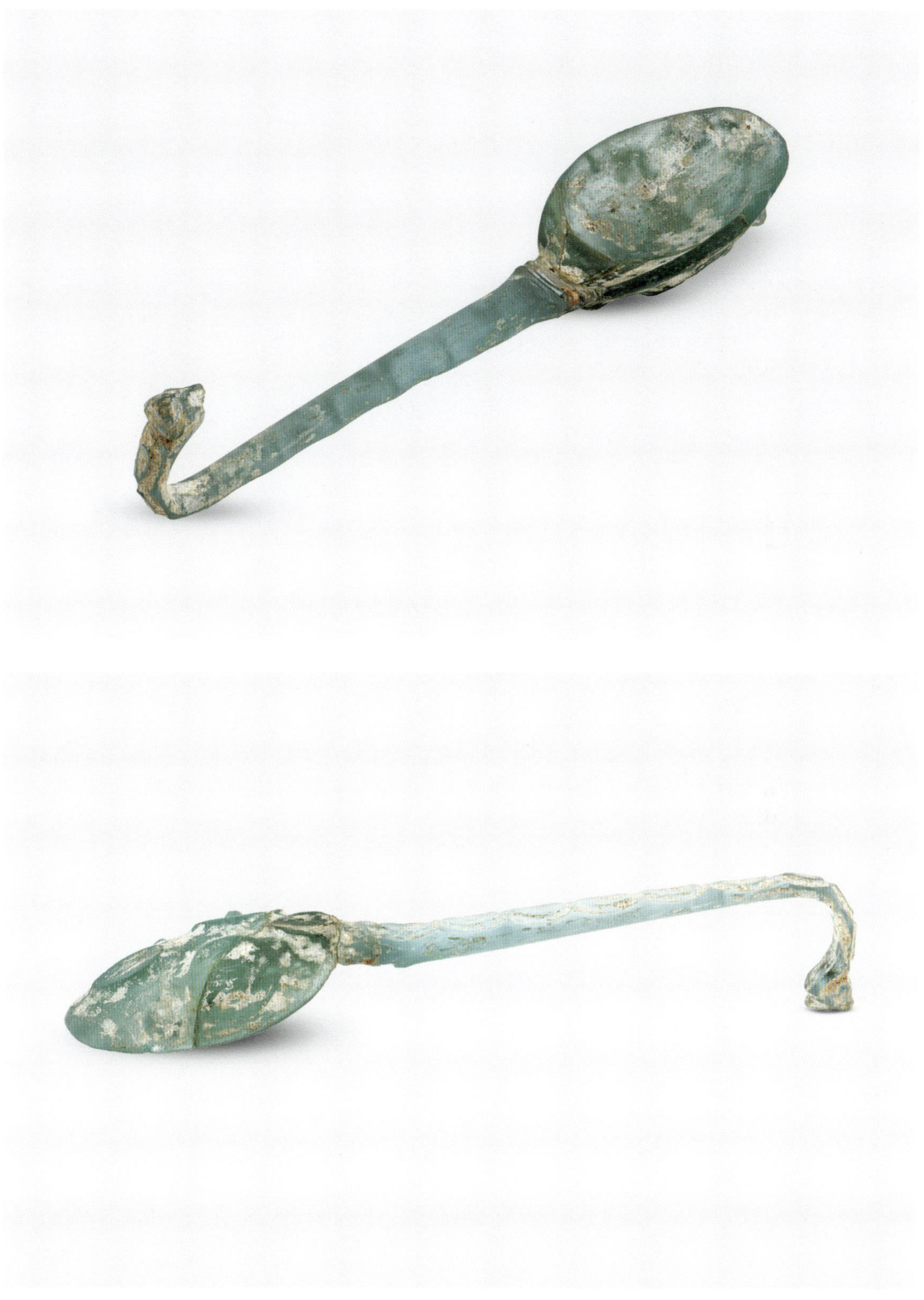

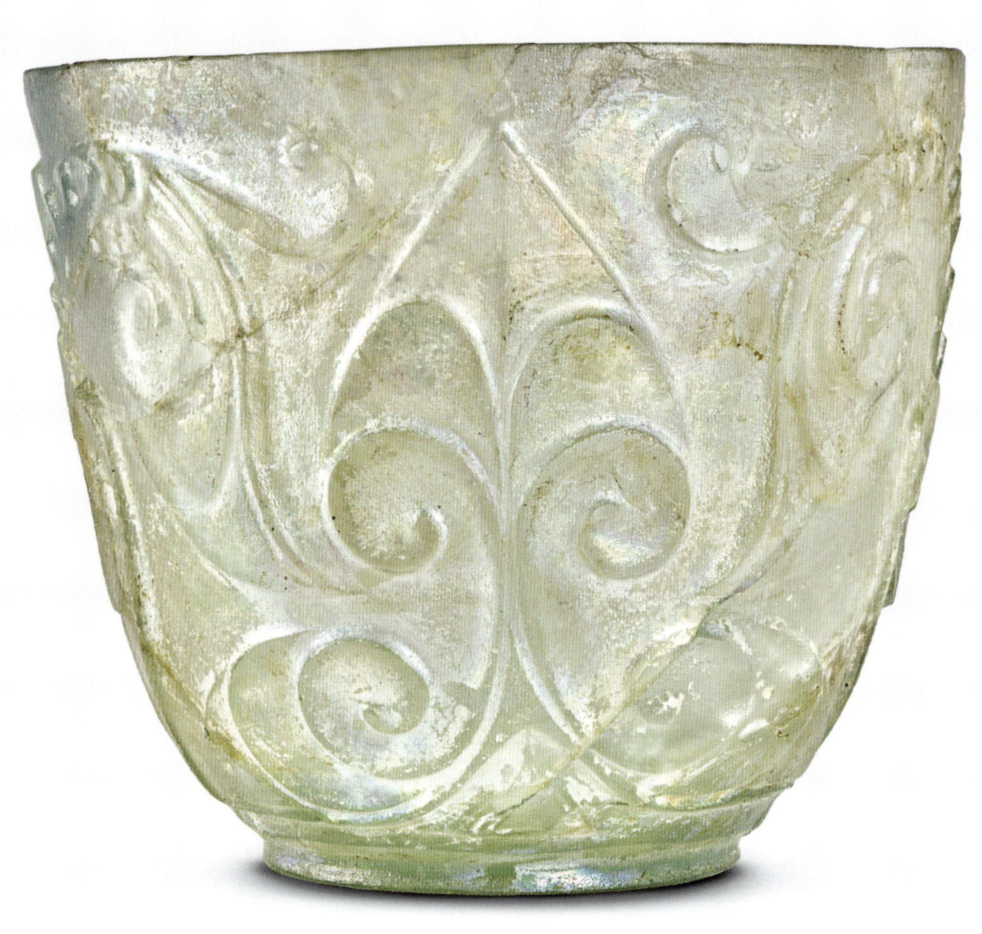

13
Cup
Probably Iraq, Abbasid period,
3rd–4th century AH/9th–10th century CE
Blown glass with wheel-cut decoration
8.6 × ø 10.3 cm
Museum of Islamic Art, GL.19.1999

This cup was likely designed to hold liquids. In Abbasid Baghdad, water from the Tigris was commonly served in small cups after meals. To keep the water cool, it was usually stored in earthenware pitchers or jars, many of which were imported from the village of Madhar, located in Iraq. In addition to water, residents of Abbasid Baghdad enjoyed *fuqqaʿ*, a spiced drink made with rose water, sugar, honey and musk. The beverage was often cooled with ice, commonly served after feasts or consumed for medicinal properties.[1]

By the 4th century AH/10th century CE, cut glass vessels like this one had reached outstanding levels of craftsmanship and were often produced as more affordable alternatives to the expensive rock crystal cups, which featured similar designs.[2] In poetry, these transparent drinking vessels were often associated with lamps or sources of life, implying that the drinker was consuming light itself. As the 5th century AH/ 11th century CE poet Asadi Tusi (d. 465 AH/1072–1073 CE) described: 'Then they retired to a garden for pleasure and feasting [...] Goblets like moons in [their hands] were sprinkling the jewels of the Pleiades'.[3] SST

1 See Ahsan, *Social Life Under the Abbasids*, p. 111.

2 Glass fragments with a similar design were excavated from the Abbasid site of Samarra in Iraq. They are held at the Museum für Islamische Kunst – Staatliche Museen zu Berlin (Sam I. 47.4, Sam I. 47.7, SamKat 246a and Sam 606). Comparable glass cups with a similar shape can be found at the Metropolitan Museum of Art, New York (x.275.3) and the David Collection, Copenhagen (24/2009). Rock crystal flasks, such as the one at The National Museum of Asian Art, Washington DC (F1949.14), feature a design similar to the object under discussion.

3 See Shalem, 'Fountains of Light', pp. 1–11 and especially p. 6.

14
Bowl
Iran (Kashan), Khwarezmid period,
6th century AH/late 12th century CE
Lustre-painted fritware
ø 18.5 cm
Museum of Islamic Art, PO.37.1999

This bowl is a type of Islamic ceramic commonly known as
'Kashan ware', a style of lustre-ware pottery associated with
Kashan, Iran, from approximately the beginning of the 5th
century AH/11th century CE until the mid-8th century AH/
mid-14th century CE. The seated figure in the centre of this
lustre-painted bowl holds a long-stemmed glass, while to the
left, a rounded vessel (possibly an ewer) floats on a floral ground.
The figure holds the goblet with his thumb touching the edge of
the flange and his forefinger underneath it. He sits cross-legged,
wearing a turban and dotted kaftan, his pose serene and his
moon-shaped face the ideal of beauty. The outside of the bowl
is covered in cobalt blue glaze and decorated with an Arabic
inscription painted in brown lustre over the blue glaze.

Countless representations of men—and occasionally
women—holding goblets by the stem appear across multiple
media, in particular ceramics and stucco. A similarly shaped
goblet appears on a lustre-painted bowl dated 575 AH
(1179–1180 CE). That image most likely represents a goblet made
of cut glass, a type that was produced in abundance in Iran.[1]
This painted bowl cleverly connects its decoration to a popular
pastime and even, quite possibly, to its function as a vessel
enjoyed during a feast. TD

Inscription:
... الاقبال و الدولت و السعاده و ...
'… Good fortune and wealth and happiness
and …'

1 Sheila Canby et al., *Court and Cosmos*,
fig. 51, p. 136.

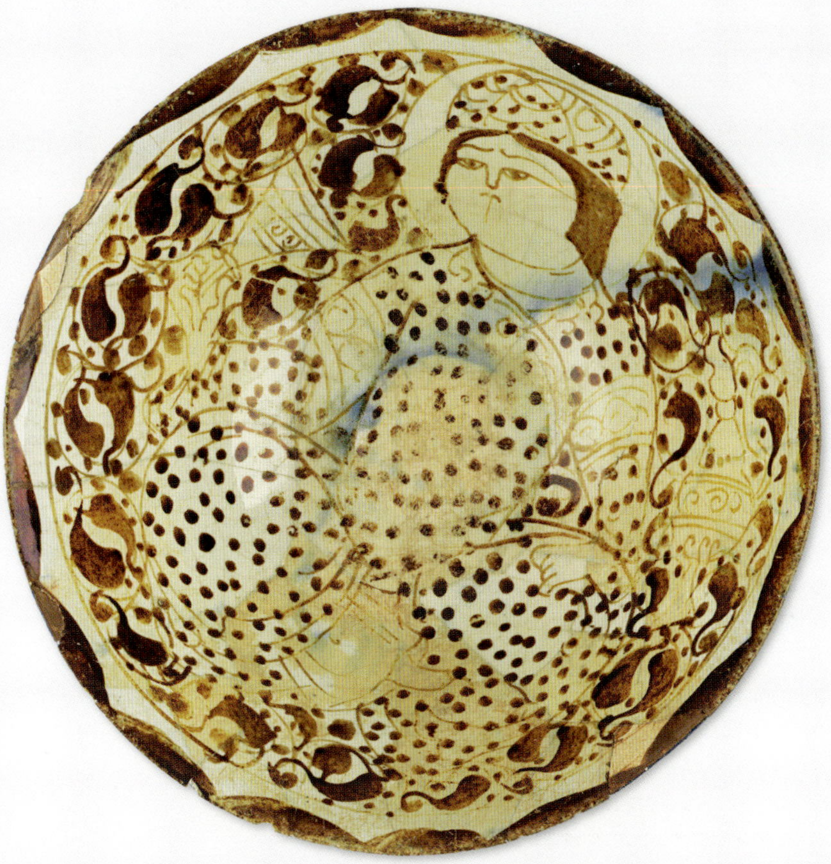

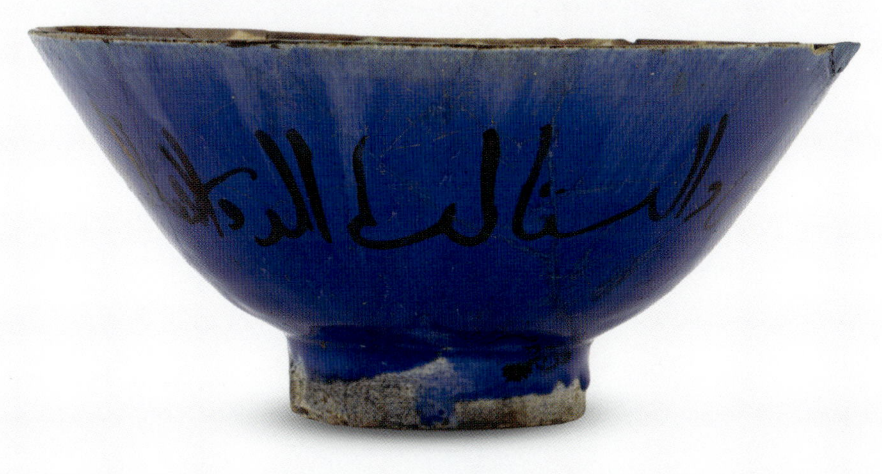

15
Rooster-headed ewer
Iran (Kashan), Khwarezmid period,
7th century AH/mid-13th century CE
Moulded and lustre-painted fritware
34 × ⌀ 17.9 cm
Museum of Islamic Art, PO.714.2007

Writing in the last quarter of the 6th century AH/12th century CE, the poet Nizami Ganjavi gives us a detailed description of a banquet to celebrate Nowruz, the Persian New Year falling on the spring equinox. In his poem *Khusrau va Shirin*, the love story of the Sasanian ruler Khusrau and the Armenian princess Shirin, Nizami mentions large braziers for burning perfumed essences, along with a jug in the shape of a cockerel, brilliant and beautiful.[1] His description closely resembles this ceramic ewer of the same period, its neck terminating in a rooster's head, with its comb well defined and the beak open to let liquid flow. Together with the sheen of the lustre paint, the deeply moulded body bestows monumentality and richness to a piece made of otherwise humble materials.

While Nizami's poetic passage provides an insight into the elite material culture of his time, the association with ancient Iranian royalty is no coincidence. Bird-shaped vessels fashioned in silver and gold have a long tradition in pre-Islamic Iran, where they were used in Zoroastrian ritual libations as well as during the Sasanian period (378 BH–30 AH/224–651 CE). Ceramic vessels with bird-headed spouts and pear-shaped bodies, dated to the Tang period (4 BH–294 AH/618–907 CE), have also been excavated in China, confirming that such vessels made their way to East Asia, at least from the Sui period (41–4 BH/581–618 CE).[2] These objects must have reached the Chinese imperial court and wider markets, most likely via diplomatic and commercial exchanges. NF

1 See Nizami Ganjavi, *Khusrau wa Shirin*, chapter 29, ll. 18–21:
که ریحان زمستان آمد آتش / زمستان گشته چون ریحان
ازو خوش خروسی کاو به وقت آواز کرده / صراحی چون
خروسی ساز کرده گهی تیهو بر آتش گاه دراج / ز رَشکِ آن
خروسِ آتشین‌تاج گهی کبک دری گه مرغ آبی / روان گشته
به نقلان کبابی

'In winter a good fire is like a flower, healing the heart with its reviving power. / From hand to hand a flagon was passed round shaped like a rooster, with a fitting sound, / Since when the drink was poured it was though its gurgling reproduced a rooster's crow / (Both francolins and partridges would feel envious of this fake bird, it seemed so real)', translation slightly adapted from Davis, trans., *Khosrow and Shirin*, p. 106.

2 See Medley, *Metalwork and Chinese Ceramics*, p. 4 ff.

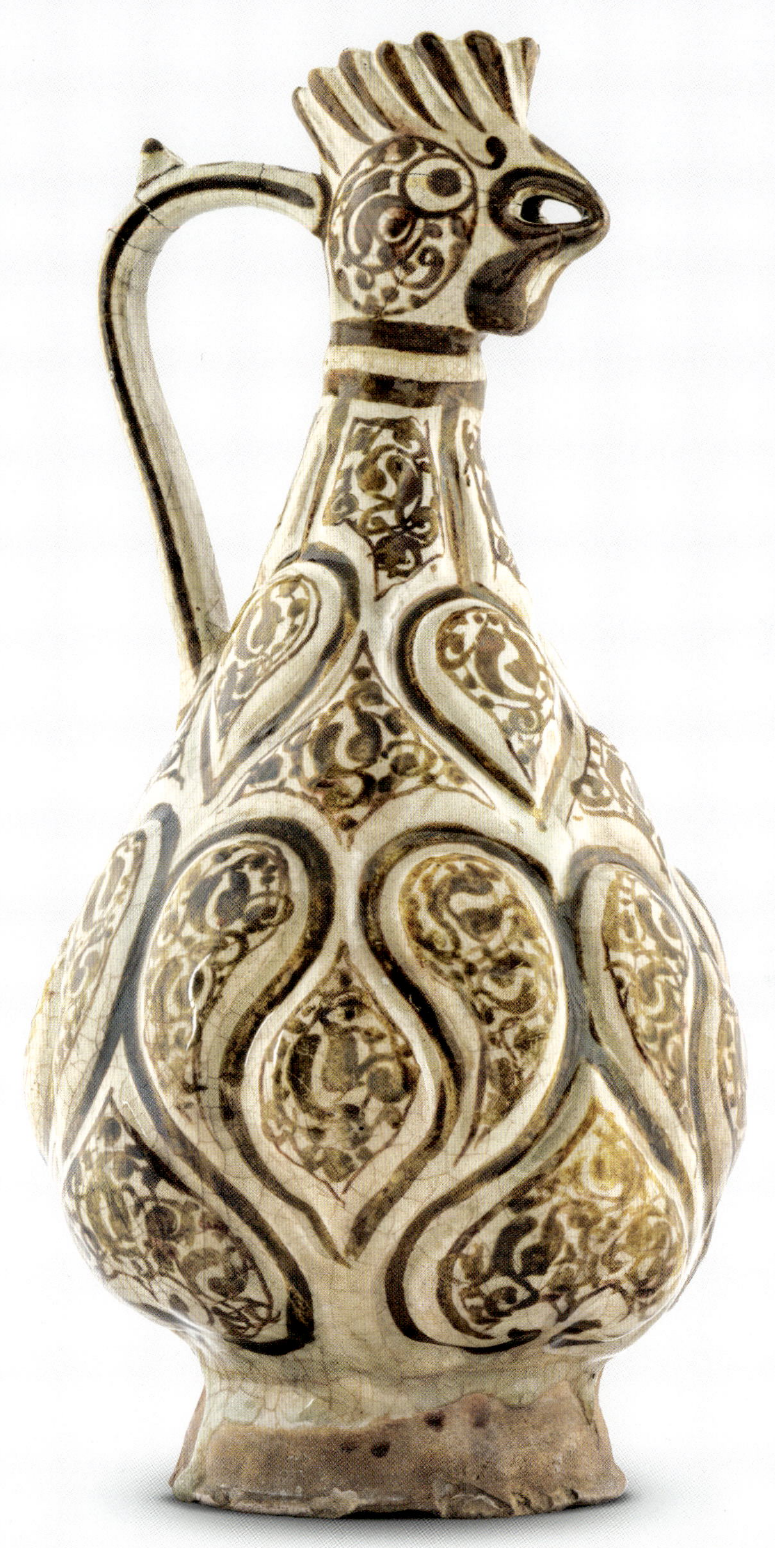

16

The Court of Pir Budaq
Iran (Shiraz), Turkmen period,
c. 859–865 AH/1455–60 CE
Opaque watercolour, gold and ink on paper
39.1 × 33.8 cm
Museum of Islamic Art, MIA.2013.150

The theme of outdoor princely gatherings with music, entertainment and copious food and drink is a classical trope of ancient Persian royal culture dating back to pre-Islamic times. Replicated in a variety of artistic media, from poetry to figurative art, this theme enjoyed enduring and widespread popularity across Iran and Central Asia even after the Arab conquest from the 2nd century AH/8th century CE onwards.[1] In this small yet lively painting, the Turkmen prince Abu al-Fath Pir Budaq (d. 871 AH/1466 CE) sits on a felt blanket placed over a carpet, canopy overhead amidst his court attendants. This painting was most likely made in Shiraz, in southwestern Iran, while Pir Budaq, eldest son of the Qara Qoyunlu Turkmen chief Jahanshah, was governor there. He was an important patron of the arts during his brief and riotous reign, which lasted until 865 AH/1460 CE.[2]

The painting allows a glimpse into the courtly material culture of the period, with its depictions of precious metalware, carpets and textiles. A few small details add a sense of intimacy and warmth to what is otherwise a celebratory royal portrait. Note the right sleeve of Pir Budaq's cobalt blue coat, removed to allow ease in drinking from his small golden cup; his tight, elongated turban, with a flap extending from its left side; the spirited dancer who sways to the sounds of the live band; and the two attendants at the bottom right corner who intently follow her every movement. The scene might capture the kind of lavish outdoor gatherings and royal banquets amply documented in historical sources and book paintings prepared for both Timurid princes and their Turkmen antagonists.

Now pasted onto a gold-sprinkled folio, the overall appearance suggests that it could have been the right page of a double-page frontispiece, either a collection of poetry (*divan*) or a work of narrative poetry (*masnavi*). The now missing left half of the frontispiece might have possibly depicted attendants and court officials busy setting up a proper banquet, as in some earlier Timurid examples dated to the late 9th century AH/third decade of the 15th century CE.[3] NF

1 See Gauthier Tolini, 'Les ressources de la Babylonie et la table de Darius le Grand (522–486)', in Lion et al., eds., *Le banquet du monarque*, pp. 145–162; Khaleghi-Motlagh, 'ADAB i. Adab in Iran'; Assadullah Souren Melikian-Chirvani, 'The Iranian Bazm in Early Persian Sources', in Gyselen and Bernus-Taylor, eds., *Banquets d'Orient*, pp. 95–120; and Luca Patrizi, 'The Metaphor of the Divine Banquet and the Formation of the Notion of Adab in Islam', in Günther, ed., *Knowledge and Education in Classical Islam*, vol. 1, pp. 516–538.

2 See David J. Roxburgh, 'Many a Wish Has Turned Dust: Pir Budaq and the Formation of Turkmen Arts of the Book', in Roxburgh, ed., *Envisioning Islamic Art and Architecture*, pp. 175–222.

3 See, for instance, the double frontispiece to Baysunghur Mirza's *Kalila wa Dimna*, dated Muharram 833 AH/ October 1429 CE in the Topkapı Sarayı Museum Library, Istanbul (r.1022, fols 1b-2a). See also the lively royal reception depicted on the left side of a double-page frontispiece from an illustrated copy of the *Shahnama* produced in Shiraz and dated 848 AH/1444 CE in The Cleveland Museum of Art (1956.10.a).

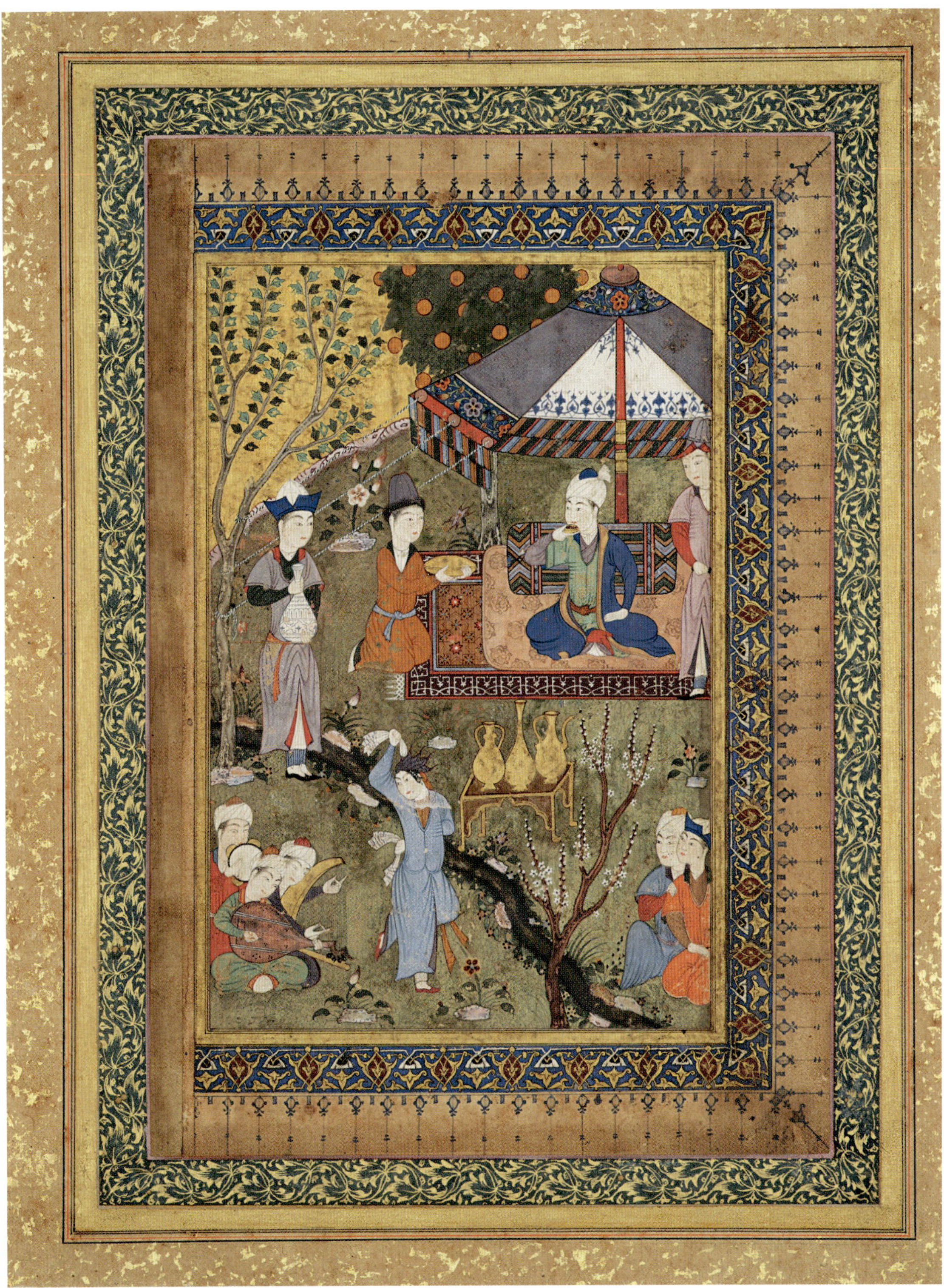

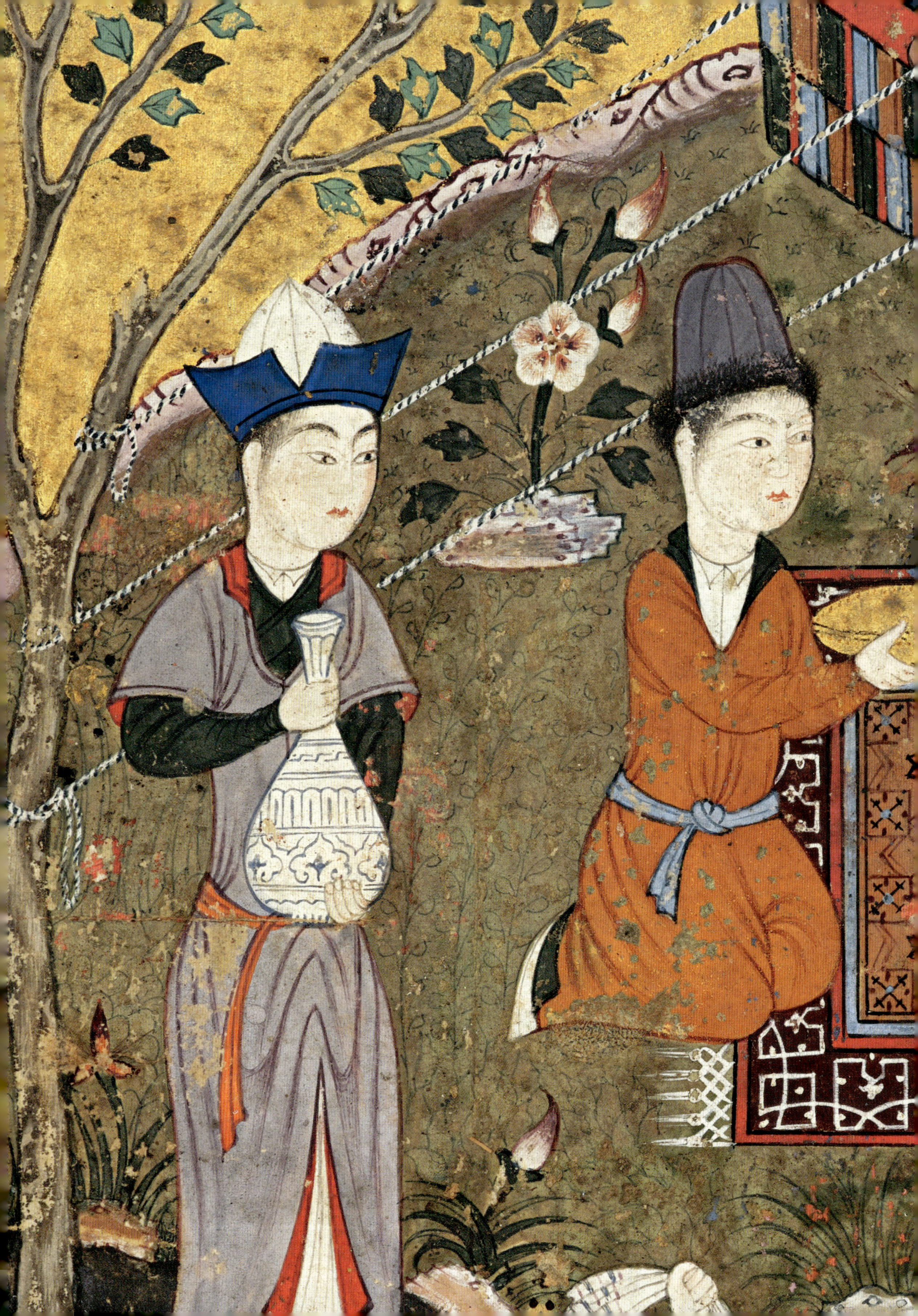

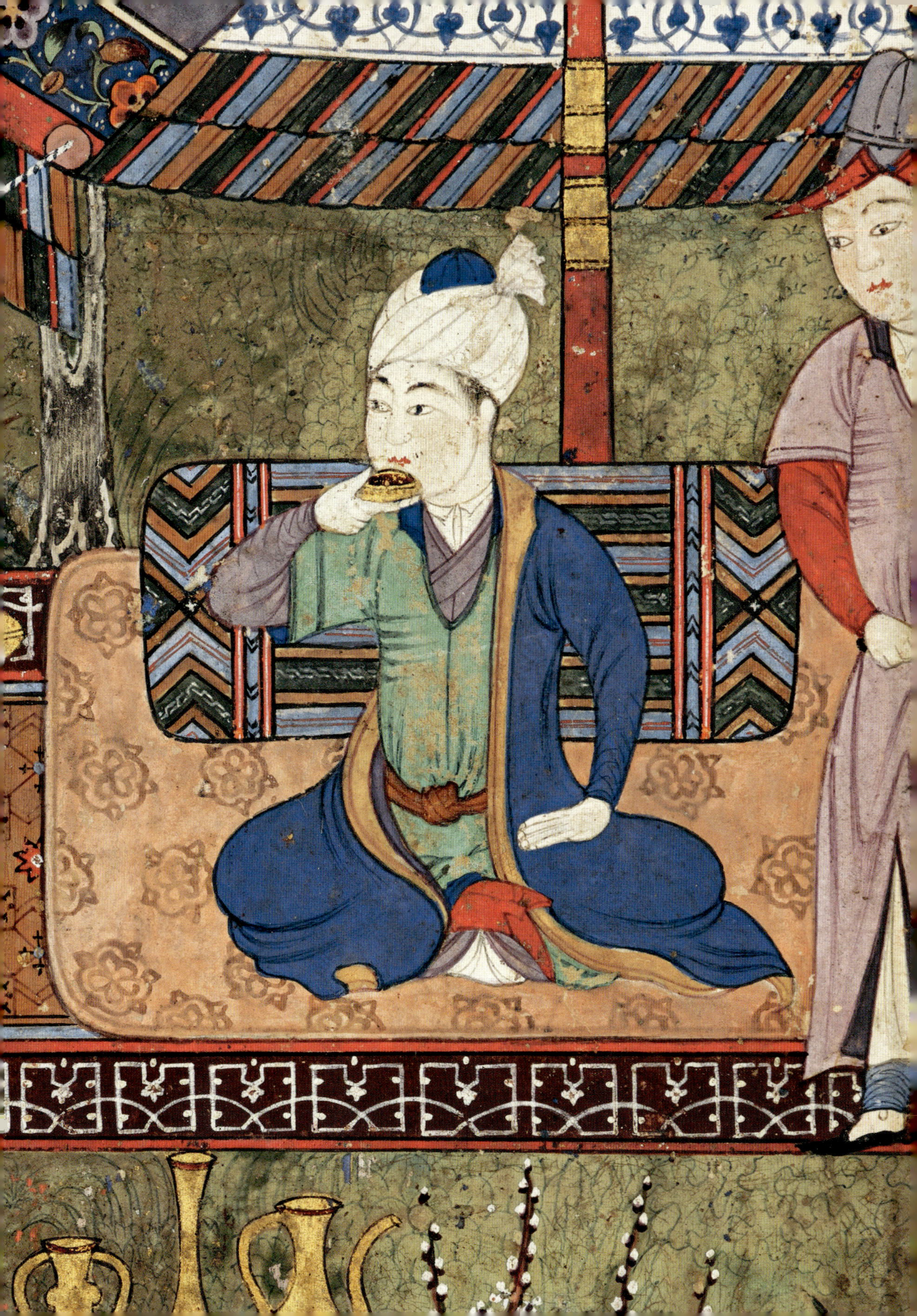

17a
Jug
Greater Khorasan (north-eastern Iran or Afghanistan),
Ghaznavid or Ghurid period, late 6th or 7th century AH/
12th or early 13th century CE
Hammered brass inlaid with gold, silver and copper
28.3 × 16.6 cm
Museum of Islamic Art, MIA.2014.502

Although this jug and tray (cat. 17b, overleaf) were not created (or acquired) as an ensemble, both in fact bear a strikingly similar decorative repertoire, suggesting that they once formed part of the same, larger dining set. Each is made from hammered brass inlaid with precious metals, and is decorated with foliate medallions and bands of *kufic* epigraphy offering good wishes to an unidentified owner.[1] The circular tray features a scalloped interior rim with a sunken base, while the smaller, bulbous jug has a multi-faceted body, cylindrical neck, and splayed foot with a domed cover terminating in a bird finial. The jug is inlaid with copper and silver, while the tray is inlaid with gold.

Stylistically, both objects are decorated with a near identical pattern: large disc-roundels filled with interlocking scrolls and a trefoil top, interspersed with small silver rosettes of single or double pointed petals (the centres of which have copper inlay). Both motifs can be found on other 'Khorasani' brasses from the period, in particular metalwork made in Herat, Afghanistan, helping to attribute these dishes to this period and to one another. The disc-roundels are also seen in contemporaneous manuscript illuminations.

1 Allan, *Metalwork Treasures from the Islamic Courts*, cat. 13, p. 52.

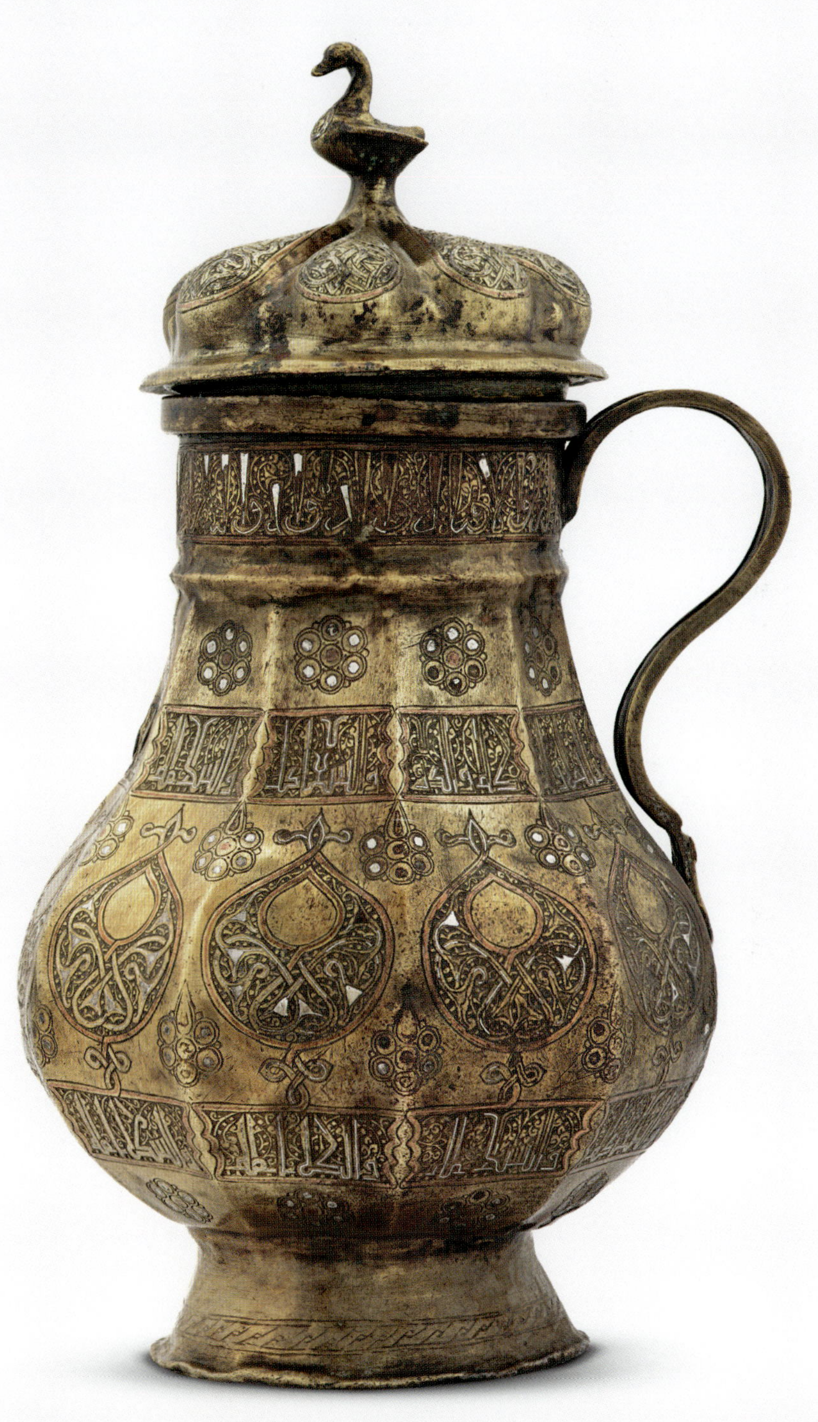

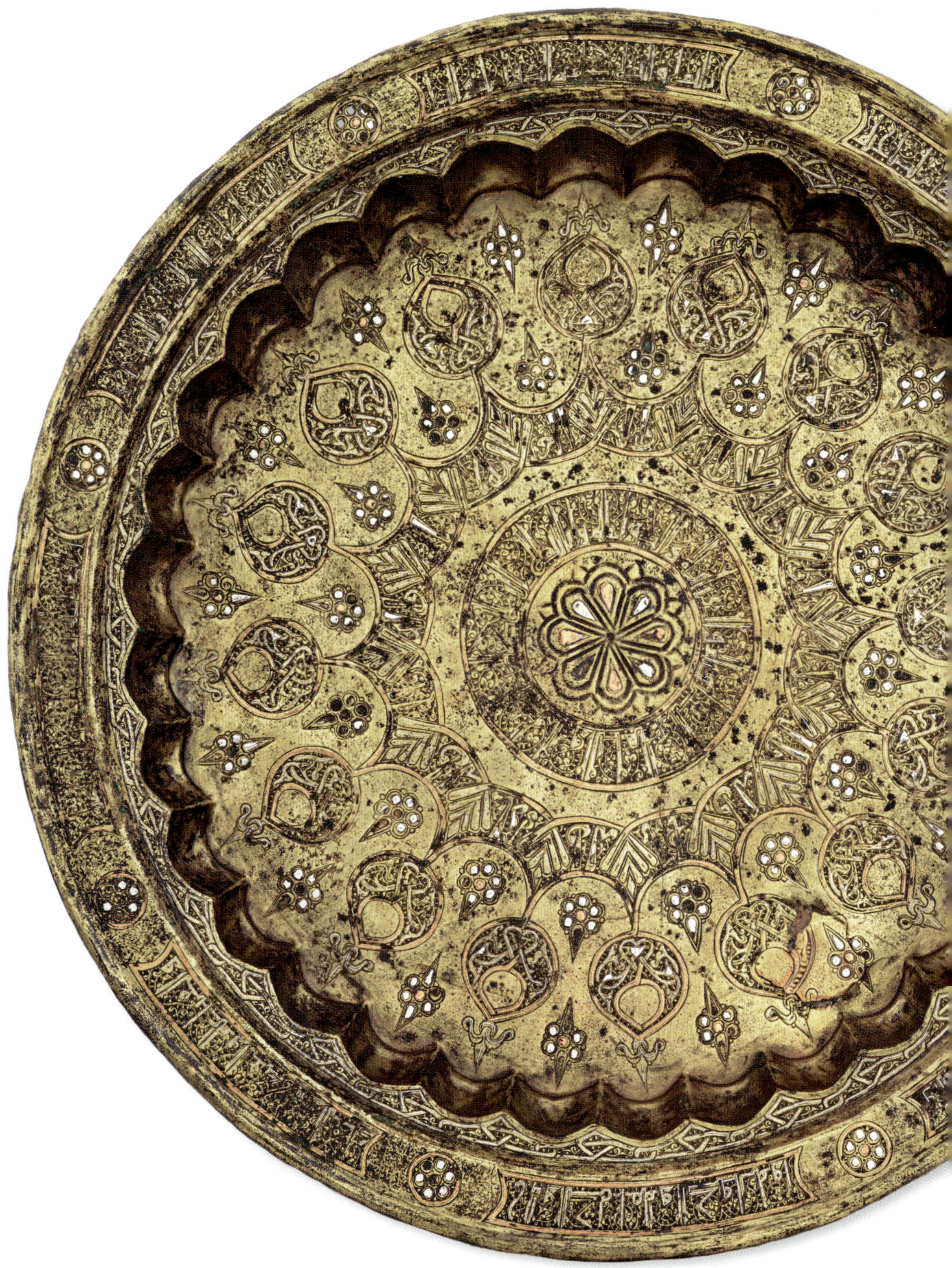

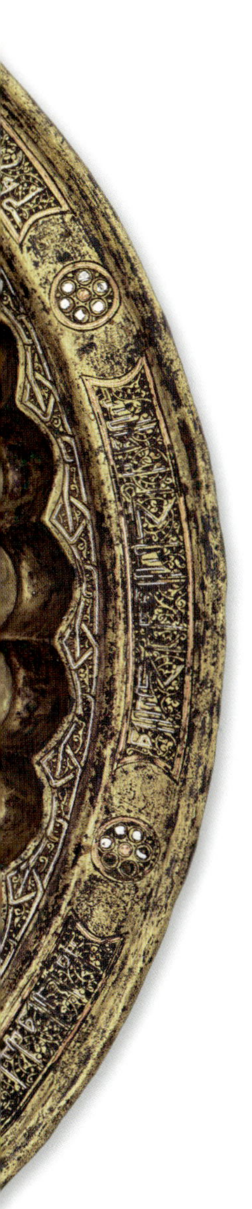

17b
Tray
Greater Khorasan (north-eastern Iran or Afghanistan),
Ghaznavid or Ghurid period, late 6th or 7th century AH/
12th or early 13th century CE
Hammered brass inlaid with gold, silver and copper
3.4 × ⌀ 35.6 cm
Museum of Islamic Art, MW.126.1999

This tray and jug (cat. 17a) would have been used together during a meal, to serve food and drink, respectively. The tray's scalloped inner rim and depressed centre suggest that it probably held solid, dried foods such as rice or pilau as opposed to liquid stews, which would have required a deeper bowl. The scalloped rim would have easily facilitated eating with one's hand, providing an edge to collect and compress the food into mouth-size bites. Several people would have sat around the tray, sharing its contents. The lidded jug, on the other hand, would have been used by one person. Both objects were either placed on a *sufra* or low portable stand. TD

18
Tray
Afghanistan, Ghaznavid period,
6th century AH/12th century CE
Hammered, incised and punched brass
35 × 23.9 × 3.3 cm
Museum of Islamic Art, MW.64.1999

A strange, composite creature occupies the central medallion of this tray—part feline, part bird of prey, it has hare-like floppy ears. All around are confronted dogs and hares set amongst vegetal tendrils and floral bursts ending in lions' heads. The rim is inscribed with an auspicious phrase in Arabic, repeated six times at even intervals. The four outer corners host interlocking birds, pheasants or peacocks. All decoration has been hammered from the back of the tray so that it stands in relief from the surface. The flat background has been incised, and then punched, creating a darker texture that enhances the three-dimensional effect of the polished elements in relief. Like other surviving examples dated roughly to the same period, this tray was most likely produced in Khorasan, a vast region comprising territories shared today by Iran and Afghanistan. This region, particularly the city of Herat, was a renowned centre for the production of high-quality metalwork. These wares tend to be decorated with silver inlay and/or moulded, hammered or incised motifs.

The uneven surface of the tray suggests it was used to serve solid foods such as fruits, sweets and nuts rather than stews or soups. Considering food was mostly consumed while seated on the floor, the shape and size of the vessel would have allowed for easy passing from one guest to another.

Despite being more affordable than gold and silver, vessels manufactured in copper alloy, and especially those inlaid with rich silver decoration, which added another element of prestige, were reserved for the most affluent households. Contemporaneous Persian literature, such as Firdausi's *Shahnama* (The Book of Kings, completed 401 AH/1010 CE) records lavish banquets in which legendary amounts of food and drink were served in similar trays. The Ghaznavid historian Abu'l Fadl Bayhaqi (d. 470 AH/1077 CE) offers in his chronicle *Tarikh-i Bayhaqi* ('The History of Bayhaqi') a rich insight into the banqueting customs at the court of Sultan Mahmud of Ghazni, who ruled in the region when this tray was made.[1] NF

Inscription:
العز الدائم
(on long side) العزّ الدائم الإقبال
'everlasting glory'
'everlasting glory, good fortune'

1 See, for instance, the episodes of the seven *majalis* of Anushirvan in Ferdowsi's *Shahnama*, a series of banquets ordered by the Iranian ruler Anushirvan, in which political issues and intellectual questions are discussed amidst copious amount of food and beverages. For the figure of Bayhaqi, see G.-H. Yusofi, 'Bayhaqi Abu'l-Fazl'.

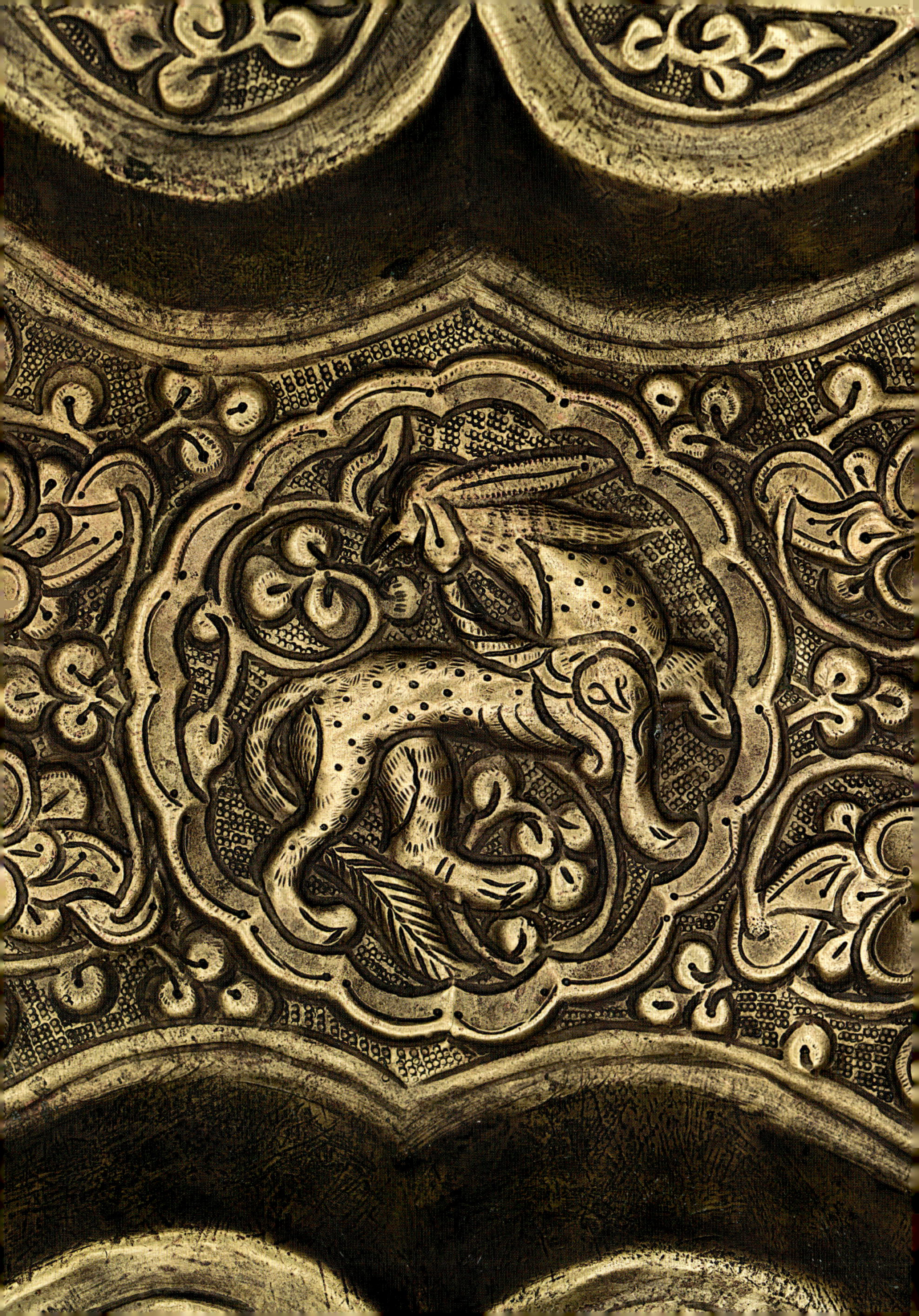

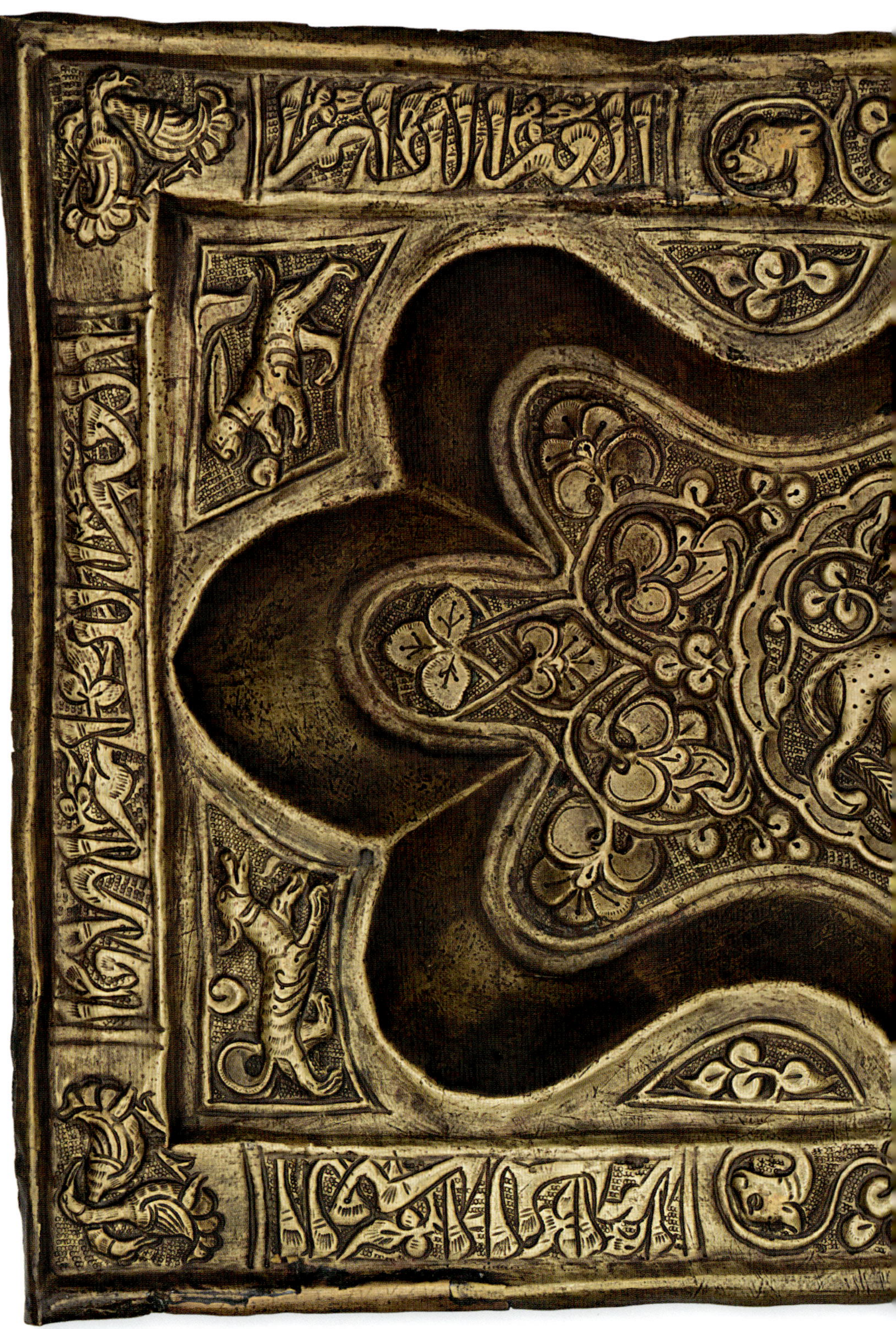

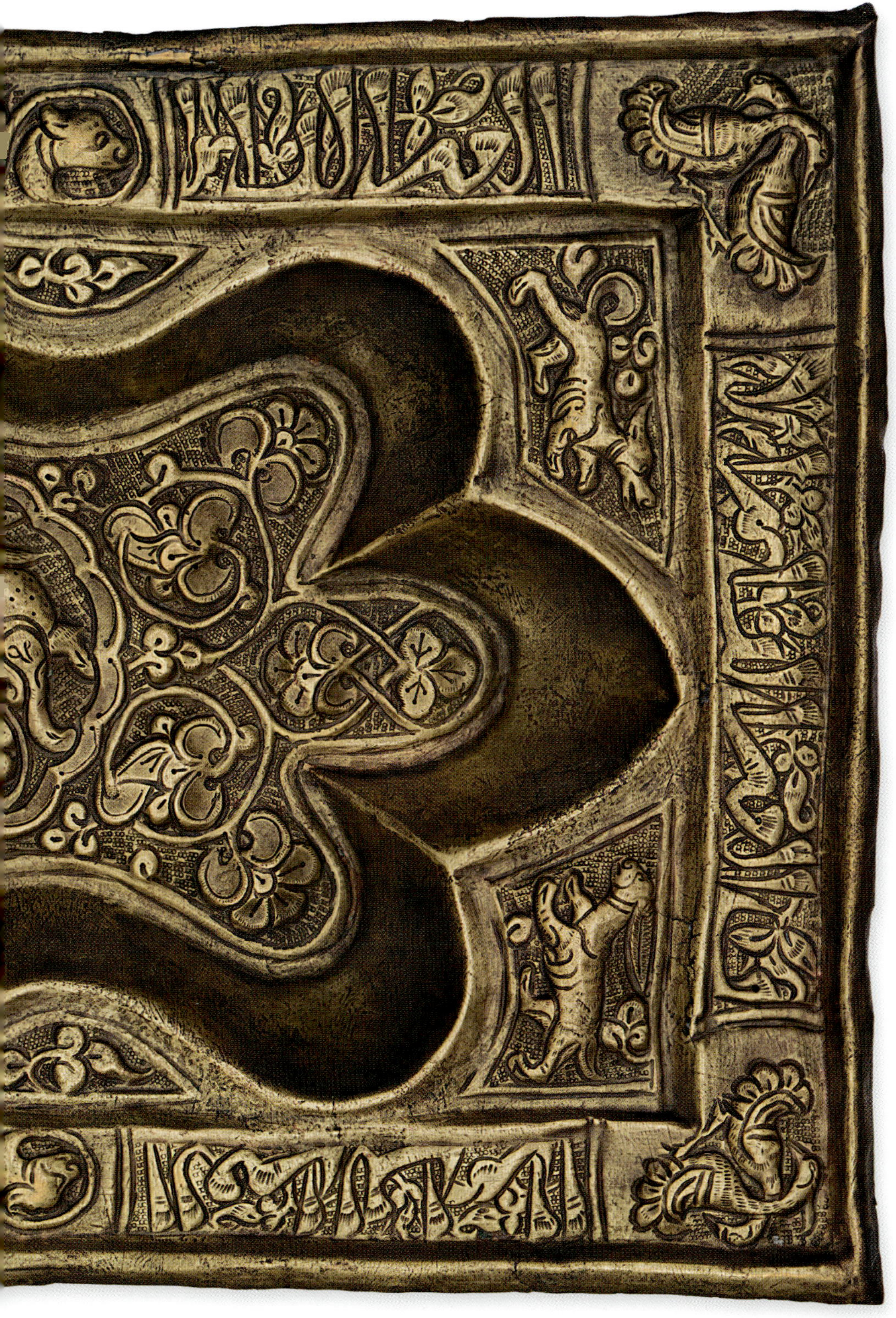

19
Ewer
Afghanistan (possibly Herat), Ilkhanid period,
late 7th–early 8th century AH/late 13th–early 14th century CE
Hammered brass inlaid with silver, copper and black compound
39.9 × ⌀ 22 cm
Museum of Islamic Art, MW.118.1999

This ewer (*aftaba* or *abdasta*) retains a powerful and luxurious presence despite having lost much of its original silver and copper inlaid decoration. It must have made quite an impression when handled during banquets in an affluent household. Based on an inscription applied to a similar ewer now at the British Museum (1848,0805.2), we know that this type of vessel was used to pour water for washing hands, an essential part of dining etiquette in cultures in which food is consumed from large communal plates. Traditionally, the right hand was used to pass dishes and to eat, a habit still practised in various regions of West and South Asia, and across Africa.[1] In elite and wealthy households, ewers such as this were accompanied by an equally lavish *tast*, a basin used to collect the water, typically scented with rose extract, musk, frankincense, sandalwood or camphor, as it was poured over a guest's hands.

This ewer belongs to a small group of similar vessels used for banquets. Its polylobed body showcases intertwined vegetal trellises alternating with a series of roundels with figural decoration, including enthroned male figures and mounted falconers and hunters accompanied by small quadrupeds. Royal figures and hunting scenes are among the most popular themes on metalwork produced for the elite in this period, motifs that have long been associated with the ideals of royalty and nobility across Eurasia. In addition to this impressive repertoire of motifs, the top part of the ewer presents a band of horsemen hunting small felines, perhaps cheetahs, which were often used as hunting auxiliaries during royal campaigns. The shoulder bears an inscription in a style regularly appearing in inlaid metalwork of the time: vertical letters terminating in small human heads, and the reserve space filled with small birds of prey. The tall slender neck shows a dense combination of diverse motifs including calligraphy, vegetal branches, bands of leaping and running animals, and hunters on horseback. A couple of seated tigers cast in relief, another recurrent feature of brass wares from this region and period, complete the rich overall decorative programme. NF

Inscription:
العافيه و السلا(مة) / والعافيه والراحة
'Health, safety, health and ease'
(on the neck)

العز والاقبال والدوامة والسعادة
والعناية والسلامة والراحة
والعال (؟)
'Glory, prosperity, longevity, happiness, (God's) care, safety, ease and wellbeing (?)' (on the shoulder)

1 In many cultures, historical as well as contemporary, the right hand is associated with cleanliness and proper manners. One Hadith reports that the Prophet Muhammad (PBUH) indicates the right hand as the proper one to eat, see Hadith no 5265, *Sahih Muslim*, vol. 5, pp. 369–370.

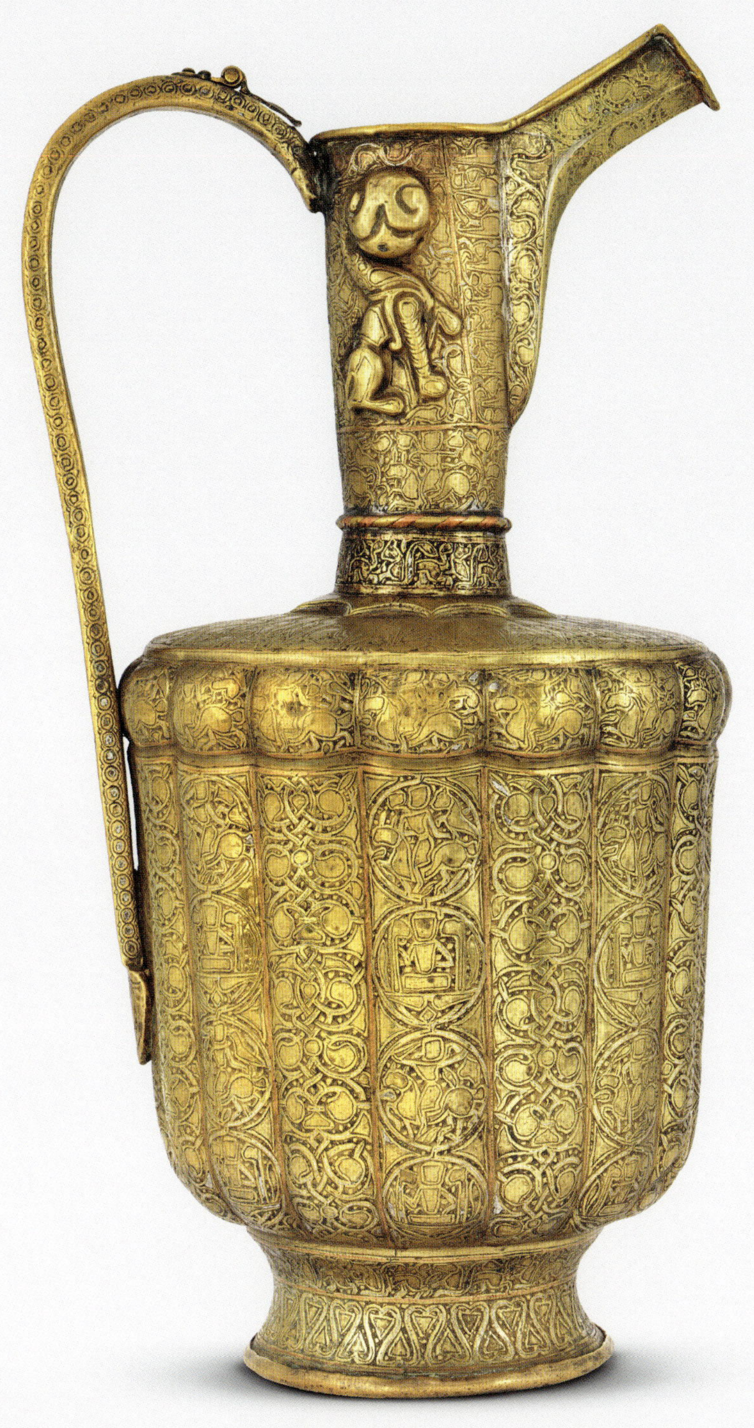

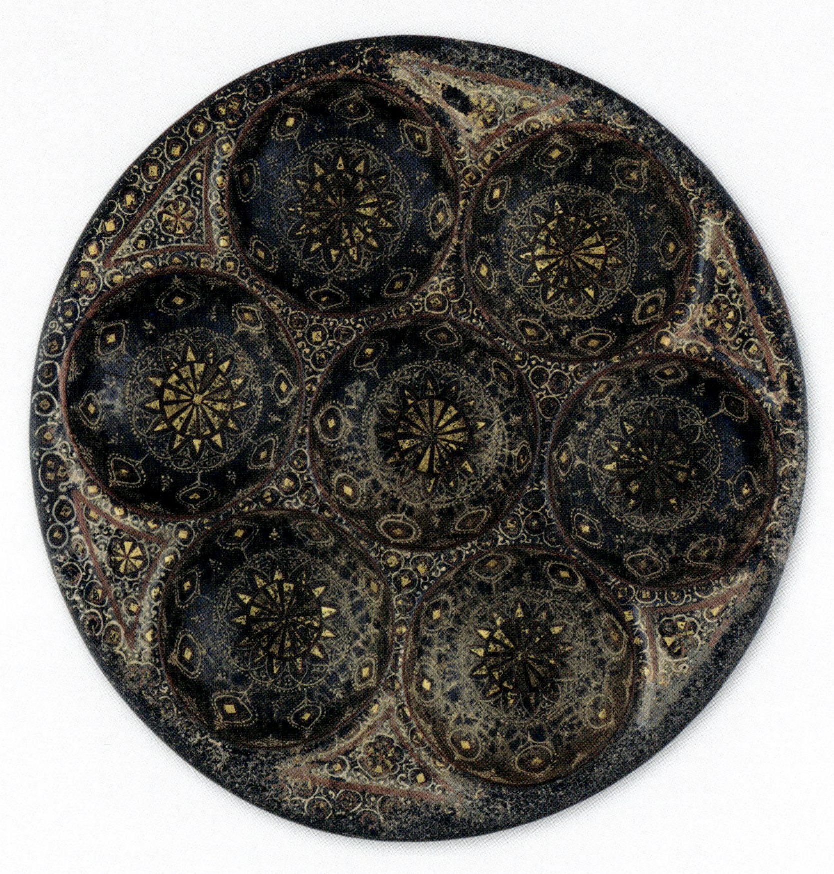

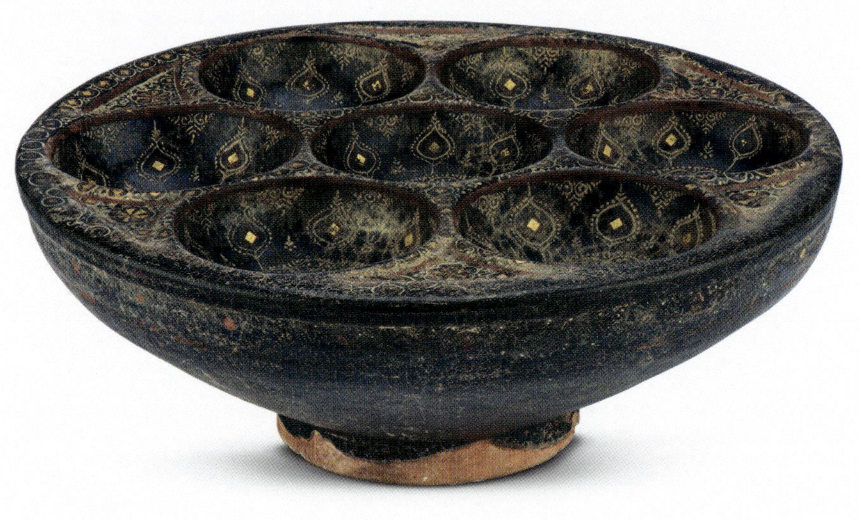

20
Dish
Iran, Ilkhanid period,
7th–8th century AH/13th–14th century CE
Press-formed, overglaze-painted
and leaf-gilded fritware (*lajvardina* ware)
13 × ⌀ 34 cm
Museum of Islamic Art, QM.2018.0591

Containers such as this were most probably used to serve a variety of small dry nibbles. They are known in Arabic as *sukkardan*, and in Persian as *shakardan*, both meaning 'sugar container', which suggests they were used specifically for sweet confectionaries. Because they include seven compartments some scholars relate the containers' use to the setting of the *Haft Sin* (Seven S's), a table display traditionally prepared for the celebration of Nowruz, the Persian New Year, with seven items starting with the letter *sin*, or 's'.

These ceramic vessels were made by joining an upper tray to a shallow bowl with a short foot. Several dated to the same period survive in museum collections, but this dish stands as a unique example decorated in the *lajvardina* technique. With a name deriving from the Persian word *lajvard*, meaning lapis lazuli, *lajvardina* wares are known for their deep blue glaze flecked with gold incrustations that resembles the texture of that precious stone. This dish has been further decorated with fine geometric and stylised vegetal motifs painted in red and white with gold highlights.

Lajvardina wares are rare because they were only produced for a short period during the reign of the Mongol Ilkhans. They were also costly to produce, requiring two firings, as described in the treatise *'Ara'es al-jawaher wa nafa'es al-ata'eb* ('Brides of Jewels and Finesses of Delights') by Abu al-Qasim 'Abdallah Kashani (d. after 724 AH/1324 CE), a Persian historian and descendant of a Kashan ceramic-making family active during the reign of Oljaytu (r. 703–716 AH/1304–1317 CE). In addition, the delicate gold decoration of *lajvardina* wares made them very fragile and easily subject to surface weathering.[1] Several tiles made in the *lajvardina* technique have been excavated in the royal complex of Takht-e Suleyman (northern Iran), suggesting that production was limited and most likely intended for the elite market. NF

1 See Holakooei et al., 'Materials and Technique of Lajvardina Ceramics'; and Allan, 'Abu'l-Qasim's Treatise on Ceramics'.

21

Two folios from a manuscript of Persian poetry
Uzbekistan (Bukhara), Shaybanid period,
10th century AH/mid-16th century CE
Gold, ink and opaque watercolour on paper
25.4 × 16.3 cm (each page)
Museum of Islamic Art, MIA.2014.327.1-2

The lines of text on the upper left corners of these folios
(see also overleaf) suggest that they originally served as a
double-page frontispiece for a collection of Persian poetry.[1]
The verses are by the Timurid poet Amir Shahi Sabzavari
(d. 857 AH/1453 CE, *ghazal* 64, vv. 1 and 3), and they describe
the pleasantry of a blooming garden and the delight of sharing
refreshments with the beloved in a lush environment. The folios
depict two couples in a verdant setting with all the conventional
elements of an ideal spring garden, a recurrent theme in
classical Persian poetry. These include a blooming meadow,
ducks swimming in a stream of water (originally in silver paint,
now tarnished), cool beverages in precious vessels, and female
musicians playing the harp (*chang*) and framed drum (*daf*),
musical instruments that also hold symbolic meaning within
love poetry. The couple in the left-hand folio are embracing;
the female holds a pomegranate, an ingredient popular in
the culinary traditions of West and Central Asia, which also
symbolises fertility and abundance.

Inscription:
بده جامی، که دیگر باغ را چشم و چراغ آمد / چمن
سرسبز شد ساقی، گل و نرگس به باغ آمد
Cupbearer, the meadow gets green,
roses and daffodils grace the garden /
Pass me a cup, because they have
brightened the garden

من و کویش، که نتوان با دل غمگین به باغ آمد / تو
کاندر پای دل خاری نداری، گشت بستان کن
And you, whose heart is full of mirth, come
walk into the garden / But I live in her
memory, for no one with a broken heart
can enter the garden

1 See, for comparison, the poetic
anthology in the Metropolitan Museum
of Art, New York (89.2.2152); an illustrated
copy of *Divan-i Shahi*, Österreichische
Nationalbibliothek, Vienna (Mixt. 399);
and a copy of Shahi's *Divan*, recently sold
at Christie's London (24 October 2024,
sale 22663, lot 64).

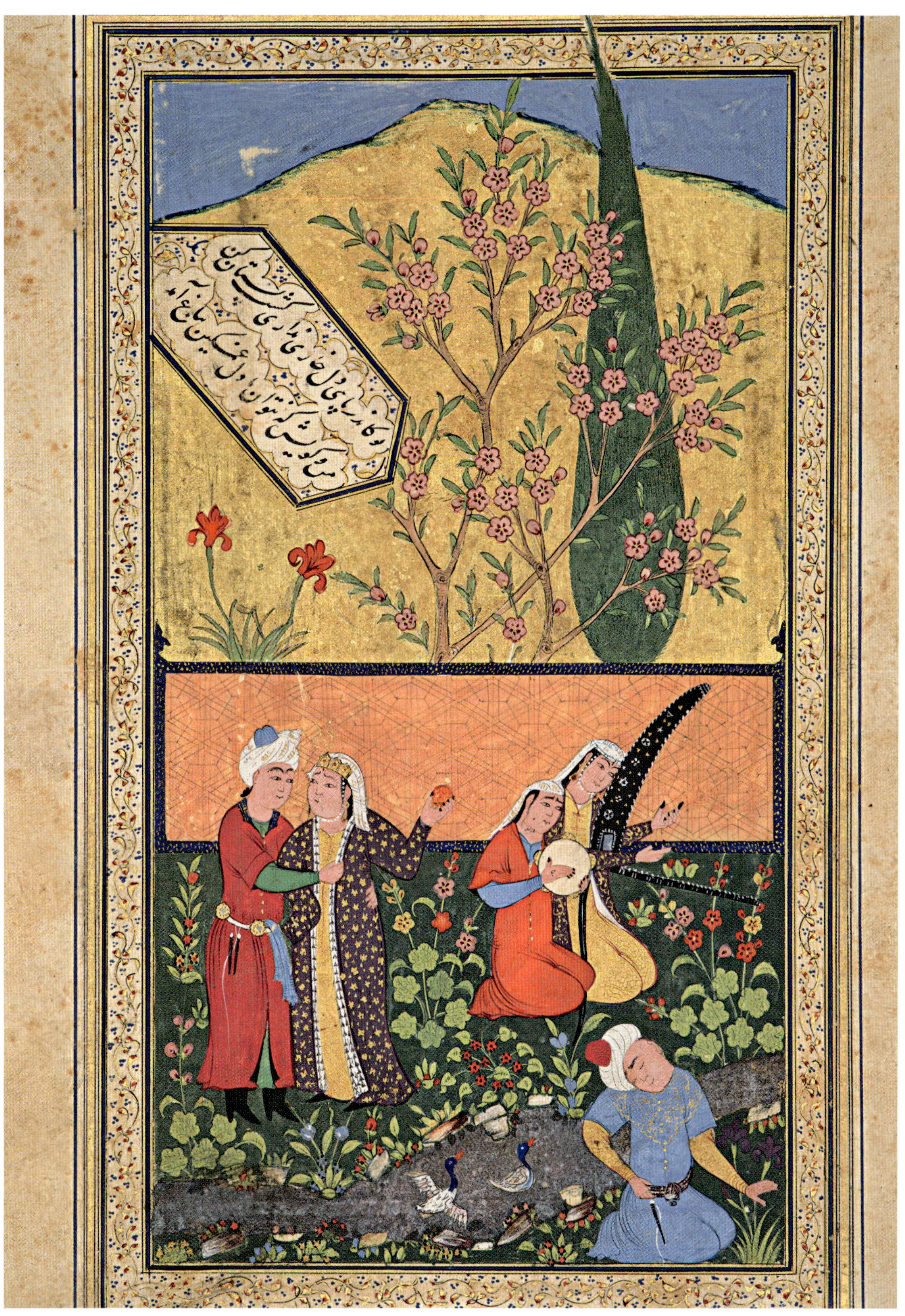

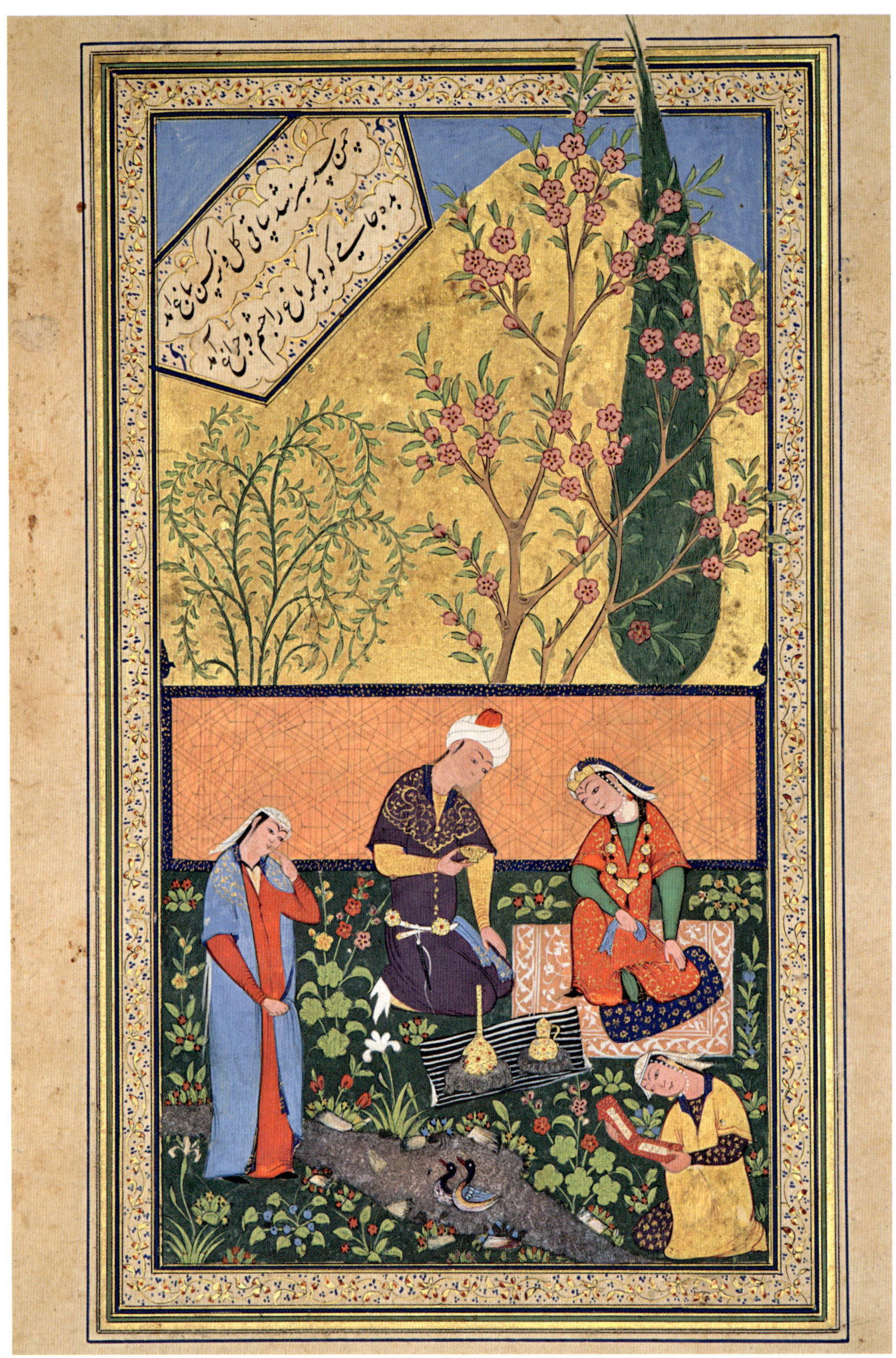

The couple in the right-hand folio appear busy in a courteous conversation, as the richly dressed gentleman sips from a small golden cup. In front of them a gilded metal tankard and a long-necked bottle encrusted with precious stones are placed on low silver tables (now tarnished grey). Made mostly in Safavid Iran, these types of vessels would have been used to serve drinks during banquets around the same period; their presence in a painting produced in Uzbek-dominated Bukhara confirms their popularity and ample circulation amongst the affluent elite of Iran and Central Asia during the 10th century AH/16th century CE. The landscape beyond the walls refers to popular themes in the Persian lyrical tradition, with cypresses (*sarv*), flowering branches, and narcissus (*narges*) that are not only elements of the landscape but also common metaphors for the beloved. NF

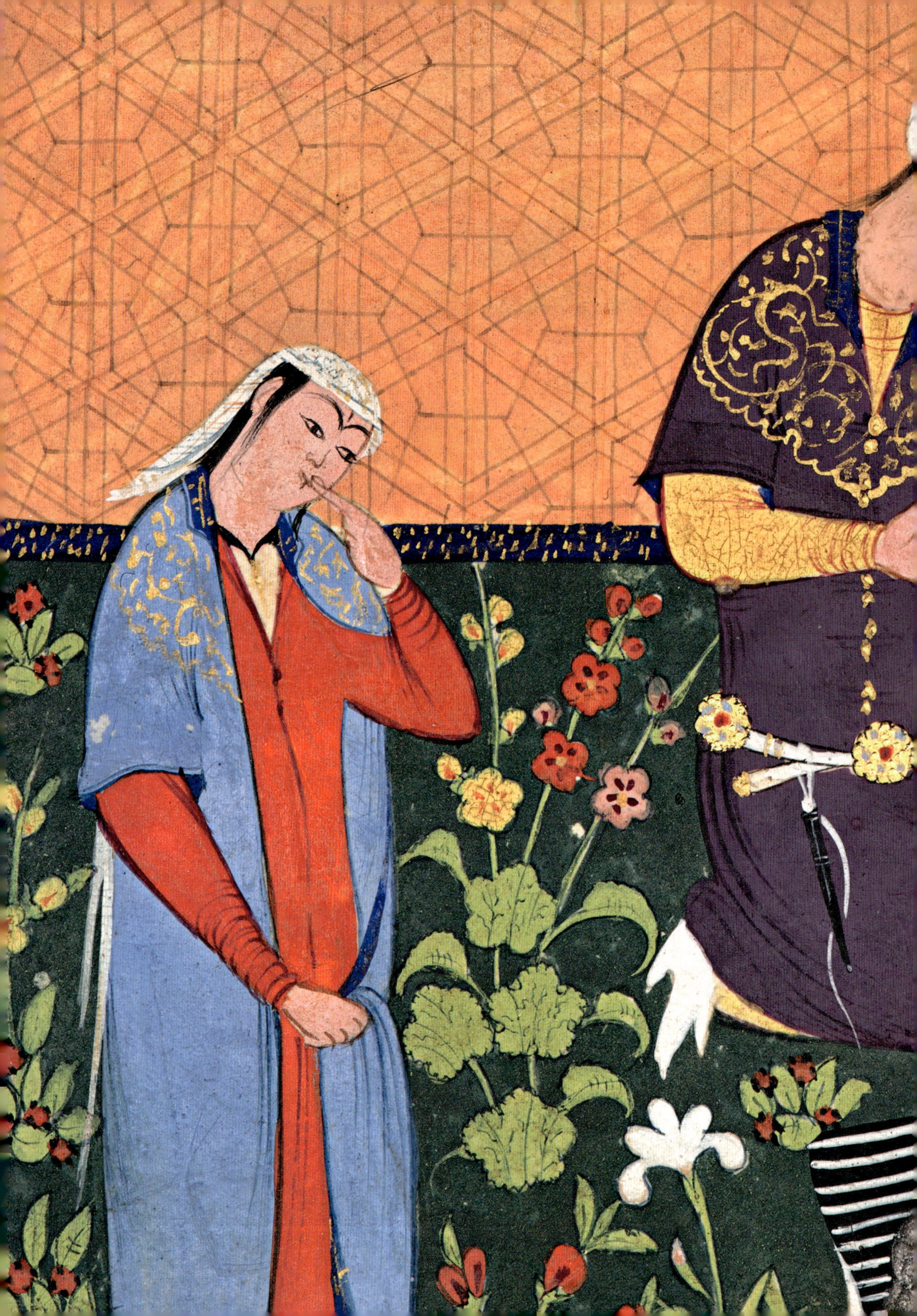

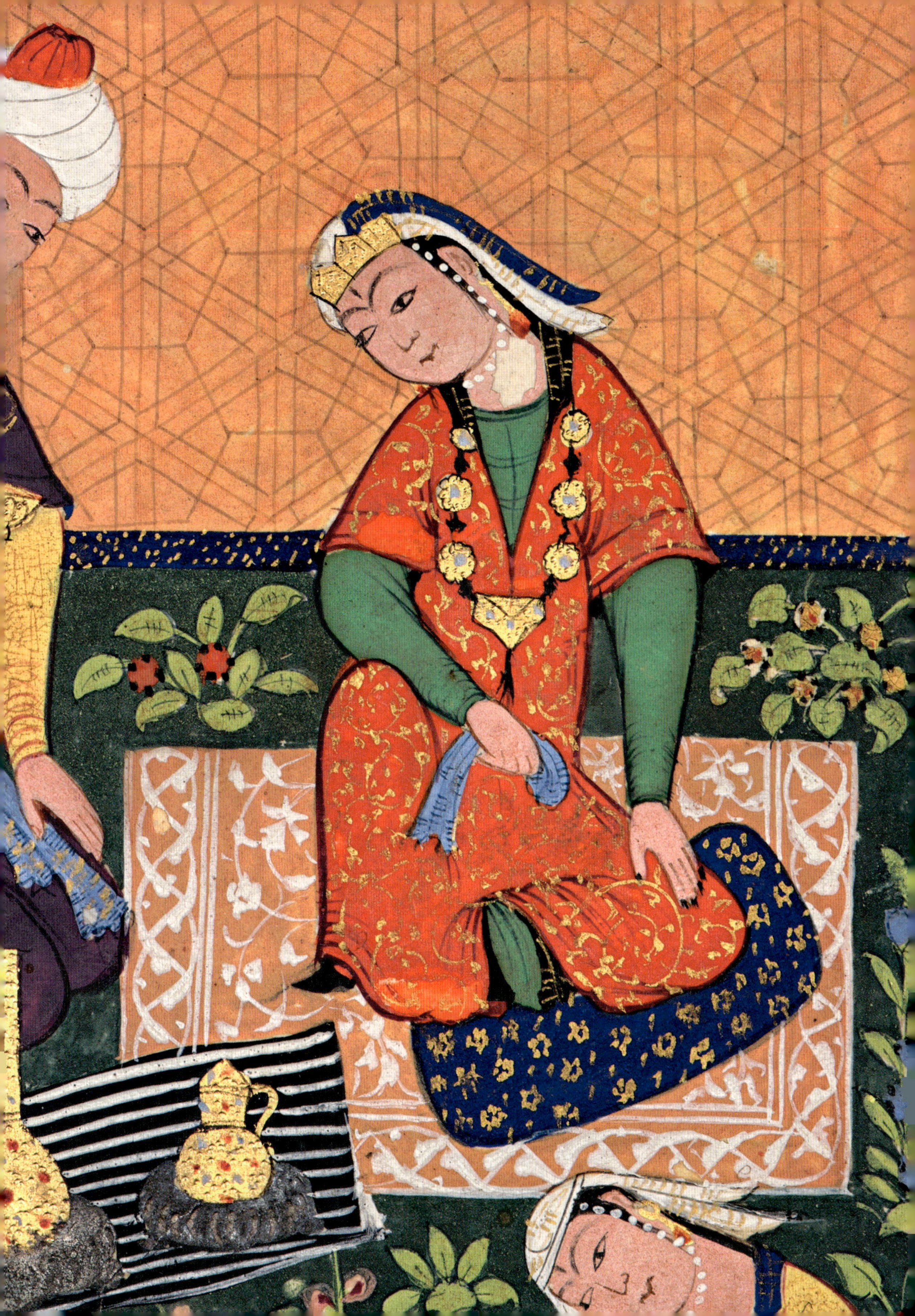

22
Ewer (*aftaba*)
India, Mughal period,
10th century AH/late 16th century CE
Cast bronze
67.5 × ⌀ 43.5 cm
Museum of Islamic Art, MW.292.2007

This monumental ewer (*aftaba* or *abdasta*) stands over 60 cm in height and is the largest known metal ewer attributed to 10th century AH/ 16th century CE Mughal India. It was probably used in a large kitchen, travelling camp or religious setting (perhaps a temple or shrine) for drinking water or washing hands, the latter typically scented with rose extracts, and poured over one's hands before and after a meal.

Drinking water was a major expense to any royal household. Emperor Akbar (r. 963–1013 AH/1556–1604 CE) reportedly only drank water sourced from the River Ganges, which was carried a considerable distance in sealed jars. In the early part of Akbar's reign, river water was mixed and cooled with saltpetre. A special department at the Mughal court, known as the *Aabdar-Khana*, was responsible for water supplied to the emperor. Cooking water, for example, came from either the Yamuna and Chenab Rivers, or was collected from rainwater. The 11th century AH/17th century CE Italian traveller Niccolao Manucci, a physician to the court of Shah Jahan (r. 1037–1069 AH/1628–1658 CE), included water bearers amongst the many departments of the royal kitchen escorted by military contingents.[1]

This vessel follows the classic Mughal ewer in form—which typically consists of a pear-shaped body, curved handle and spout, a tall neck and a crescent shaped top. The earliest attributed example of an *aftaba* dates to 8th century AH/14th century CE Turkey or Iran. This piece is fashioned from six parts of cast bronze: a bulbous body; splayed pedestal foot; cylindrical neck with a collared rim; dome-shaped lid with a floral knob; 'S' shaped handled; and slender spout. The lid is secured to the handle by a metal tongue that swivels on a pin attached to the handle. The ewer's body is undecorated except for three fine lines etched in parallel around the middle, and zoomorphic heads at each end of the spout and handle. A small, illegible inscription—possibly in Persian or Devanagari script—is etched onto the upper shoulder. Originally, this ewer may have been accompanied by a large basin used to collect the water poured over a guest's hands when washed. TD

1 Husain, *The Emperor's Table*, p. 14.

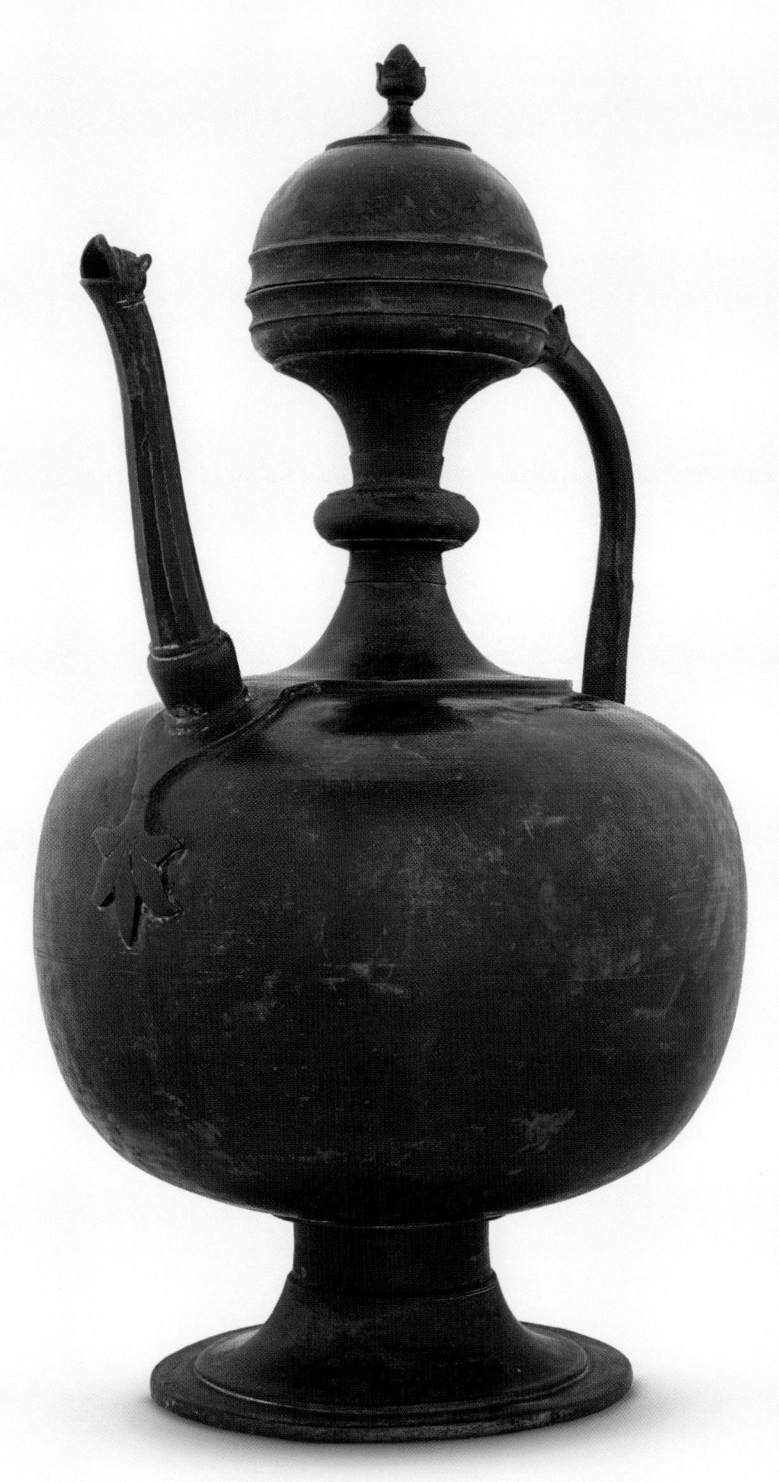

23
Cow and calf painting
Attributed to Dasavanta
India, Mughal period, 10th century AH/late-16th century CE
Opaque watercolour, ink and gold on paper
Painting: 19.3 × 11.7 cm, folio: 30.5 × 20 cm
Museum of Islamic Art, MS.33.2007

The advent of Mughal rule in North India resulted in a great
fusion of culinary traditions, including Indian, Persian and Turkish
cuisines. Based on the list of recipes provided in the *Ain-i Akbari*,
Emperor Akbar's (r. 963–1013 AH/1556–1604 CE) official court
chronicle, sheep, goat, rice, wheat, barley and lentils appeared
frequently, along with fresh milk and yoghurt. Akbar was known
to start every meal with milk or yoghurt. He also followed a strict
system of cooked dishes, avoiding meat on Fridays and Sundays,
the first day of every month of the solar year, and during the
month in which he was born (*Aban*).[1] Milk products, however,
were always allowed to be consumed. This tender painting
illustrates a cow with its suckling calf. The painting, although
unsigned, has been attributed to the Hindu artist Dasavanta,
a prominent painter in Akbar's royal atelier. TD

1 Husain, *The Emperor's Table*, p. 16.

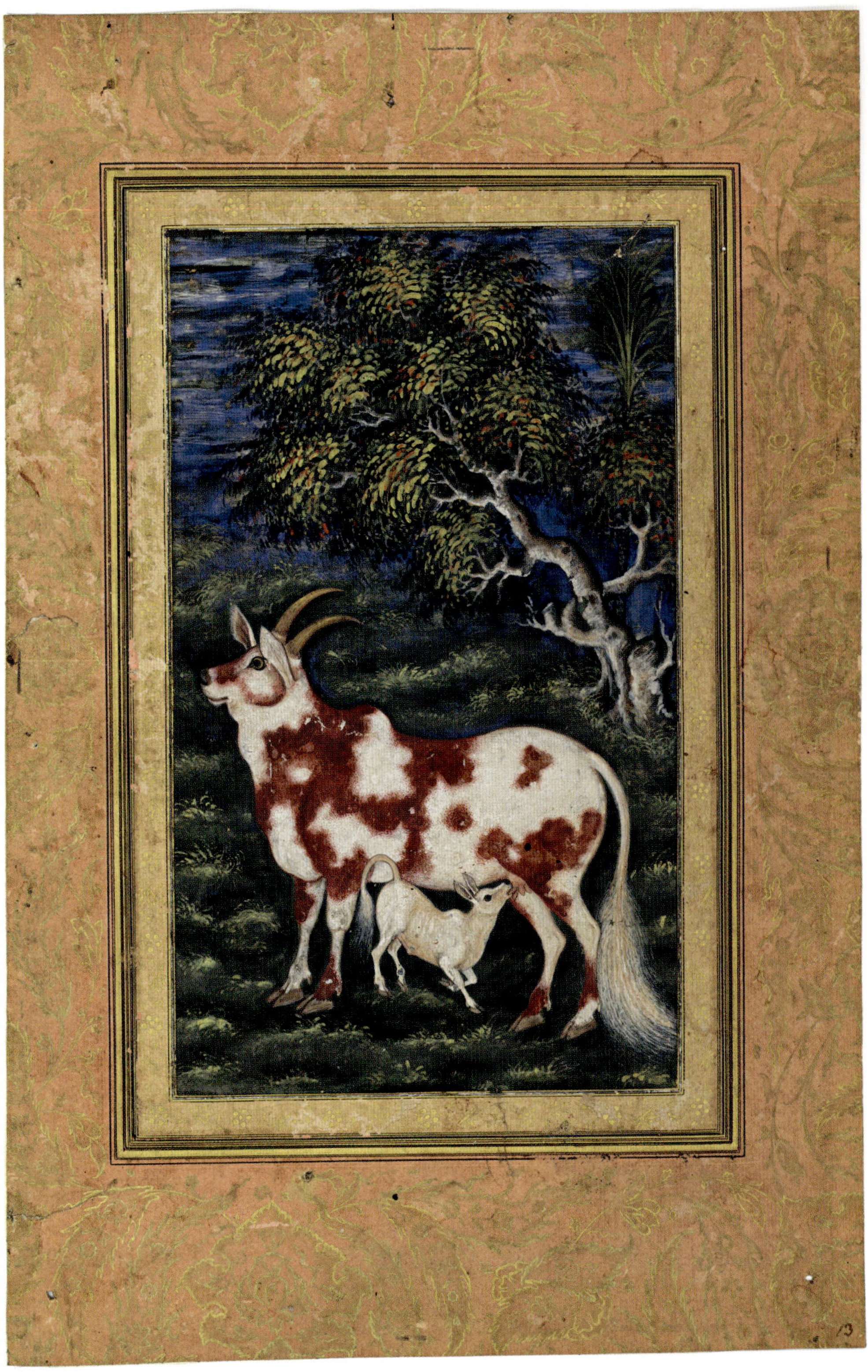

Portrait of the Mughal Emperor Jahangir
Attributed to Balchand
India, Mughal period, *c.* 1030 AH/1620 CE
Opaque watercolour, ink and gold on paper
22.3 × 17.3 cm
Museum of Islamic Art, MS.771.2011

Perhaps intended as a preparatory drawing for a larger, ceremonial painting, this delicate sketch of the Mughal emperor Jahangir (r. 1013–1037 AH/1605–1627 CE) reflects his powerful status. He is dressed in regal attire, his head encircled by a halo, and his hand rests on a lion's head.[1] To his left stands an attendant offering a lidded cup on a small tray, similar in size to the one shown overleaf.[2]

Jahangir spent most of his time between the Punjab (Lahore) and Kashmir, where a large number of cooks had migrated from Samarqand, bringing with them their own culinary traditions. Like his father, Akbar, Jahangir also adopted specific culinary doctrines, such as only eating vegetarian food (*sufiyana*) on Sundays and Thursdays and dining in the company of yogis and *Shrivatri* (those who worship the deity Shiva). According to his memoirs, he preferred black partridge and a dish called *dopiyazah* of *nilgai* (black antelope) as well as fish. He was also known to be a great promotor of horticulture, in particular fruits.[3]

Inscription:
جهانت بكام و فلک يار باد/جها[ن] آفرينت نگهدار باد
بكام تو بادا همه كار تو/خداوند گيتى نگهدار تو
بنده درگاه، عمل بالچند

'May the world be as you like, and the universe be a friend to you/May the creator of the universe protect you/May everything related to you be the way you like/May God keep you [from harm]
Servant of God, Made by Balchand'[4]

1 The present drawing was most certainly produced after 1022 AH/1614 CE as the emperor's ears are pierced; this, according to the *Jahangirnama* happened on the twelfth of Shahrivar (August 26th) of that year.

2 See an example in the Los Angeles County Museum of Art (M.83.1.5).

3 Thackston, ed. and trans., *The Jahangirnama*, pp. 184–185.

4 The author thanks Mohammed Farsimadan for his reading and translation of the inscription. The first couplet comes from a poem by Sa'di, while the second couplet is attributed to Sa'di, Ferdowsi and Daqiqi.

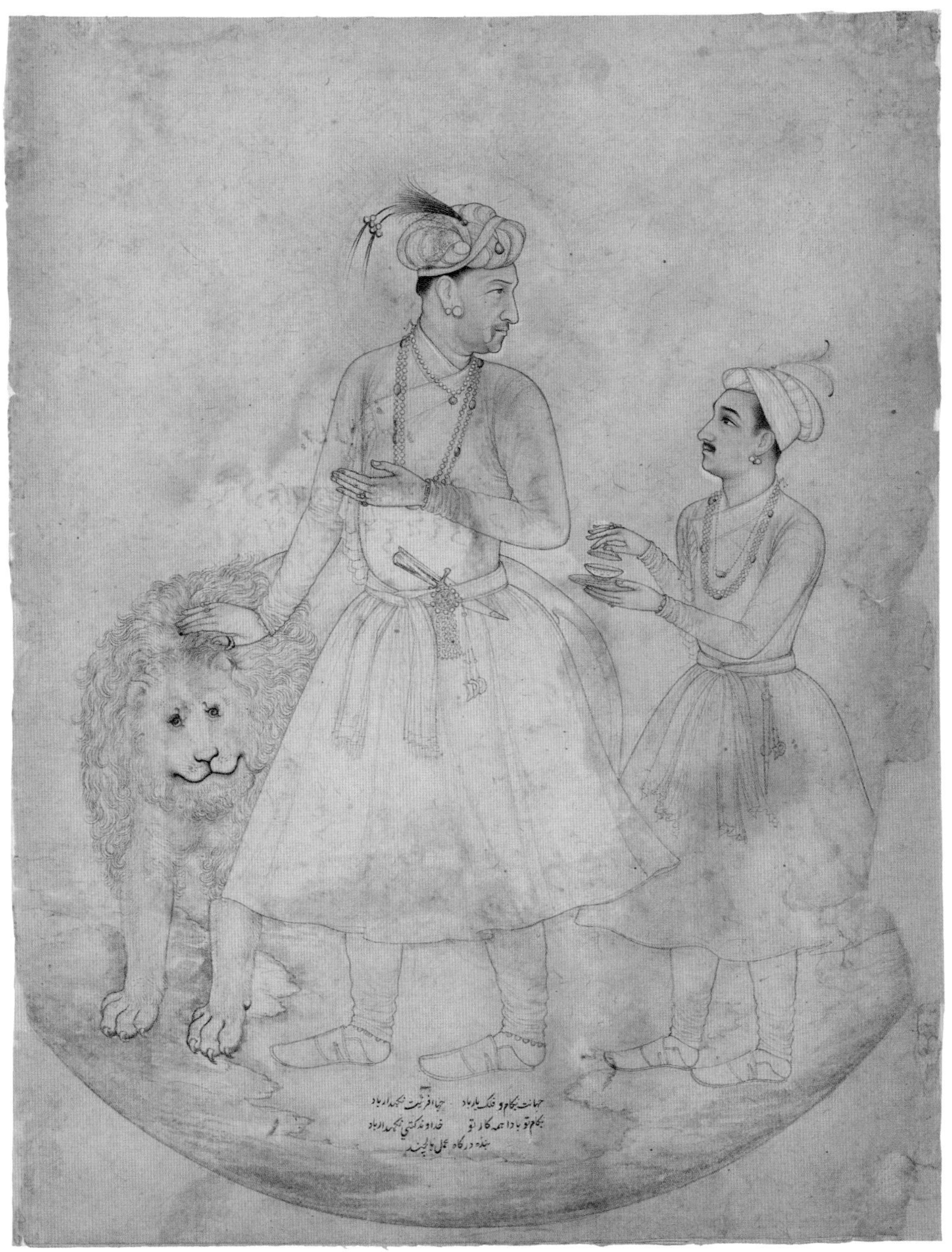

جهان بکام و فلک یار باد   جهان آفرینت نگهدار باد
بکام تو بادا همه کار تو   خداوند گیتی نگهدار باد
بنده درگاه عمل بالہند

24b
Cup
India, Mughal period,
mid-11th century AH/17th century CE
Carved jade
2.0 × 8.3 × 5.4 cm
Museum of Islamic Art, GL.172.2003

Small jade cups such as this one were produced in large quantities at the Mughal court, not only because the Mughals inherited the taste for fine jades from their ancestors, the Timurids, but also because they believed that foods served in jade dishes helped detect poison by immediately changing colour. This cup has been delicately carved into the shape of a leaf, with a shallow, rounded body, thin, semi-translucent sidewalls, and a handle shaped like a tightly curled acanthus leaf. The interior is smoothly polished, while the exterior has a raised midrib and faintly indicated veins. Jades of this lighter colour and restrained decoration are typically dated to the mid-11th century AH/mid-17th century CE or later. TD

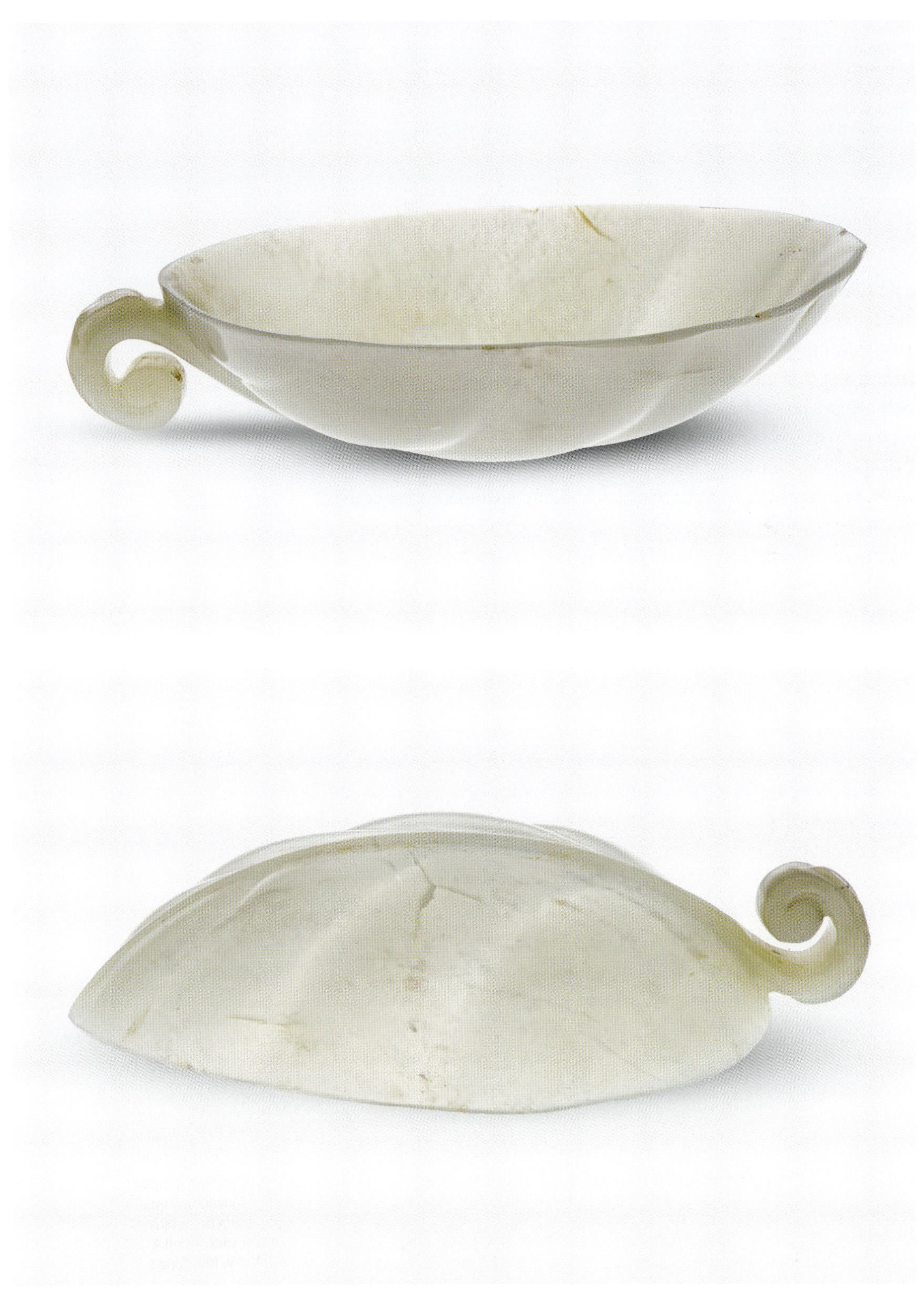

25
Tent panel (*qanat*)
Northern India, Mughal period,
12th century AH/18th century CE
Block-printed, painted and mordant-dyed cotton
505 × 124 cm
Museum of Islamic Art, TE.81.2003

The *Akbarnama*, the account of Akbar's reign (r. 963–1013 AH/
1556–1604 CE) authored by Abu al-Fazl, discusses the role of
bazm (banqueting) as equal to *razm* (fighting). In describing
Akbar as an emperor who knew the 'niceties of banquet', the
text underscores that Mughal kingship and governance were
as much rooted in military conquest as they were in feasting.[1]
Feasts were a tool for strengthening bonds, and were bound by
elaborate rules of etiquette: they should be hosted in a garden
or on the banks of waterbodies, and adorned by colourful gold-
embroidered or chintz-printed *sufra*s.[2] In the same text, Abu al-
Fazl notes that tents were 'an excellent dwelling place, a shelter
from heat and cold [...] as the ornament of royalty'.[3] The textiles
used for these shelters not only created the perfect environment,
but also reflected the ruler's wealth and majesty.

This elegant panel was probably made for a princely or royal
tent. It would have been joined to a series of similar panels
that enclosed an outdoor space within a palace compound, or,
used as a moveable screen to divide the inside of a tent when
travelling. As it was customary for the Mughal rulers to move
throughout their empire, whether to regulate affairs or administer
justice, to engage in warfare or partake in the private pleasure
of hunting (*shikar*), these portable panels helped create an ideal
(and impressive) interior space. This panel is painted with a large
poppy plant against a white ground strewn with cloud bands
beneath a yellow ground arch. The borders, as well as the flowers
and leaves of the plant, are block-printed from small individual
blocks, while the stems have been drawn and painted by hand.[4]
Although generally attributed to North India, several places were
known to have made printed cotton textiles at the time, such as
Golconda in the Deccan and the cities of Burhanpur, Agra, and
Sironj, all within the Mughal dominions. TD

1 Abu al-Fazl 'Allami, *The Akbarnama*,
vol. 3, p. 78.

2 Neha Vermani, 'Convivial Politics:
An Overview of Feasting at the Mughal
Court', in Komaroff, ed., *Dining with the
Sultan*, p. 92.

3 See the notes for lot 31, Christie's,
12th June 2018, available online at https://
www.christies.com/en/lot/lot-6142480.

4 Comparable examples are held by the
Calico Museum, Ahmedabad (801a) and
the Baroda State Museum and Picture
Gallery, Vadodara (I.A. 764). See also
Sotheby's, 10th June 2020, lot 143.

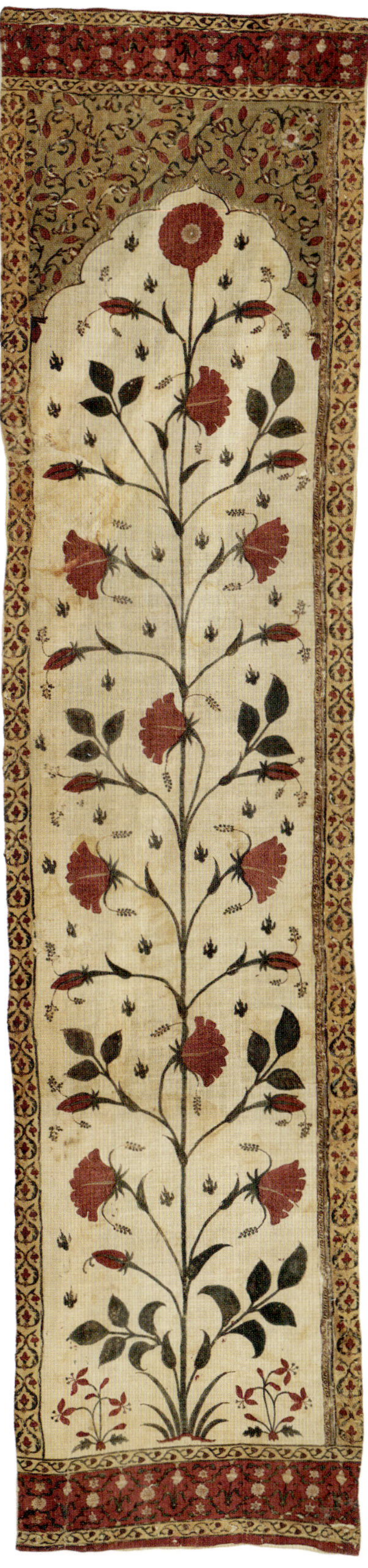

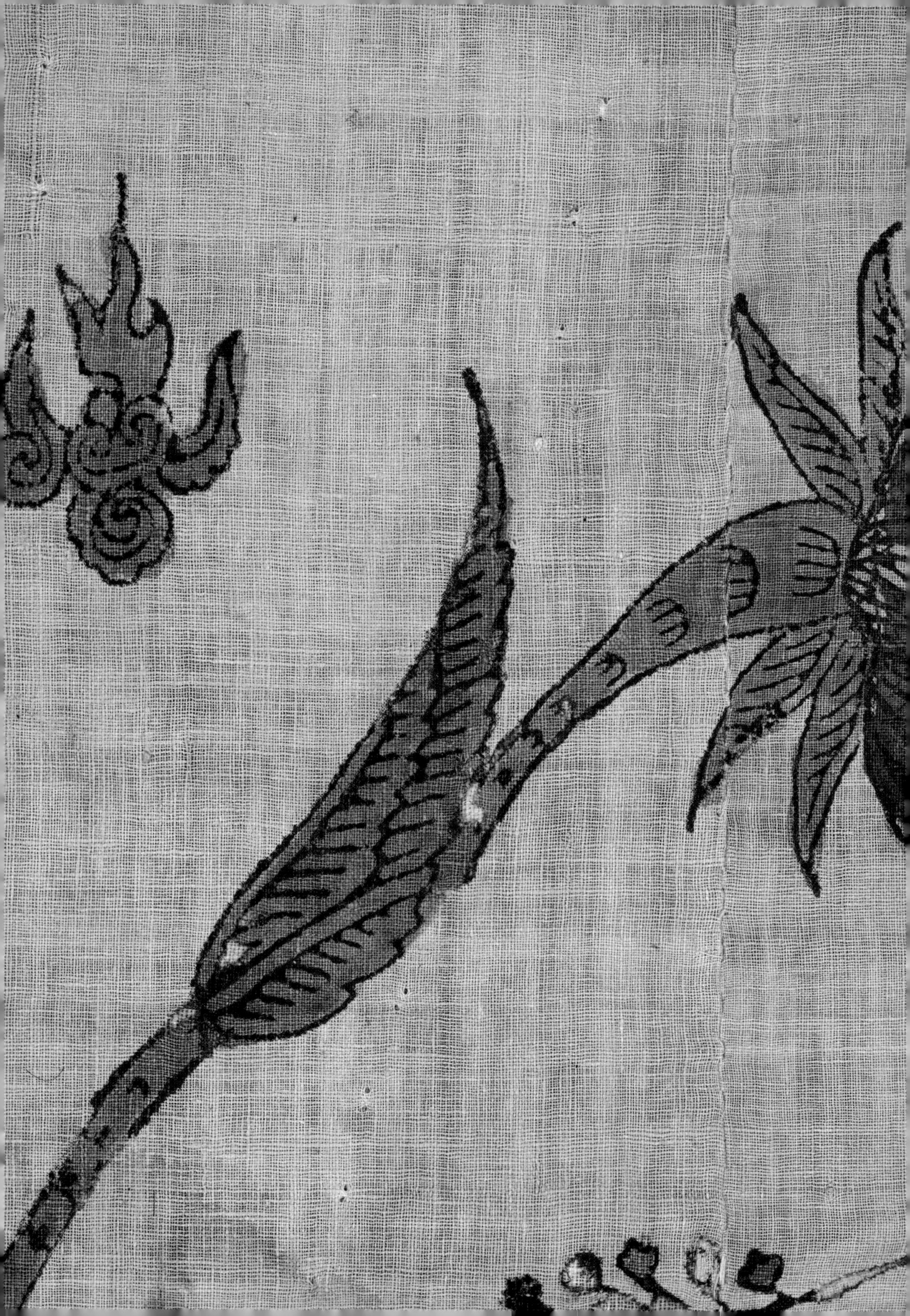

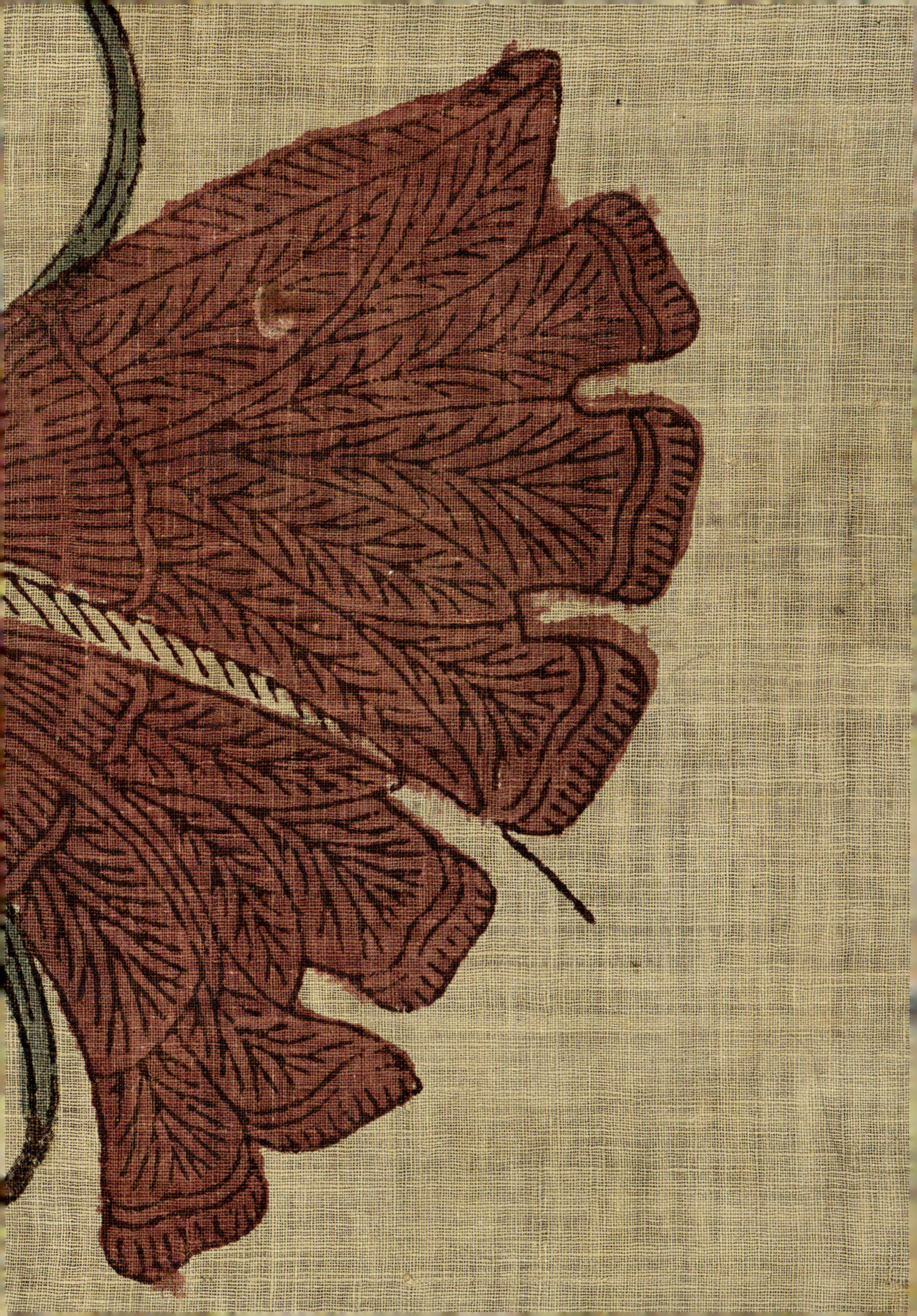

26
Lidded jar
India (Jaipur or Delhi), Mughal period,
13th century AH/19th century CE
Enamelled copper set with diamonds
H. 12.2 cm
Museum of Islamic Art, JE.219.2003

The Mughal emperors paid considerable attention to the
adornment of dining. Their foods were always rich, colourful,
and decorated with gold and silver leaves—some even made
to look like gems and jewels with fruits cut into the shape of
flowers—while their tables were elaborately set with the finest
serving vessels. According to Emperor Akbar's 10th-century
AH/late 16th-century CE official chronicle, the *Ain-i Akbari*, the
royal kitchen had its own budget with a department dedicated
to expenses related to the emperor's table, which included food
preparation, serving utensils, and tableware.[1] In the same text,
in a section dedicated to courtly crafts, a detailed description is
given to the art of enamelling, a technique that was introduced
by either Portuguese or Italian goldsmiths working in Goa at the
time; by the 13th century AH/19th century CE, the technique had
become widespread throughout South Asia.[2] This enamelled,
baluster-shaped jar is further decorated with large table-cut
diamonds set in the traditional *kundan* technique, whereby the
stones are foil backed and set into metal collets using high-carat
gold foil (as opposed to being soldered).

Within the Mughal court, jewel encrusted objects such as
this would have decorated the tables of important ceremonies
and events, often accompanied by other fine wares made from
gold, jade and porcelain. According to the *Mirzanama*, a late
11th-century AH/17th-century CE manual on Mughal codes of
conduct, jewel-studded jugs were explicitly included amongst
the objects advised to adorn the dining venue.[3] This jar may
have been used to serve *paan*, a digestif and stimulant made of
chopped betel nut, lime and spices typically offered at the end
of a meal to freshen the mouth. TD

1 Husain, *The Emperor's Table*, p. 15.

2 Abu al-Fazl 'Allami, *The Ain-i Akbari*,
vol. 3, p. 346.

3 See *Mirzanama*, British Library, London
(Add 16, 819), fols. 89b-95b, referenced in
Komaroff, ed., *Dining with the Sultan,* p. 92,
footnote 9.

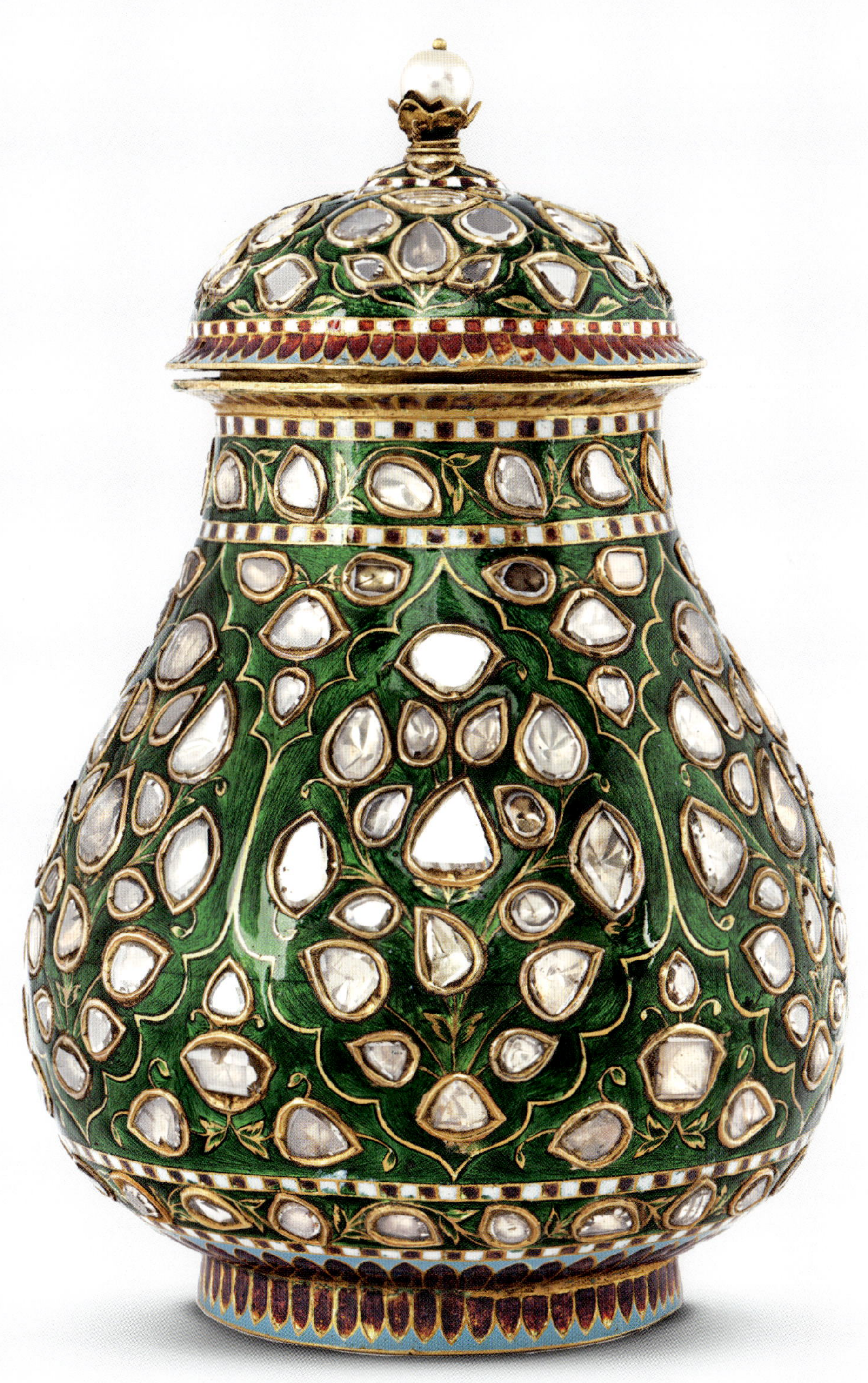

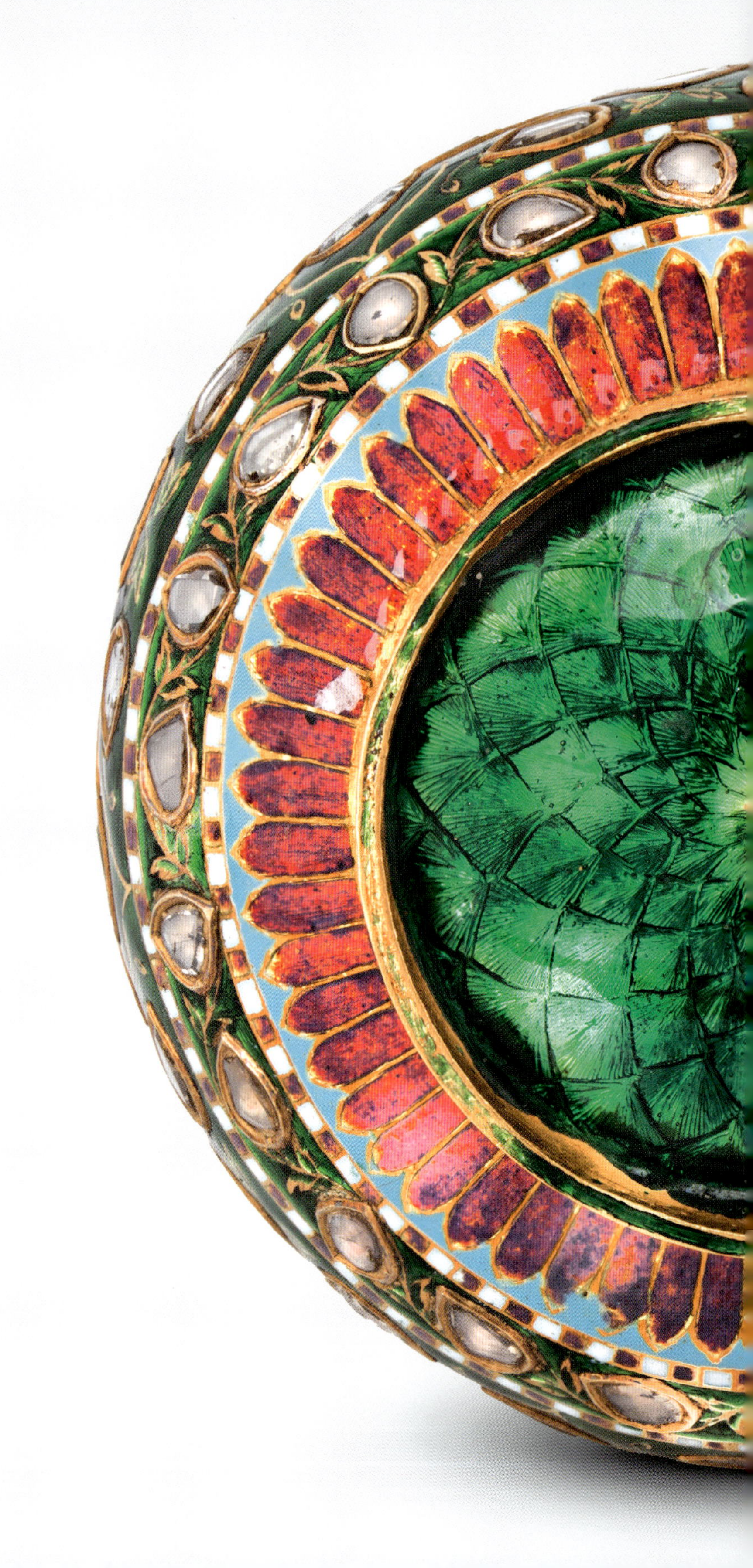

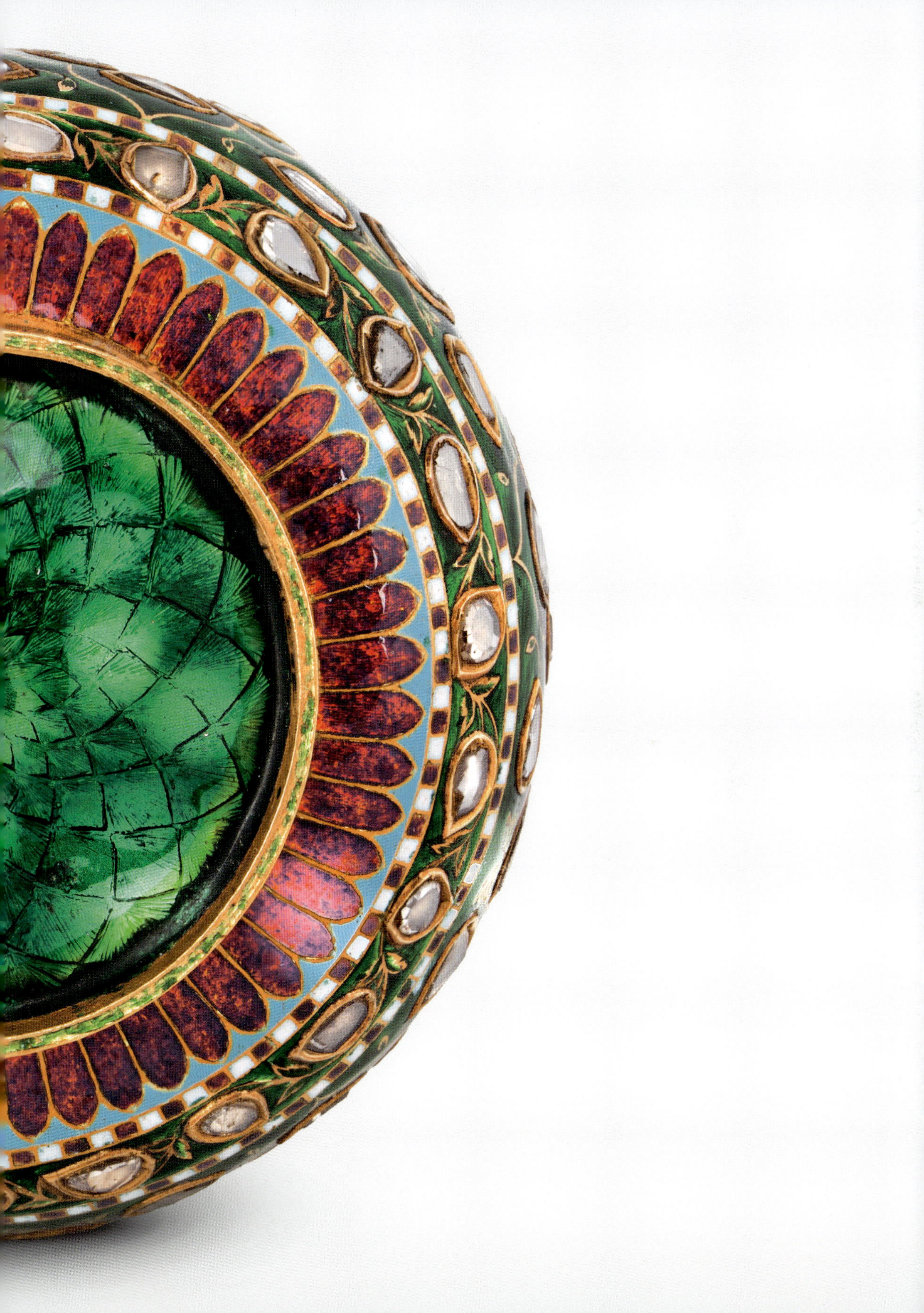

27

Dish with grapevines
Turkey (Iznik), Ottoman period,
c. 877–881 AH/1525–1530 CE
Underglaze-painted fritware
7 × ⌀ 40.3 cm
Museum of Islamic Art, PO.46.1999

Inspired by the refined designs of blue-and-white ceramics of the Chinese Yuan dynasty, the Ottoman Sultan Mehmed II (r. 855–886 AH/1451–1481 CE) supported the production of ceramics at Iznik, in western Anatolia (modern-day Turkey). Iznik wares soon became widely popular in elite Ottoman households, where they were used for decoration,[1] to show wealth, and also to serve the contemporary cuisine of stews, pilafs and soups.

In this piece, the grape clusters and floral patterns are directly inspired by Chinese blue-and-white porcelains of the Ming dynasty (769–1054 AH/1368–1644 CE). The distinctive 'wave and rock' motif found around the rim, however, is drawn from the earlier Yuan period (669–769 AH /1271–1368 CE) designs. Fruits are often represented on Iznik dishes, but the grape motif was the most common, inspired by Chinese porcelains and also by plants grown in the region. One departure from Ming prototypes is the vibrant turquoise that appears on this dish. RA

1 Gonnella, et al., *Museum of Islamic Art*, pp. 339, 352.

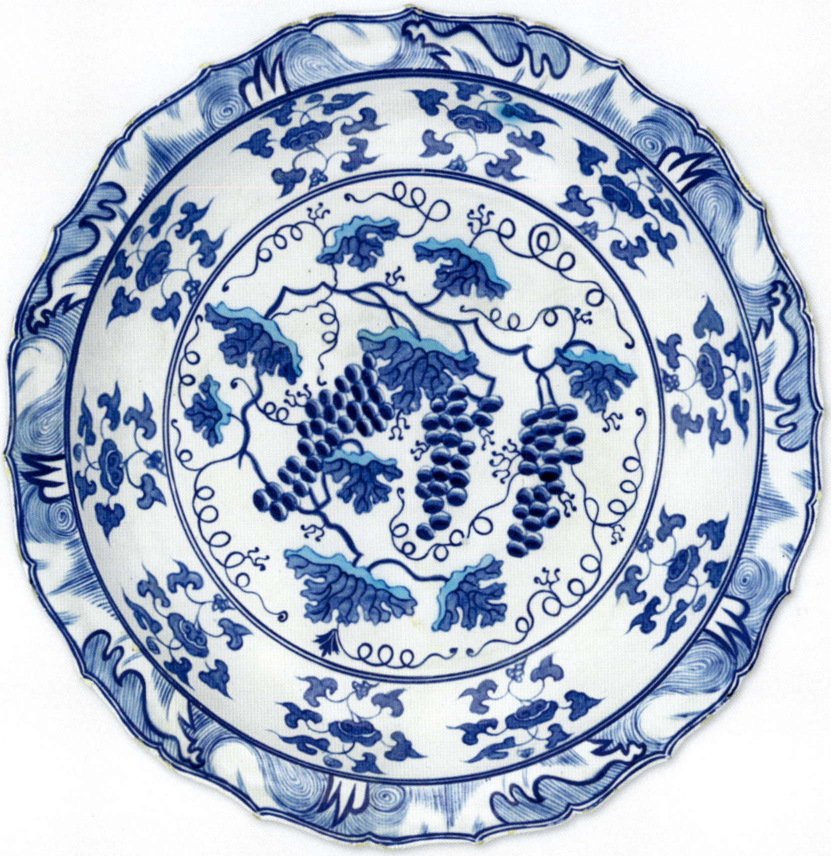

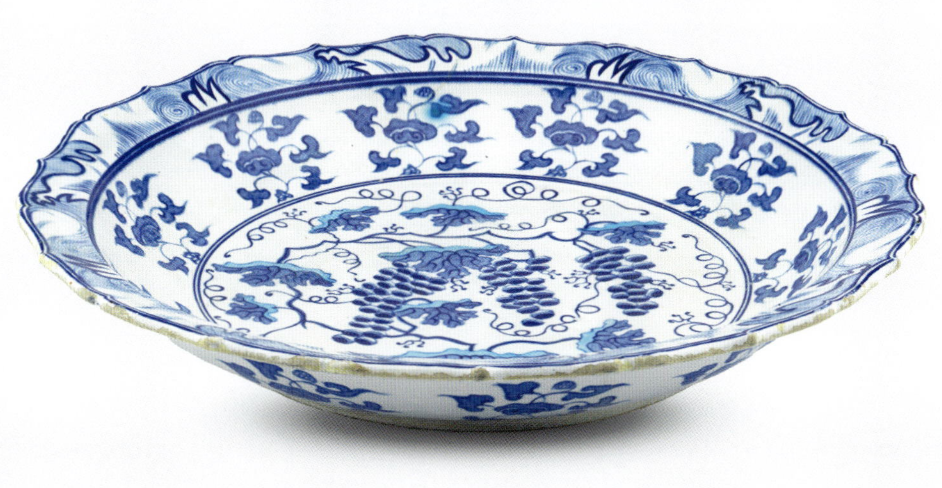

28

Bottle (*surahi*)
Turkey (Iznik), Ottoman period,
10th century AH/late 16th century CE
Underglaze-painted fritware
44.5 × ø 20.7 cm
Museum of Islamic Art, PO.10.1997

Under the rule of Sultan Suleiman the Magnificent (926–973 AH/ 1520–1566 CE), Iznik pottery reached new heights in quality due to a growing demand from the Ottoman elite and the imperial court. These Iznik pieces, made from fritware (a combination of quartz, clay, and ground glass) and decorated with intricate underglaze painting, marked a significant shift from earlier Ottoman pottery production. They were additionally much lighter in weight, making them easier to use as tableware. Iznik wares symbolised wealth and were often exchanged as gifts, but they were even more commonly used by the elites as tableware to serve a variety of dishes.

This bottle's impressive size, slender neck, and slightly flaring mouth are complemented by the vibrant depictions of animals including deer, hares, leopards and partridges. The decoration also incorporates floral motifs such as tulips and carnations. The inclusion of animals is quite rare in Iznik pottery, and this imagery clearly references the exchanges between the earlier Chinese Tang dynasty (1st–4th century AH/7th–10th century CE) and the Ottoman Empire.

This bottle was probably produced around the 990s AH/1580s CE, a period when Iznik pottery production blossomed and new pigments such as red and green were introduced. It also includes turquoise and cobalt blue, which were especially favoured colour combinations just before the introduction of red, green and purple. The bottle would have been used in Ottoman households to store and pour water and other beverages. RA

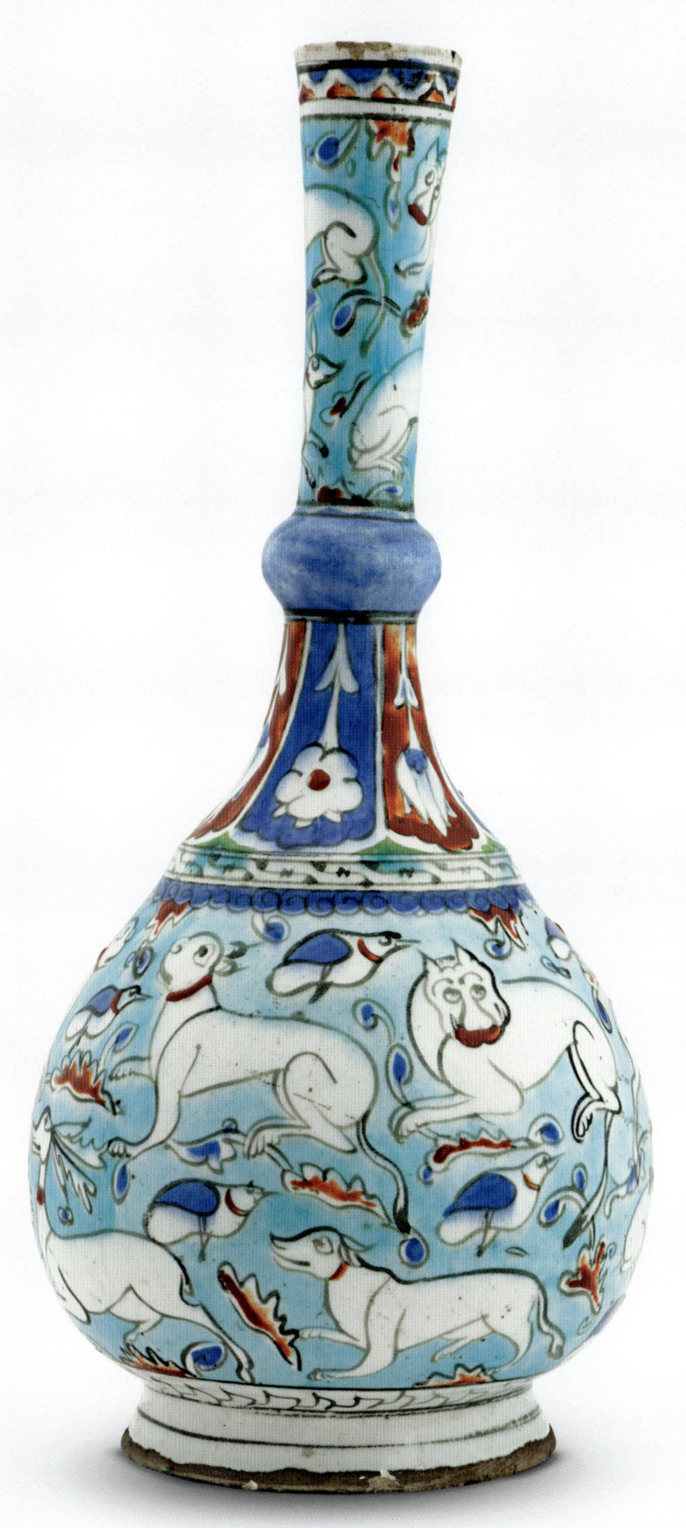

29
Spoons
Turkey, Ottoman period,
13th century AH/19th century CE
Carved tortoiseshell, ebony and ivory pierced
and mounted with copper alloy pins
L. 19.5 – 26.5 cm
Museum of Islamic Art, IV.29.2002

The spoon holds a distinctive place in Turkish culture, particularly because it was, until the 13 century AH/19th century CE, the only utensil present on the table aside from plates. This gave the spoon a wide range of uses. This set of spoons are crafted from costly materials such as coral, ivory, tortoiseshell and horn, with one featuring a silver handle. These materials found their way into Ottoman decorative arts during the 10th century AH/16th century CE, after the Ottomans gained control of the lucrative Indian Ocean trade routes that were previously dominated by the Portuguese. These spoons were likely used for enjoying sherbet, a popular fruit-based dessert, although similar spoons were also employed for serving rice, fruit stews and preserves from communal dishes. Reserved for the opulent tables of Istanbul's royalty and elite, these spoons would have been a mark of luxury and refinement.

Beyond their practical use, spoons also carried symbolic significance in Ottoman culture. In parts of Anatolia, spoons were incorporated into folk dances and even hung as decorative ornaments in homes. The spoon also had a role in matters of marriage. It was considered improper for young men and women to openly discuss marriage with their fathers, so they expressed their intentions subtly. For instance, a spoon placed in the middle of a dish of rice, or an extra spoon laid at the table, signalled a desire to marry.[1] In this way, spoons became more than just practical tools; they were imbued with cultural meaning, playing a role in both everyday life and special occasions. TS

1 Arif Bilgin, 'Spoon Up Some Pilaf: Spoons in the Turkish Culture', in Erke, ed., *Turkish Cuisine with Timeless Recipes*, p. 17.

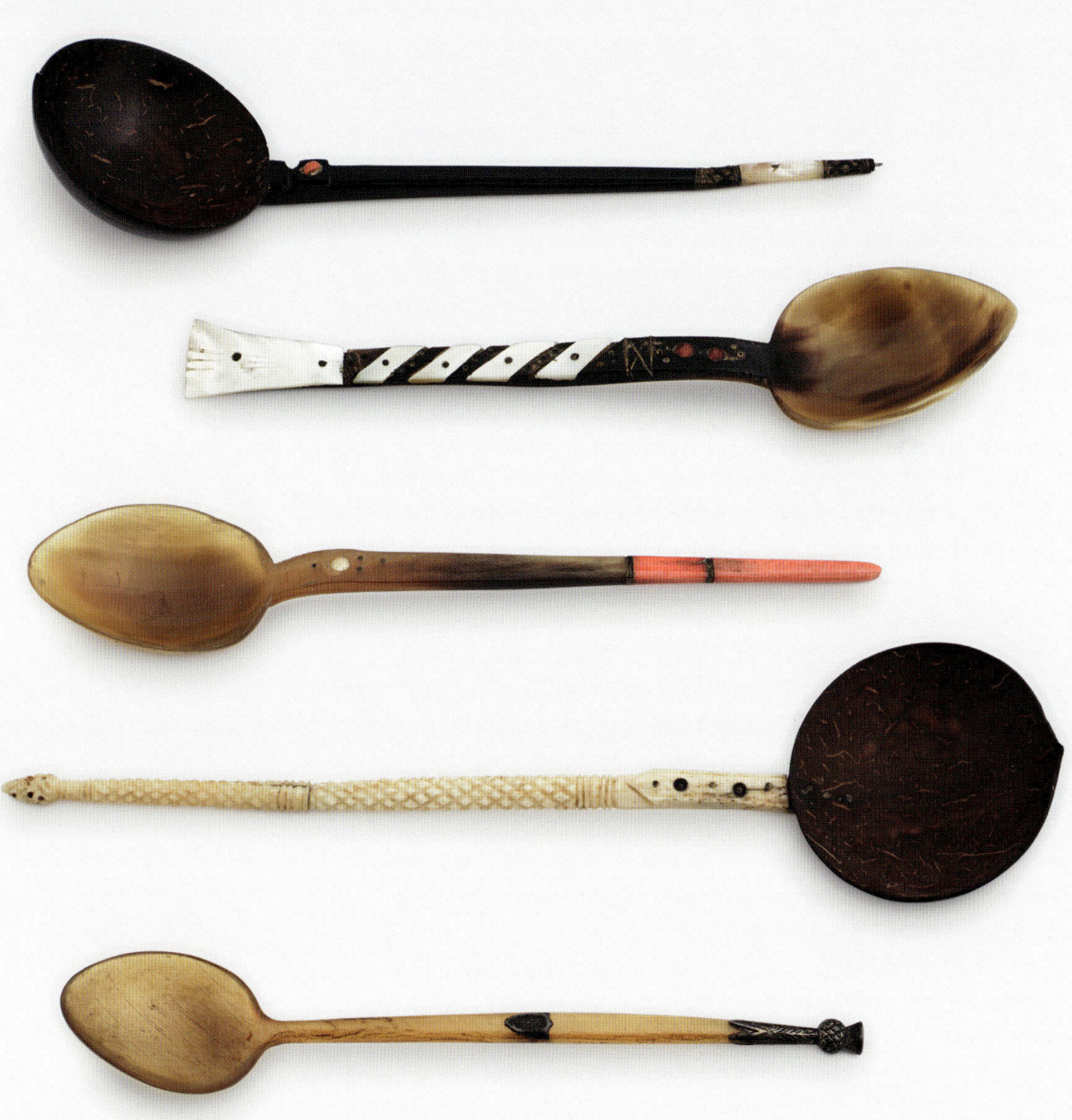

Robe (kaftan)
Turkey, Ottoman period,
13th century AH/19th century CE
Woven silk with metallic embroidery
150.7 × 151.5 cm
Museum of Islamic Art, TE.186.2003

This kaftan exemplifies the role of male clothing in the imperial Ottoman court of the 13th–14th centuries AH/19th–20th centuries CE. Although kaftans were worn by both men and women, certain features distinguish them by gender. Men's kaftans like this one, of green velvet embroidered in gilt metal thread, often had front openings, extended to floor-length, and were decorated with large-scale patterns. They were typically paired with matching baggy trousers (*şalvar*) and an inner shirt (*gömlek*) that buttoned from the elbow to the wrist, and had adjustable cuffs.

While this kaftan dates to the 13th century AH/19th century CE, its design and function are part of a long-standing tradition of ceremonial Ottoman attire that evolved over centuries. From the 9th–10th century AH/15th–16th century CE onward, such garments served as markers of status, power, and cultural continuity. This type of clothing was typically worn at the most important occasions in the Ottoman state calendar, including the two Eid celebrations, circumcision ceremonies, and major state or diplomatic events. For example, in 990 AH/1582 CE, Sultan Murad III (r. 982–1004 AH/1574–1595 CE) celebrated the circumcision of his son, Prince Mehmed, with a lavish festival that extended over fifty days, one of the longest and most extravagant events of the Ottoman era.[1] It attracted dignitaries from across the Empire, as well as esteemed guests from beyond its borders, all of whom would have been dressed in rich attire. Guests also dressed in beautifully adorned robes at banquets, as seen in paintings of the period. In an illustration to the *Nusretname*, for instance, Lala Mustafa Pasha, a former Grand Vizier of the Ottoman Empire (r. 988 AH/1580 CE), hosts an opulent feast for several state officials, all of whom are dressed in robes similar to this example.[2] TS

1 Terzioğlu, 'The Imperial Circumcision Festival of 1582: An Interpretation', p. 84.

2 Oberling and Smith, *The Food Culture of the Ottoman Palace*, p. 83.

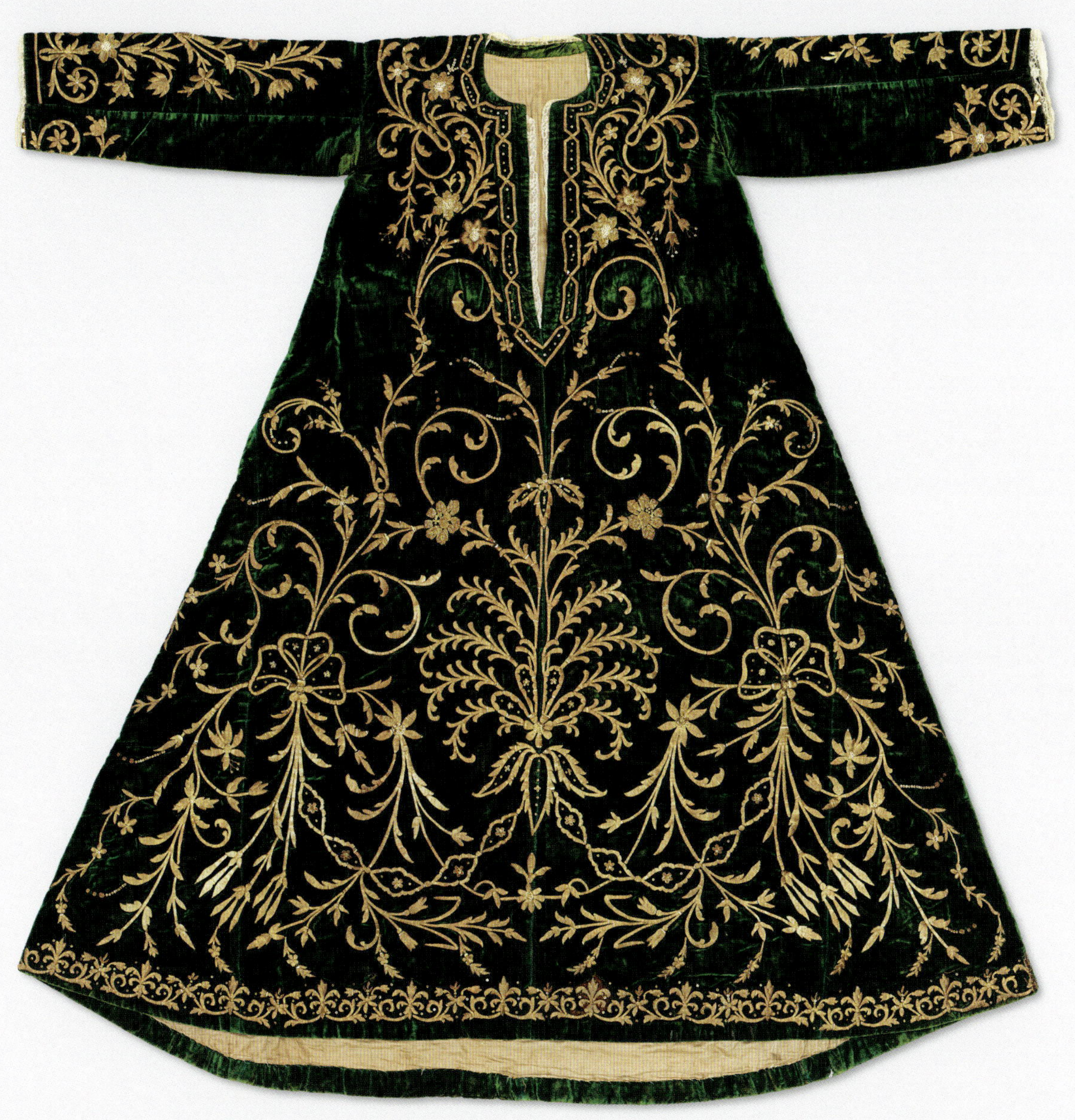

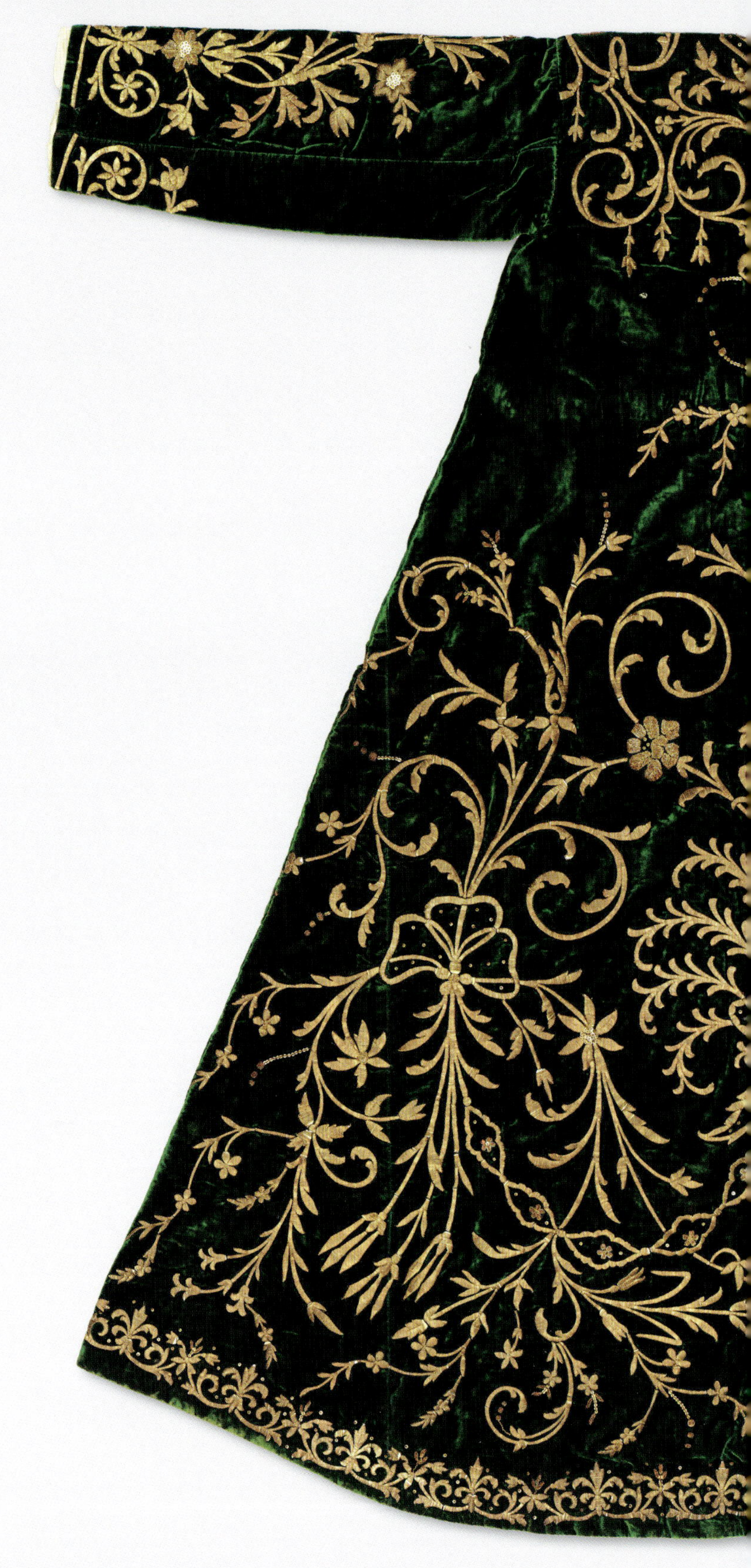

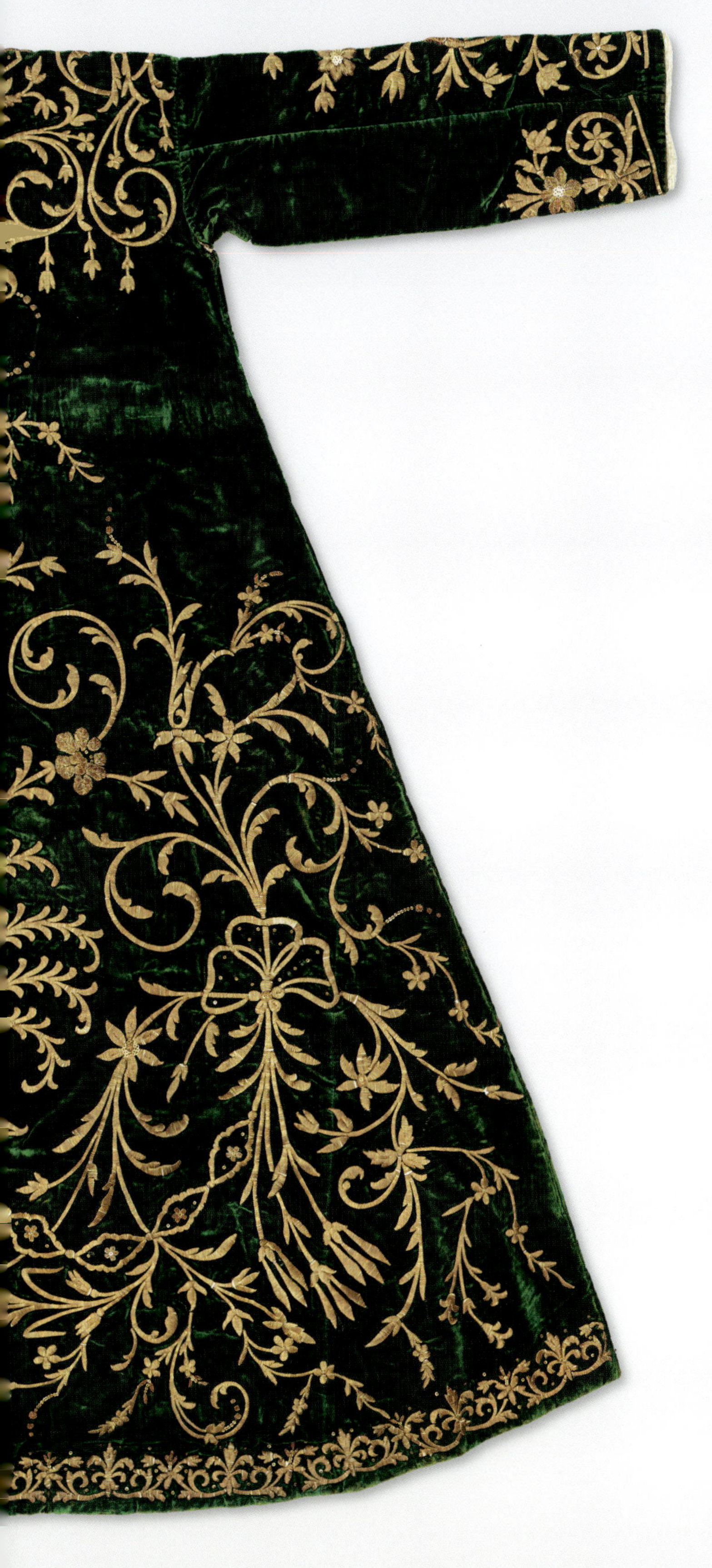

Bibliography

Abdulla, Maryam Mohammed, *Khafayif* (Doha: Self-published, 1993)

Ahsan, Muhammad Manazir, *Social Life Under the Abbasids* (London and New York: Longman, 1979)

Akgün, Sevim Demir and Levent Öztürk. 'Cuisine and Dishes in Use During the Prophet Muhammed Era (A.D. 569–632)', *European Journal of Islamic Studies* 9/4 (2018), pp. 81–85

Al-Bukhari, Muhammad Ibn Isma'il, *Sahih al-Bukhari: The Translation of the Meanings of Sahih al-Bukhari, Arabic-English*, trans. Muhammad Muhsin Khan, 9 vols (Riyadh: Darussalam, 1997)

Al-Tamimi, Aisha Mohammad, *Mawaed Shaabia Qataria* (Doha: Roza Publishing House, 2023)

Al-Tirmidhi, Muhammad Ibn 'Isa, *English Translation of Jami' At-Tirmidhi Compiled by: Imam Hafiz Abu 'Eisa Mohammad Ibn 'Eisa At-Tirmidhi*, trans. Abu Khaliyl, 6 vols (Riyadh: Darussalam, 2007)

Al-Washsha, Abu Tayyib, *Le Livre de brocart ou La société raffinée de Bagdad au Xe siècle: (al-Kitab al-Muwashsha)*, trans. Siham Bouhlal (Paris: Éditions Gallimard, 2004)

'Allami, Abu al-Fazl ibn Mubarak, *The Ain-i Akbari,* trans. H.F. Blochmann and H.S. Jarrett, 3 vols (Calcutta: The Asiatic Society of Bengal, 1873–1894)

'Allami, Abu al-Fazl ibn Mubarak., *The Akbarnama*, ed. and trans. Henry Beveridge, 3 vols (Calcutta: The Asiatic Society of Bengal, 1907–1939)

Allan, James W, 'Later Mamluk Metalwork–II: A Series of Lunch-Boxes', *Oriental Art* N.S. 17/2 (1971), pp. 156–164

Allan, James W, 'Abu'l-Qasim's Treatise on Ceramics', *Iran* 11 (1973), pp. 111–120

Allan, James, ed., *Islamic Art in the Ashmolean Museum, Part Two* (Oxford: Oxford University Press, 1995)

Allan, James W, *Metalwork Treasures from the Islamic Courts* (Doha and London: Museum of Islamic Art with The Islamic Art Society, 2002)

Alymbaeva, Aida Aalyed, *Food and Identity in Central Asia* (Halle (Saale): Max Planck Institute for Social Anthropology, 2017)

Andrews, Jean, 'Diffusion of Mesoamerican Food Complex to Southeastern Europe', *Geographical Review* 83/2 (1993), pp. 194–204

Anjum, Nazer Aziz, 'Ship Construction in Mughal India', *Proceedings of the Indian History Congress* 70 (2009–10), pp. 297–309

Ashtor, Eliyahu, *A Social and Economic History of the Near East in the Middle Ages* (Los Angeles: University of California Press, 1976)

Babaie, Sussan, ed., *Iran after the Mongols* (London and New York: I.B. Tauris, 2019)

Basir, Tariq and Soumya Datta, 'Bread, Freedom or Social Justice? An Empirical Investigation into the Determinants of the Arab Spring', *Democratization* 31/4 (2023), pp. 1–19

Bayhaqi, Khawja Abulfazl Muhammad ibn Husein, *Tarikh-i Bayhaqi*, ed. and annot. Manuchihr Danishpazhu (Tehran: Intisharat-i Hirmand, 1997)

Bazin, Marcel, Christian Bromberger, Daniel Balland, and Ṣogra Bazargan, 'Berenj', *Encyclopeadia Iranica* IV/2, pp. 147–163; available online at https://www.iranicaonline.org/articles/berenj-rice (accessed 25 September 2024)

Bottéro, Jean, *Mesopotamian Culinary Texts*, trans. Jerrold Cooper (Winona Lake, IN: Eisenbrauns, 1995)

Canby, Sheila, Deniz Beyazit, Martina Rugiadi and A.C.S. Peacock, *Court and Cosmos: The Great Age of the Seljuks* (New York: The Metropolitan Museum of Art, 2016)

Chekhab Abudaya, Mounia and Nur Sobers-Khan, 'Acts of Devotion in Late Ottoman Prayer Books: Examination of an Illustrated Manuscript in the Collection of The Museum of Islamic Art, Doha', *Muqarnas* 41 (in press)

Dağyeli, Jeanine, 'Wheat the Magnificent: Revisiting a Central Asian Agricultural Ritual', *Paideuma: Mitteilungen zur Kulturkunde* 64 (2018), pp. 203–226

Dalal, Radha, Sean Roberts and Jochen Sokoly, eds., *The Seas and the Mobility of Islamic Art* (The Biennial Hamad Bin Khalifa Symposium on Islamic Art) (New Haven: Yale University Press, 2021)

Dankoff, Robert, and Sooyong Kim, *An Ottoman Traveller. Selections from the Book of Travels of Evliya Çelebi* (London: Eland Publishing, 2011)

Desmet-Grégoire, Hélène., 'Bread', *Encyclopaedia Iranica*, 4/4, pp. 444–447; available online at https://www.iranicaonline.org/articles/bread-persian-nan (accessed 23 September 2024)

Diffie, Bailey and George Winius, *Foundations of the Portuguese Empire, 1415–1850: Europe and the World in the Age of Expansion* (Minneapolis: University of Minnesota Press, 1977)

Dmitriev, Kirill, Julia Hauser and Bilal Orfali, eds., *Insatiable Appetite: Food as Cultural Signifier in the Middle East and Beyond.* (Leiden: Brill, 2020)

Erke, Ebru, ed., *Turkish Cuisine with Timeless Recipes* (Ankara: Republic of Turkey Ministry of Culture and Tourism, 2022)

Farridnejad, Shervin and Touraj Daryaee, eds., *Food for Gods, Food for Mortals: Culinary and Dining Practices in the Greater Iranian World* (Irvine, CA: University of Irvine, 2022)

Flandrin, Jean-Louis and Massimo Montanari, eds., *Food: A Culinary History from Antiquity to the Present* (New York: Columbia University Press, 1999)

Folsach, Kjeld von, *Art from the World of Islam in The David Collection* (Copenhagen: F. Hendriksens Eftf., 2001)

Folsach, Kjeld von, 'A Number of Pigmented Wooden Objects from the Eastern Islamic World', *Journal of the David Collection* 1 (2003), pp.73–96

Ganjavi, Nezami, *Khosrow and Shirin*, trans. Dick Davis (Washington, DC: Mage Publishers, 2023)

Gelder, Geert Jan van, *Of Dishes and Discourse: Classical Arabic Literary Representations of Food* (New York: Routledge, 2011)

Glück, Heinrich, *Die indischen Miniaturen des Hamzae-Romanes im Österreichischen Museum für Kunst und Industrie in Wien und in anderen Sammlungen* (Leipzig, Zürich and Vienna: Amalthea Verlag, 1925)

Gonnella, Julia, et al, ed., *Baghdad: Eye's Delight* (Doha and Milan: Qatar Museums and Silvana Editoriale, 2022)

Gonnella, Julia, Mounia Chekhab Abudaya, Tara Desjardins, Nicoletta Fazio, Simone Struth, eds., *Museum of Islamic Art: The Collection* (Doha and London: Qatar Museums and Thames & Hudson, 2022)

Günther, Sebastian, ed., *Knowledge and Education in Classical Islam: Religious Learning between Continuity and Change* (Leiden: Brill, 2020)

Gutiérrez Lloret, Sonia, 'Panes, hogazas y fogones portátiles. Dos formas cerámicas destinadas a la cocción del pan en Al-Andalus: el hornillo (*tannūr*) y el plato (*tābaq*)', *Lucentum* 9–10 (1991), pp. 161–175

Gyselen, Rika and Marthe Bernus-Taylor, eds., *Banquets d'Orient* (*Res Orientales IV*) (Bures-sur-Yvette: Le Groupe pour l'Étude de la Civilisation du Moyen-Orient, 1992)

Hallett, Jessica, 'Iraq and China: Trade and Innovation in the Early Abbasid Period', in *China-Mediterranean Sea: Routes and Exchange of Ceramics Prior to the 16th Century, Taoci: Revue Annuelle de la Société Française d'Étude de la Céramique Orientale* 4 (2005), pp. 21–29

Heine, Peter, *The Culinary Crescent: A History of Middle Eastern Cuisine* (London: Gingko, 2018)

Helou, Anissa, *Feast: Food of the Islamic World* (New York: Harper Collins Publishers, 2018)

Holakooei, Parviz, Moslem Mishmastnehi, Ali Moloodi Arani, Stefan Röhrs and Ute Franke, 'Materials and Technique of Lajvardina Ceramics from the Thirteenth to Fourteenth Century Iran', *Archaeological and Anthropological Sciences* 15/3 (2023), article 33

Husain, Salma, *The Emperor's Table: The Art of Mughal Cuisine* (New Delhi: Lustre Press and Roli Books, 2008)

Ibn al-Hajjaj, Imam Abul Hussain Muslim, *Sahih Muslim*, trans. Nasiruddin al-Khattab, 5 vols (Riyadh: Darussalam, 2020)

Ibn Ḥawqal, Muhammad, *Configuration de la terre (Kitab Surat Al-Ard)*, trans. Tome J.H. Kramers and G. Wiet (Paris: G.P. Maisonneuve & Larose, 1964)

Ibn Mubārak Shāh, *The Sultan's Feast: A Fifteenth-Century Egyptian Cookbook*, ed. and trans. Daniel Newman (London: Saqi Books, 2020)

Idris, Mardjoko. 'Prohibition in Qur'an: Structure and Meaning', *Sunan Kalijaga: International Journal of Islamic Civilization* 2/1 (2019), pp. 59–79

Irwin, John and Margaret Hall, *Indian Painted and Printed Fabrics* (Ahmedabad: Calico Museum of Textiles, 1971)

Karizaki, Vahid Mohammadpour, 'Ethnic and Traditional Iranian Breads: Different Types, and Historical and Cultural aspects', *Journal of Ethnic Foods* 4/1 (March 2017), pp. 8–14

Kashani, Ali Akbar Khan Ashpazbashi, *Sufra-yi at'ima* (Tehran: Bunyad-i Farhang-i Iran, 1974)

Khaleghi-Motlagh, Djalal, 'ADAB i. Adab in Iran', *Encyclopaedia Iranica*, 1/4, pp. 432–439; available online at http://www.iranicaonline.org/articles/adab-i-iran (accessed 18 December 2024)

Klein, Yaron, 'Abū Ṭayyib al-Washshāʾ and the Poetics of Inscribed Objects', *Journal of the American Oriental Society* 138/1 (January-March 2018), pp. 1–28

Krahl, Regina, John Guy, J. Keith Wilson and Julian Raby, eds., *Shipwrecked: Tang Treasures and Monsoon Winds* (Washington, DC: Arthur M. Sackler Gallery, Smithsonian Institution, 2010)

Komaroff, Linda, ed., *Dining with the Sultan: The Fine Art of Feasting* (Los Angeles: Los Angeles County Museum of Art and DelMonico Books, 2023)

Lemonier, Aurélien and Maryam Al Thani, eds., *Art Mill Museum 2030* (Milan and Doha: Silvana Editoriale and Qatar Museums, 2023)

Levanoni, Amalia, 'Food and Cooking during the Mamluk Era: Social and Political Implications', *Mamluk Studies Review* 9/2 (2005), pp. 201–222

Lewicka, Paulina B, *Food and Foodways of Medieval Cairenes* (Leiden: Brill, 2011)

Lion, Brigitte, Catherine Grandjean and Christophe Hugoniot, eds., *Le banquet du monarque dans le monde antique* (Tours: Presses universitaires François-Rabelais and Presses universitaires de Rennes, 2013)

Medley, Margaret, *Metalwork and Chinese Ceramics* (London: The Percival David Foundation of Chinese Art and University of London, 1972)

Mendelsohn, Loren D, 'The *Tacuinum Sanitatis*: A Medieval Health Manual', *Petits Propos Culinaires* 99 (2013), pp. 69–89

Mez, Adam, *The Renaissance of Islam*, trans. S. Khuda Bakhsh and D.S. Magoliouth. (Patna: Jubilee Printing and Publishing House, 1937)

Mir, Mustansir, 'Bread', *Encyclopaedia of Qur'an*, 1, pp. 255–256

Moayyad, Heshmat, 'Boshāq Aṭ'ema', *Encyclopaedia Iranica*, 4/4, pp. 382–383; available online at https://www.

iranicaonline.org/articles/boshaq-atema (accessed on 25 September 2024)

Nasrallah, Nawal, ed. and trans., *Annals of the Caliphs' Kitchens: Ibn Sayyār al-Warrāq's Tenth-Century Baghdadi Cookbook* (Leiden: Brill, 2010)

Nasrallah, Nawal, trans., *Treasure Trove of Benefits and Variety at the Table: A Fourteenth-Century Egyptian Cookbook* (Leiden and Boston: Brill, 2018)

Oberling, Gerry and Grace Martin Smith, *The Food Culture of the Ottoman Palace* (Ankara: Republic of Turkey Ministry of Culture and Tourism, 2001)

O'Kane, Bernard, A.C.S. Peacock and Mark Muehlhaeusler, eds., *Inscriptions in the Medieval Islamic World* (Edinburgh: Edinburgh University Press, 2023)

Pasqualone, Antonella. 'Traditional Flat Breads Spread from the Fertile Crescent: Production Process and History of Baking Systems', *Journal of Ethnic Foods* 5/1 (March 2018), pp. 10–19

Perry, Charles, ed. and trans., *Scents and Flavors: A Syrian Cookbook* (New York: NYU Press, 2017)

Pope, Arthur Upham and Phyllis Ackermann, *A Survey of Persian Art*. 6 vols (Oxford: Oxford University Press, 1938–1939)

Qajar, Nadir Mirza, *Khurak ha-yi Irani: bi farsi-yi sara* (Tehran: Intisharat-i Danishgah Tehran, 2007)

Ramazani, N, 'Āb-Gūšt', *Encyclopaedia Iranica*, 1/1, pp. 47–48; available online at https://www.iranicaonline.org/articles/ab-gust (accessed on 25 September 2024)

Roxburgh, David J, ed., *Envisioning Islamic Art and Architecture: Essays in Honor of Renata Holod* (Leiden & Boston: Brill, 2014)

Saba, Matthew D, 'Abbasid Lusterware and the Aesthetics of 'Ajab', *Muqarnas* 29 (2012), pp. 187–212

Shalem, Avinoam, 'Fountains of Light: The Meaning of Medieval Islamic Rock Crystal Lamps', *Muqarnas* 11 (1994), pp. 1–11

Spengler III, Robert N, *Fruit from the Sands: The Silk Road Origins of the Foods We Eat* (Oakland, CA: University of California Press, 2019)

Sorokin, Pitrim A, *Man and Society in Calamity: The Effects of War, Revolution, Famine, Pestilence upon Human Mind, Behavior, Social Organization and Cultural Life* (New York: E. P. Dutton & Company, 1943)

Stromberg, Matt, 'New Show of Islamic Art Explores the Pleasure of Eating Together', *Hyperallergic*, published 19 December 2023; available online at https://hyperallergic.com/862806/new-show-of-islamic-art-at-lacma-explores-the-pleasure-of-eating-together/ (accessed 23 September 2024)

Tamari, Vera, 'Ninth–Tenth Century White Mesopotamian Ceramic Ware with Blue Decoration' (Unpublished M. Phil thesis, University of Oxford, 1984)

Terzioğlu, Derin, 'The Imperial Circumcision Festival of 1582: An Interpretation', *Muqarnas* 12 (1995), pp. 84–100

Thackston, Wheeler M., ed. and trans., *The Jahangirnama: Memoirs of Jahangir, Emperor of India* (Oxford: Oxford University Press, 1999)

The Encyclopaedia of Islam. New edn. prepared by a number of leading orientalists. Edited by an editorial commmittee consisting of B. Lewis, Ch. Pellat, J. Schacht, et al. (Leiden, Brill, 1954–1991)

Al-Tujībī, Ibn Razīn, *The Exile's Cookbook: Medieval Gastronomic Treasures from al-Andalus and North Africa,* ed. and trans.Daniel Newman (London: Saqi Books, 2023)

Watson, Andrew M, *Agricultural Innovation in the Early Islamic World: The Diffusion of Crops and Farming Techniques, 700–1100* (Cambridge: Cambridge University Press, 1983)

Watson, Oliver, *Ceramics from Islamic Lands* (London: Thames & Hudson, 2004)

Watson, Oliver, 'Revisiting Samarra: The Rise of Islamic Glazed Pottery', *Beiträge zur Islamischen Kunst und Archäologie* 4 (2014), pp. 123–142

Wiet, Gaston. *Catalogue Genéral du Musée Arabe du Caire, Objects En Cuivre.* 1932 (republished Cairo: L'Organisation Égyptienne Générale du Livre, 1984)

Yusofi, G.-H, 'Bayhaqi Abu'l-Fazl', *Encyclopaedia Iranica*, III/8, pp. 889–894; available online at https://

www.iranicaonline.org/articles/bayhaqi-abul-fazl-mohammad-b (accessed 18 December 2024)

Zidan, Boussy, 'Cross-Cultural Exchange Between the Islamic World and Europe through the 10th–12th Centuries AH/ 16th–18th Centuries CE (Iznik Ceramic and Italian Maiolica as a Case Study)', *Journal of the General Union of Arab Archaeologists* 4/2 (2019), pp. 1–46

Following page
Yahya Barmaki Is Received by Ishaq the Muslim (detail), folio from the *Akhbar-i Barmakiyan* (Chronicle of the Barmakid dynasty), India, Mughal period, 11th century AH/ early 17th century CE, opaque watercolour, ink and gold on paper, 40 × 27.5 cm. Museum of Islamic Art, Doha, MIA.2014.375.1

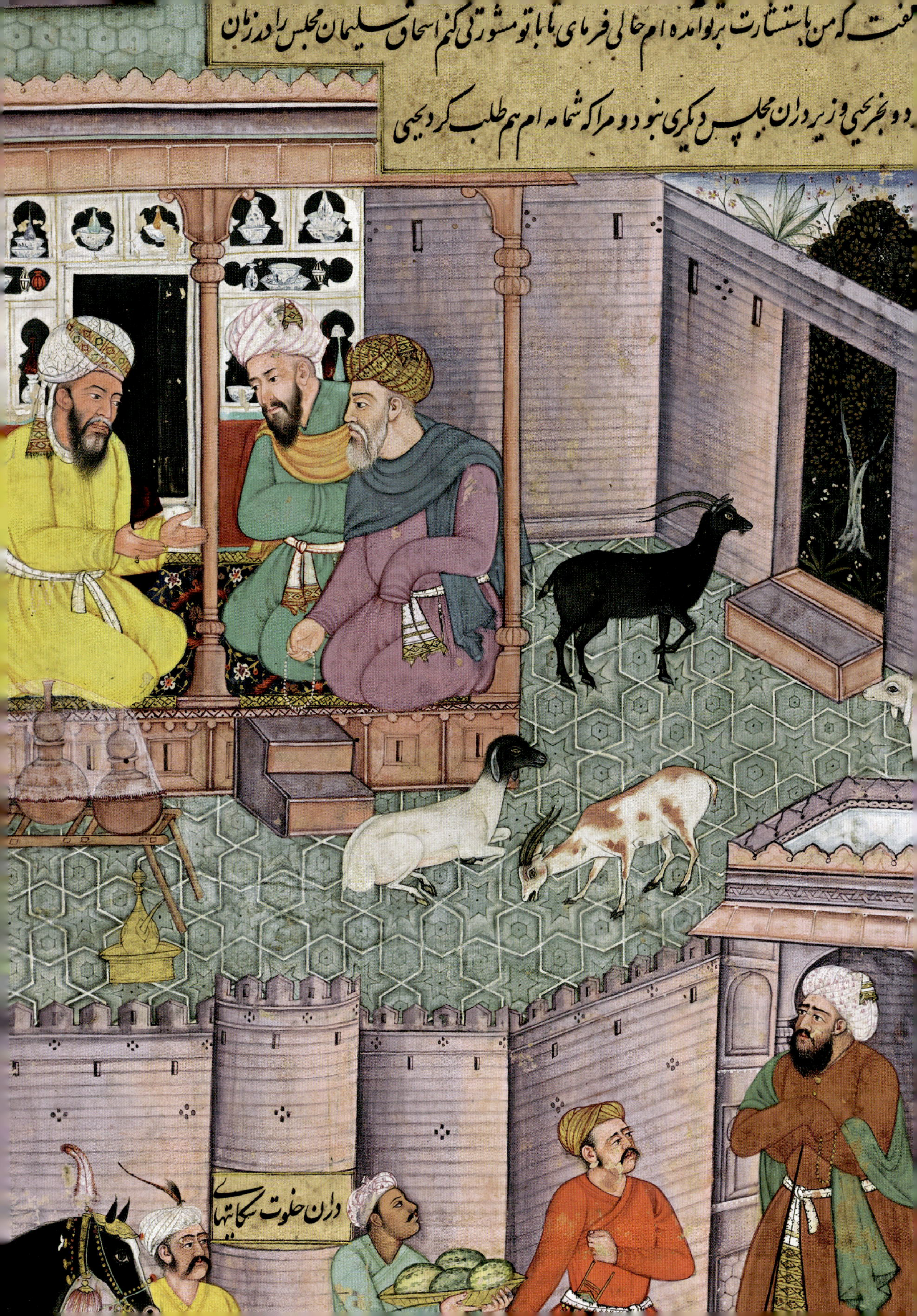
گفت که من با تو بشارت برتو آمده ام حالی فرمای یا با تو مشورتی کنم اسحاق سلیمان مجلس را در زان
دو نجر نجی و زیر درآن مجلس دیگری نبو د و مرا که شمامه ام هم طلب کرد یحیی
درآن خلوت سگانیهای

Exhibited Works

The following is a full list of exhibited works, organised according to the structure of the exhibition and content presented in the labels. All objects are from the collection of the Museum of Islamic Art, Doha, unless otherwise stated.

Manuscript copy of the Qur'an
Iran, Abbasid period, 7th century AH/
13th century CE
Ink, opaque watercolour and gold on paper with leather binding
47 × 34.5 cm (closed); 66 × 85.5 cm (open)
MS.783.2011
Cat. 1, pp. 62, 65

Manuscript copy of the Qur'an
Egypt (Cairo), Mamluk period,
8th century AH/14th century CE
Ink, opaque watercolour and gold on paper
49 × 35.2 cm (closed)
MS.415.2007

Manuscript copy of the Qur'an
Iran, Ilkhanid period, 7th century AH/
13th century CE
Ink, opaque watercolour and gold on paper
35 × 29.5 cm (closed)
MS.710.2010

Hajj certificate
Central Asia or South Asia,
1223 AH/1808 CE
Ink and gouache on paper
56.3 × 78.8 cm
MS.740.2011

**Manuscript of the *Dala'il al-Khayrat*
('Guide to Benevolent Deeds')**
Written by Muhammad al-Jazuli
Copied by Mehmed Emin and illuminated by Hafiz Mehmed Nuri
Istanbul, Ottoman period,
dated 1216 AH/1801 CE
Ink, opaque watercolour and gold on paper
23.4 × 16.7 cm (closed)
MS.427.2007
Cat 2b, p. 69

**Manuscript of the *En'am-i Sherif*
('The Noble En'am')**
Copied by Haci Mehmed Resim and illuminated by Haci Ahmed Ayasofia
Istanbul, Ottoman period,
dated 1294 AH/1877 CE

Ink, opaque watercolour and gold on paper
24.8 × 17 cm (closed)
MS.399.2007
Cat. 2a, p. 67

Bowl
Iran, Samanid period, 4th century AH/
10th century CE
Slip-painted and glazed earthenware
ø 25.5 cm
PO.658.2007

Bowl
Iran, Samanid period, 4th century AH/
10th century CE
Slip-painted and glazed earthenware
H. 10.7 cm; ø 20.7 cm
MIA.2014.516

Bowl
Iran, Samanid period, 4th century AH/
10th century CE
Slip-painted and glazed earthenware
ø 27.8 cm
PO.1099.2011

Prayer rug
Central Iran, Safavid period,
10th century AH/16th century CE
Wool, silk and metallic thread
180 × 112 cm
CA.85.2011

**Two folios from *'Aja'ib al-Makhluqat
wa Ghara'ib al-Mawjudat*
(The Wonders of Creation and
the Oddities of Existence)**
Written by Zakariya al-Qazwini
Syria, Mamluk period, 7th century AH/
13th century CE
Opaque watercolour and ink on paper
44 × 33.5 cm
MS.647.71; MS.647.62

**Illustration of the venous system
from a treatise on the anatomy of the
human body (probably the *Tashrih-i
Mansuri*)**
Author most commonly known as Mansur ibn Ilyas
Probably Iran, Safavid period,
10th century AH/16th century CE
Ink on paper
25.5 × 32.4 cm
MS.650.2

Letters about wheat and medicine
Egypt, Fatimid period,
5th–6th century AH/11th–
12th century CE
Ink on paper
11.1 × 8.4 cm; 19.5 × 30 cm
MS.516.2003.4; MS.515.2003.231

Mortar (*havan*)
Western Iran, late Seljuk or early Ilkhanid period, late 6th–early 7th century AH/12th–early 13th century CE
Cast copper, tin, zinc and lead alloy
14.9 cm × ø 20.2 cm
MIA.2014.74
Cat. 9, p. 85

Mortar and pestle
Spain, Taifa Kingdoms,
6th century AH/12th century CE
Cast bronze
9.5 × 18.6 cm; 29 × 5.3 cm
MW.432.2007; MW.434.2007

Zebu cow and calf figurine
Syria (Raqqa), Ayyubid period,
7th century AH/13th century CE
Turquoise-glazed fritware
29.5 × 38 × 16.9 cm
PO.788.2008
Cat. 3, p. 71

Albarello
Iran (Kashan), Khwarezmid or Mongol period, 7th century AH/
13th century CE
Cobalt-glazed and moulded fritware
27 × ø 16.5 cm
PO.715.2007

Two albarelli
Spain (Manises), Kingdom of Castile and Leon, 8th–9th century AH/
14th–15th century CE
Lustre-painted earthenware
36.3 × ø 16.8 cm; 33.5 × ø 15.2 cm
MIA.2013.147.1; PO.1092.2011

Albarello with portrait of Ibn Sina
Italy (Palermo), 10th century AH/
16th century CE
Tin-glazed earthenware (*maiolica*)
30.5 × ø 14.2 cm
PO.1086.2011
Cat. 7, p. 79

***Tacuinum Sanitatis* ('Almanac of
Health')**
Italy, Sicily, *c.* 1475 CE
Ink and opaque watercolour on paper
39.3 × 28.1 cm (closed)
Museum of Islamic Art Library, Qatar Museums, Doha, RS79.L64.14[75]
Cat. 8, pp. 80, 82–83

Storage jar
Iraq, Abbasid period, 2nd–3rd century AH/
8th–9th century CE
Turquoise-glazed earthenware
47.5 × ø 33 cm
PO.218.2003

Bowl with bird
Iraq, Abbasid period, 4th century AH/
10th century CE
Lustre-painted and glazed earthenware
6.4 × ø 22.2 cm
MIA.2013.74

Bowl with date palm
Iraq (probably Basra), Abbasid period,
3rd century AH/9th century CE
Earthenware, with opaque white
and cobalt blue glazes
ø 20.1 cm
PO.566.2007
Cat. 4, p. 73

Bowl with fish
Iraq or Iran, Abbasid period,
3rd century AH/9th century CE
Polychrome painted ('splashware')
earthenware
7 × ø 22 cm
PO.565.2007

Storage jar
Syria, Mamluk period, 8th century AH/
14th century CE
Underglaze painted fritware
34.9 × ø 27.8 cm
PO.738.2007
Cat. 5, p. 75

Tray with ship ('junk')
India (Surat or Cambay), Mughal period,
10th–11th century AH/late 16th–
early 17th century CE
Lacquered and gilded turned wood
ø 75 cm
WW.110.2007
Cat. 6, pp. 76–77

**First edition of *Den rechte(n) Weg aus
zu fahren von Lissbona gen Kallakuth*
('The Correct Way to Sail from Lisbon
to Calcutta')**
Vasco Da Gama (author)
Nuremberg, Johann Weissenburger,
1506 CE
Ink and opaque watercolour on paper
20 × 14.8 cm (closed)
Lusail Museum, Qatar Museums, Doha,
LB.154

**First edition of *New Kreüterbuch*
('New Herbal')**
Switzerland (Basel), 1543 CE
Leonhart Fuchs (Botanist), Heinrich
Füllmaure, Albert Meyer and Veit Rudolf
Speckle (illustrators)
Opaque watercolour and ink on paper
39.7 × 26.8 × 9.2 cm (closed)
General Collection, Qatar Museums,
Doha, STM.NH.BO.0034

**Mappemonde dréssée sur les
relations les plus nouvelles** ('World Map
Drawn Up on the Most Recent Relations')
Louis-Charles Desnos (cartographer
and publisher), Paris, 1766 CE
Opaque watercolour and ink on paper
53 × 77 cm
Qatar National Library, Doha,
HC.MAP.00510

**First edition of *De historia stirpium
commentarii insignes*
('Notable Commentaries on the
History of Plants')**
Switzerland (Basel), 1542 CE
Leonhart Fuchs (Botanist), Heinrich
Füllmaure, Albert Meyer, Veit Rudolf
Speckle (illustrators)
Opaque watercolour and ink on paper
40.1 × 27.4 × 8.5 cm (closed)
General Collection, Qatar Museums,
Doha, STM.NH.BO.1441

Ramadan Feast
VCUarts Qatar Student Project, 2024
Papier mâché, hand painted
10 × 2.5 m
Collection of Mathaf: Arab Museum
of Modern Art, Doha, MATL.2024.2

Cauldron
Caucasus or Eastern Turkey, Timurid
period, 8th century AH/14th century CE
Cast bronze
80.5 × ø 70 cm
MW.147.2000

Bucket
Iran (Khurasan), Seljuq or Khwarezmid
period, 6th–7th century AH/
12th–13th century CE
Cast bronze with silver inlay
25.8 × 19.7 × ø 19.7 cm
MW.149.1999

Brazier
Iran or Central Asia, Mongol or
Ilkhanid period, 7th–8th century AH/
13th–14th century CE
Hammered and chiselled cast iron
with velvet
25.2 × 53.2 cm
MIA.2014.81
Cat. 10, p. 87

Cooking in a Landscape
Afghanistan (Herat), Safavid period,
c. 987 AH/1580 CE
Opaque watercolour and ink
on paper
29 × 20 cm
MIA.2013.151

Rulers feasting and enjoying entertainment
Manuscript of the *Shahnameh*
(Book of Kings) by Firdawsi
Copied by Hidayat Allah Shirazi
Iran (Shiraz), Safavid period, dated
991AH/1583 CE
Opaque watercolour, ink, and gold on paper
40.5 × 27.5 cm (closed)
MS.639

**Two folios from a manuscript
of Persian poetry**
Uzbekistan (Bukhara), Shaybanid period,
10th century AH/mid-16th century CE
Opaque watercolour, ink, and gold
on paper
21 × 10.8 × 0.7 cm
MIA.2014.327.1; MIA.2014.327.2
Cat. 21, pp. 115, 116

Tray stand
Syria, Ayyubid period, 7th century AH/
late 13th century CE
Hammered brass inlaid with silver
24.8 × ø 25.6 cm
MW.110.1999

Tray
Made for Sultan al-Nasir Muhammad
bin Qala'un (r. 693–741 AH/1293–1341 CE,
with interruptions)
Egypt or Syria, Mamluk period,
8th century AH/early 14th century CE
Hammered brass inlaid with gold and silver
11.5 × ø 110 cm
MW.35.1998

Lunchbox
Egypt or Yemen, Mamluk period,
9th century AH/15th century CE
Hammered brass inlaid with silver
17.8 × 28 × 27.6 cm
MW.157.2000
Cat. 11, p. 89

Jug and tray
Greater Khorasan (north-eastern Iran or
Afghanistan), Ghaznavid or Ghurid period,
late 6th or 7th century AH/12th or early
13th century CE
Hammered brass inlaid with gold, silver
and copper
28.3 × 16.6 cm; 3.4 × ø 35.6 cm
MIA.2014.502; MW.126.1999
Cat. 17, pp. 103, 104–105

Tray
Afghanistan, Ghaznavid period,
6th century AH/12th century CE
Hammered, incised and punched brass
35 × 23.9 × 3.3 cm
MW.64.1999
Cat. 18, pp. 107, 108–109

Ewer
Afghanistan (possibly Herat), Ilkhanid
period, late 7th–early 8th century AH/
late 13th–early 14th century CE
Hammered brass inlaid with silver,
copper and black compound
39.9 × ø 22 cm
MW.118.1999
Cat. 19, p. 111

Bowl
Syria or Mesopotamia, Abbasid period,
3rd century AH/9th century CE
Blown glass with scratch-engraved
decoration
4 × ø 17.1 cm
GL.62.2003

Two cups
Egypt and Iran, Abbasid period,
3rd–4th century AH/9th–10th century CE
Blown glass and wheel-cut decoration
8 × ø 8 cm; 8.6 × ø 10.3 cm
GL.44.2002; GL.19.1999 (Cat. 13, p. 92)

Spoon
Possibly Iran or Iraq, Saminid or
Abbasid period, 3rd–4th century AH/
9th–10th century CE
Blown glass with wheel-cut
decoration
3.8 × 20.3 × 4.6 cm
GL.527.2011
Cat. 12, p. 91

Beaker
Iran, Abbasid period, 3rd–4th century AH/
9th–10th century CE
Blown glass with wheel-cut
decoration
15.8 × ø 9.8 cm
GL.337.2007

Robe
Uzbekistan (Bukhara), 14th century AH/
20th century CE
Woven and block-printed velvet (*ikat*)
122 × 163 cm
CO.35.1999

Cup with deer
Iran (Kashan), Khwarezmid period,
dated 594 AH/1197 CE
Lustre-painted fritware
11.9 × ø 16.4 cm
MIA.2013.82

Flask
Iran (Kashan), Ilkhanid period,
7th century AH/mid-13th century CE
Lustre-painted fritware
ø 19 cm
PO.138.2000

Rooster-headed ewer
Iran (Kashan), Khwarezmid period,
7th century AH/mid-13th century CE
Moulded and lustre-painted
fritware
34 × ø 17.9 cm
PO.714.2007
Cat. 15, p. 97

Bowl with figure holding a cup
Iran (Kashan), Khwarezmid period,
6th century AH/late 12th century CE
Lustre-painted fritware
ø 18.5 cm
PO.37.1999
Cat. 14, p. 95

Dish
Iran, Ilkhanid period, 7th–8th century AH/
13th–14th century CE
Press-formed, overglaze-painted
and leaf-gilded fritware (*lajvardina* ware)
13 × ø 34 cm
QM.2018.0591
Cat. 20, p. 112

Dish
Iran, Safavid period, 11th–early 12th
century AH/second half of the
17th century CE
Underglaze-painted fritware
ø 48.3 cm
PO.647.2007

Two bottles
Iran, Safavid period, 11th century AH/
17th century CE
Underglaze-painted fritware
29 × ø 18.3 cm; 53 × ø 9.5 cm
PO.1095.2011; MIA.2014.162

Dish
Iran (Kerman), Safavid period,
11th century AH/17th century CE
Overglaze-painted fritware
ø 28.6 cm
PO.101.1999

'Gombroon ware' bowl
Iran (Bandar Abbas), Safavid period,
11th century AH/17th century CE
Pierced, painted and glazed porcelain
9.4 × ø 19.7 cm
MIA.2014.175

The Court of Pir Budaq
Iran (Shiraz), Turkmen period,
c. 859–865 AH/1455–60 CE
Opaque watercolour, gold and ink
on paper
39.1 × 33.8 cm
MIA.2013.150
Cat. 16, pp. 99, 100–101

***Feast in Homage of Kay Khosraw after
His Enthronement***
Folio from the *Shahnameh* (Book of Kings)
by Firdawsi
Made for Shah Isma'il II (r. 983–984 AH/
1576–1577 CE)
Attributed to Burji
Iran (Qazwin), Safavid period, dated 984
AH/1577 CE
Opaque watercolour, gold, and ink on paper
41 × 29 cm
MIA.2013.91

***Nushirvan Records His Sage Counsel
for Hurmuzd***
Folio 654r from the *Shahnameh* (Book of
Kings) of Shah Tahmasp (r. 930–984 AH/
1524–1576 CE)
Attributed to Muzaffar 'Ali
Iran (Tabriz), Safavid period,
c. 930 AH/1530 CE
Opaque watercolour, gold and ink on paper
47.4 × 31.2 cm
MIA.2014.75

Robe
Iran, Safavid or Zand period,
12th century AH/18th century CE
Woven silk with metallic wrapped threads
102 × 111 cm
CO.170.2003

Tent panel (*qanat*)
Northern India, Mughal period,
12th century AH/18th century CE
Block-printed, painted and
mordant-dyed cotton
505 × 124 cm
TE.81.2003
Cat. 25, pp. 129, 130–131

Coat
India, 13th century AH/19th century CE
Woven silk with metallic wrapped threads
134.5 × 178 cm
CO.49.1999

***Yahya Barmaki Is Received by Ishaq
the Muslim***
Folio from the *Akhbar-i Barmakiyan*
(Chronicle of the Barmakid dynasty)
India, Mughal period, 11th century AH/
early 17th century CE
Opaque watercolour, ink and gold on paper
40 × 27.5 cm
MIA.2014.375.1

A Prince Visiting a Sage
India, Mughal period, 11th century AH/
early 17th century CE
Opaque watercolour, ink and gold on paper
40.6 × 29 cm
MS.292.2007

Cow and calf painting
Attributed to Dasavanta
India, Mughal period, 10th century AH/
late-16th century CE
Opaque watercolour, ink and gold on paper
Painting: 19.3 × 11.7 cm, folio: 30.5 × 20 cm
MS.33.2007
Cat. 23, p. 123

***Six Wise Men Including Mian Mir
and Mullah Shah in Discussion,***
folio from the Ardeshir album
Attributed to La'lchand
India, Mughal period, 11th century AH/
mid-17th century CE
Opaque watercolour, ink and gold
on paper
55.9 × 35 cm
MS.826.2012
p. 4

Portrait of the Mughal Emperor Jahangir
Attributed to Balchand
India, Mughal period, c. 1030 AH/1620 CE
Opaque watercolour, ink and gold on paper
22.3 × 17.3 cm
MS.771.2011
Cat. 24a, p. 125

Cup
India, Mughal period, mid-11th century
AH/17th century CE
Carved jade
2.0 × 8.3 × 5.4 cm
GL.172.2003
Cat. 24b, p. 127

Spoon
India, 12th–13th century AH/
18th–19th century CE
Gold set with rubies, diamonds
and emeralds
14.4 × 3.6 cm
JE.225.2011

Lidded jar
India (Jaipur or Delhi), Mughal period,
13th century AH/19th century CE
Enamelled copper set with diamonds
H. 12.2 cm
JE.219.2003
Cat. 26, pp. 133, 134–135

Ewer (*aftaba*)
India, Mughal period,
10th century AH/late 16th century CE
Cast bronze
67.5 × ø 43.5 cm
MW.292.2007
Cat. 22, p. 121

Dish with grapevines
Turkey (Iznik), Ottoman period,
c. 877–881 AH/1525–1530 CE

Underglaze-painted fritware
7 × ø 40.3 cm
PO.46.1999
Cat. 27, p. 137

**Manuscript copy of the *Diwan
of 'Ali Shir Niva'i***
Copied by 'Abdallah ibn Sheikh
Murshid al-Shirazi
Turkey, Ottoman period, dated
1008 AH/1600 CE
Opaque watercolour, gold and ink
on paper
25 × 17.2 × 3.9 cm (closed)
MS.584.2007

Robe
Turkey, Ottoman period,
13th century AH/19th century CE
Woven silk with metallic embroidery
150.7 × 151.5 cm
TE.186.2003
Cat. 30, pp. 143, 144–145

Bottle (*surahi*)
Turkey (Iznik), Ottoman period,
10th century AH/late 16th century CE
Underglaze-painted fritware
44.5 × ø 20.7 cm
PO.10.1997
Cat. 28, p. 139

Dish
Turkey (Iznik), Ottoman period,
10th century AH/late 16th century CE
Underglaze-painted fritware
6 × Ø 29.8 cm
PO.125.1999

Tankard
Turkey (Iznik), Ottoman period,
10th century AH/late 16th century CE
Underglaze-painted fritware
18.5 × 16 × ø 12 cm
PO.100.1999

Jug
Signed by Husayn ibn Mubarakshah
Afghanistan (Herat), dated 988 AH/
1485 CE
Cast brass inlaid with gold and silver
13 × 14.1 cm
MW.471.2007

Jug
Turkey or the Balkans, Ottoman period,
10th century AH/16th century CE
Gilded silver
102 × ø 10.1 cm
MW.43.1998

Jug
Turkey (Iznik), Ottoman period,
10th century AH/mid-16th century CE

Underglaze-painted fritware
17.7 × 16.6 × ø 15 cm
PO.151.2002

***Reception of Ottoman Ambassador
Yusuf Muttahir Agha by Gabriel
Bethlen, Prince of Transylvania
(1580–1629 CE)***
Unknown artist, 11th century AH/
early 17th century CE
Oil on canvas
60 × 87 cm
Lusail Museum, Qatar Museums, Doha,
OM.1006

Cuisinier Turc **(Turkish chef)**
*Les quatre premiers livres des
navigations et pérégrinations orientales*
('The Four First Books of Eastern
Navigations and Wanderings')
Nicolas de Nicolay (author)
Lyon, Guillaume Rouillé (printer/publisher),
dated 1567 CE
Opaque watercolour and ink on paper
34.5 × 25 cm (closed)
Lusail Museum, Qatar Museums, Doha,
OM.957

Spoons
Turkey, Ottoman period,
13th century AH/19th century CE
Carved tortoiseshell, ebony and ivory
pierced and mounted with copper alloy pins
L. 19.5 – 26.5 cm
IV.29.2002
Cat. 29, p. 141

Napkin (*yağlik*) with galleon ships
Turkey, Ottoman period,
12th century AH/18th century CE
Metal-embroidered silk and linen
70 × 73 cm
MIA.2013.102

Bowl
China (Canton), Qing Dynasty,
dated 1281 AH/1865 CE
Enamelled and gold-painted porcelain
15.7 × 37 × ø 20 cm
PO.666.2007

Three coffee cup holders (*zarfs*)
Iran (Tehran), Qajar period,
13th century AH/19th century CE
Enamelled and gilded metal alloy
5.2 × 5.2 × ø 3.3 cm
JE.229.2012.1, JE.229.2012.3, JE.229.2012.5

Spoon
Iran, Qajar period, 13th century AH/
19th century CE
Gilded cast brass
5 × 7.2 × 48.5 cm
MW.642.2011

Market paintings from a Qajar album
Iran, Qajar period, 13th century AH/
late 19th century CE
Gouache on paper
38.2 × 31.1 cm (each page)
MS.772.2011.3, MS.772.2011.2 (p. 50),
MS.772.2011.34

Un mercato in Oriente
(A Market in the East)
Alberto Pasini (1826–1899)
Probably Istanbul, dated 1881
Oil on canvas
54.6 × 65.4 cm
Lusail Museum, Qatar Museums,
Doha, OM.715

La kasbah rouge **(The Red Kasbah)**
Jacques Majorelle (1886–1962)
Marrakesh, dated 1924
Oil on canvas
122.5 × 102.5 cm
Lusail Museum, Qatar Museums, Doha,
OM.890

Scène de marché avec ânes
(Market Scenery with Donkeys)
Mohammed Ben Ali Rbati (1861–1939)
Morocco
Watercolour and pencil on paper
69.6 × 82.3 cm
Collection of Mathaf: Arab Museum
of Modern Art, Doha, MAT.2013.13.5

View of the Port of Algiers
Jean-Jacques Midderigh (1877–1970)
Algeria, 1920–1930
Chromolithographic print on paper
116.2 × 42 cm
Qatar National Library, Doha,
HC.GM.P.2019.0119

Consommez l'huile d'olive de Tunisie
(Consume olive oil from Tunisia)
Jean Piaubert (1900–2002)
Paris, Damour Publicité (publisher), *c.* 1930
Chromolithographic print on paper
160 × 120 cm
Qatar National Library, Doha,
HC.GM.P.2019.0209

Ville de Boufarik. Concours agricole
Nord-Africain (Algérie). Du 14 au 25 mai
1927 **(City of Boufarik. North African**
Agricultural Competition, from May
14–27, 1927)
Léon-Georges-Jean-Baptiste Carre
(1878–1942)
Algiers, Imprimerie Baconnier
(publisher), 1927
Chromolithographic print on paper
106.6 × 76.5 cm
Qatar National Library, Doha,
HC.GM.P.2019.0141

Syndicat d'Initiative et de Tourisme
de Tanger. Tanger. Son site, son climat
(Tangier Initiative and Tourism Union.
Tangier. Site and Climate)
Jacques Majorelle (1886–1962)
Algiers, Imprimerie Baconnier
(publisher), 1924
Chromolithographic print on paper
105 × 75.1 cm
Qatar National Library, Doha,
HC.GM.P.2019.0144

Maquettes
Abdulrahman Al-Mulla (b. 1965)
Qatar, 2024
Clay, sand, white gypsum and wood
36.8 × 42.5 × 35.8, 34 × 75.4 x 43.7,
37.7 × 42.6 × 33
Collection of the artist

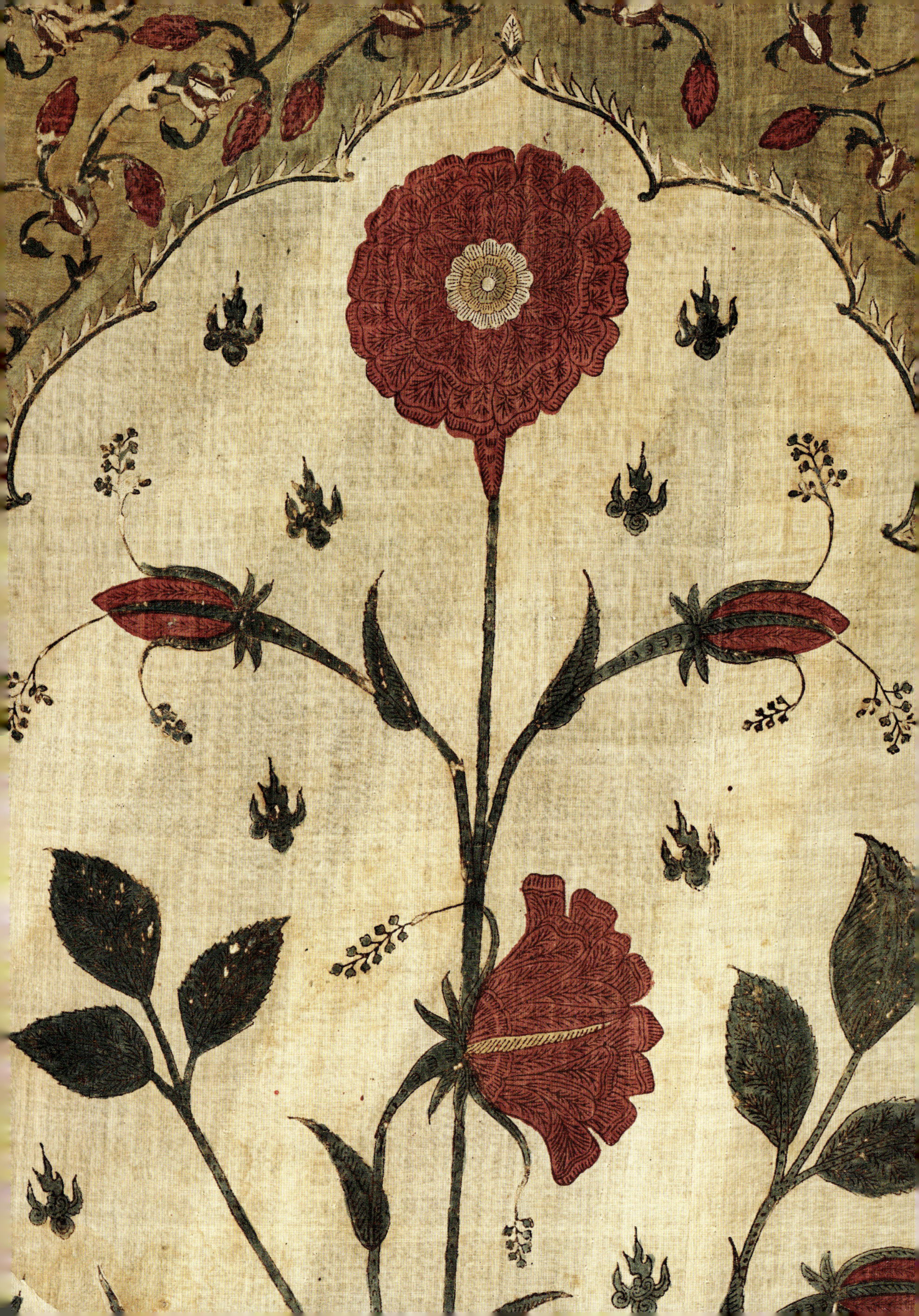

About the Contributors

Reem Aboughazala (RA) joined the Museum of Islamic Art, Doha in 2018 as a Curatorial Assistant. She has been involved in the Museum's relaunch project as well as several publication and exhibitions, including *Set in Stone: Gems and Jewels from Royal Indian Courts* (2019–2020), *Beautiful Memories of Palestine* (2021) and *Baghdad: Eye's Delight* (2022). She studied Art History at Virgina Commonwealth University School of the Arts in Qatar and received her MA in Museum and Gallery Practice from University College London, Qatar.

Mounia Chekhab Abudaya (MCA) is the Deputy Director of Curatorial Affairs at the Museum of Islamic Art, Doha. She completed her PhD in Islamic Art History and Archaeology at the Pantheon Sorbonne University, Paris. Her expertise is in the Western Mediterranean, manuscripts and pilgrimage-related devotional materials in the Islamic world. At MIA, she has curated several exhibitions including *Hajj: The Journey through Art* (2013–2014) in collaboration with the British Museum.

Tara Desjardins (TD) is Senior Curator of Decorative Arts & Design at the Lusail Museum, Doha. She was previously the curator of South Asia at the Museum of Islamic Art where she curated the exhibition *Set in Stone: Gems and Jewels from Royal Indian Courts* (2019–2020) and contributed to *Baghdad: Eye's Delight* (2022) and *Fashioning an Empire: Textiles from Safavid Iran* (2023–2024). She holds a PhD from the School of Oriental and African Studies (SOAS), University of London and an MA in Art Business from the Sotheby's Institute of Art, London. She has previously held curatorial positions at the San Diego Museum of Art and the Victoria & Albert Museum, London. Her research has been published by the *Journal of Glass Studies*, *Artibus Asiae*, and Yale University Press. She is also the author of *Mughal Glass: The History of Glassmaking in India* (Roli Books, 2024).

Nicoletta Fazio (NF) is Curator of Iran and Central Asia at the Museum of Islamic Art, Doha. An art historian and medievalist by training, she received her PhD in Global Art History from the University of Heidelberg (Germany). Prior to joining the curatorial team in Doha, she was Junior Curator at the Museum *für* Islamische Kunst, Berlin. At MIA she has worked on several exhibition projects, most recently *Baghdad: Eye's Delight* (2022) and *Fashioning an Empire: Textiles from Safavid Iran* (2023–2024).

Linda Komaroff is Curator of Islamic Art at LACMA. In addition to *Dining with the Sultan: The Fine Art of Feasting* (2023), her past Islamic art exhibitions at LACMA include the NEH-supported *The Legacy of Genghis Khan: Courtly Art and Culture in Western Asia, 1256-1353* (2002–2003) and *Gifts of the Sultan: The Arts of Giving at the Islamic Courts* (2011–2012). Her research and publications focus primarily on the Iranian world, with a special emphasis on decorative arts.

Daniel Newman is Professor and Chair of Arabic Studies at the University of Durham (UK). He has translated a number of works of Arabic literature, from both the premodern and modern eras, including *The Sultan's Feast: A Fifteenth-Century Egyptian Cookbook* (2020). His website eatlikeasultan.com, on medieval Arab cooking, combines his interest in food and history. It is a serious resource for the study of food and foodways and includes recipes for fishes he has tested by cross-checking multiple Arabic texts.

Teslim Sanni (TS) is a Curatorial Research Assistant at the Museum of Islamic Art, Doha. He holds a BA in Art History from Virginia Commonwealth University and an MA in Islamic Art and Architecture from Hamad Bin Khalifa University. His research explores Islamic art and material culture, with a particular focus on its intersections with African cultural identity. At MIA, Teslim Sanni contributes to the development of exhibitions, authors catalog texts, and supports educational initiatives, striving to make the museum's collection more accessible and engaging for diverse audiences. Alongside his research work, Teslim Sanni also teaches the survey of global art history to first-year students at Virginia Commonwealth University School of The Arts in Qatar.

Simone Struth (SST) is curator of Central Islamic Lands at the Museum of Islamic Art, Doha. She was responsible for the Online Collection Project and the new permanent galleries dedicated to the Indian Ocean trade and the spread of Islam to China and Southeast Asia. She has also contributed to major MIA publications including *Museum of Islamic Art: The Collection and Baghdad: Eyes Delight*. An Islamic art historian by training, she studied in Munich (LMU) and Cairo. Specialising in Abbasid art, she completed her PhD on Abbasid stucco material from Samarra. Before joining MIA, Simone Struth worked for the Samarra Project (MOSYS 3D) at the Museum für Islamische Kunst, Berlin.

Opposite page
Tent panel (detail, see page 128)

Her Excellency Sheikha Al Mayassa
bint Hamad bin Khalifa al Thani
Chairperson, Qatar Museums

Mohammed Saad Al Rumaihi
Chief Executive Officer, Qatar Museums

Sheikh Faisal bin Abdulaziz Al Thani
*President, Museum of Islamic Art and
Chairman, Board of Directors of Ahli Bank*

Shaika Nasser Al-Nassr
Director, Museum of Islamic Art

THE EXHIBITION

*A Seat at the Table: Food and Feasting
in the Islamic World*
20 May – 8 November 2025
Museum of Islamic Art, Doha

Organised by the Museum of Islamic Art,
in collaboration with the Los Angeles
County Museum of Art

Curators
Tara Desjardins, Senior Curator,
Decorative Arts and Design, Lusail Museum
Teslim Sanni, Curatorial Affairs Researcher

Curatorial Affairs
Mounia Chekhab Abudaya, Deputy
Director of Curatorial Affairs

Exhibition Management
Mercedes Navarro Tito, Elisa Maduro,
Lolwa Alsolaiti, Aleesha Suleman

Collections Management
Manal Al-Marri, Shaikha Al-Kaabi,
Errol Ituriaga, Jordani Goni Vercher,
Romeo Fuentes

Conservation
Reem Al Khuzaei, Serhat Karakaya,
Stefan Masarovic, Dominika Kostolnikova,
Maja Bacic

Digital Assets
Marc Pelletreau, Samar Kassab,
Chrysovalantis Lamprianidis, Christian
Sánchez

Translation to Arabic
Salam Shughry
Dr Suliman Alomirat

Learning and Outreach
Salem Abdulla Al Aswad, Anwar Efaifa,
Noora Al Meadadi, Rodha Mohammed,
Aisha Al Nameh, Susan Parker Leavy
and their teams

*Operations, Security and Facilities
Management*
Abdulla Al Dosari, Ahmad Al Kalbani,
Nasser Al Meanis and their teams,
Larry Fabriga, Rolan Tuazon, John Albert
Matinong, Christopher Mata Maningo
(MIA FM Team)

Galleries
Joseph Conrad Encinares, Reynaldo
Batungbakal, Ovel Salvador Mangune,
Romel Dela Vega

Events
Faraz Ahmed

QM Marketing and Communications
Stephanie Cliffe, Mohammed Khamis
Al-Abdulla, Hanan Saif, Lamis Nassar,
Malak Latrous, Wasay Mir, Varsha Eriyari,
Isobel Smith. Zeina Gammoh, Aneta
Perevska, Dana Al Shebani, Fatema
Al Yousuf (MIA). Dana Al Mana (MIA),
Mohamed Saheel, Norhan Mohamed,
Shatsy Mahmoud Awad, Sima Muderris,
Reem Aouir. Loubna Zeidan, Reem
Shaddad, Vrinda Abilash, Ali Alzuheiri.
Ali Al-anssari, Aimen Jan, Wadha
Al Mesalam, Shaikha Ahmed Ali

QM Publications
Randa Takieddine, Tracy Anne Goulding

Qatar Creates
Khalid Gharaibeh, Anas El Khateeb,
Moamen Ahmadien, Lina Hajo, Nisrine
Sajide, Nihal Nooh, Athul Narayanan

QC+
Rocemele Cayetano, Mariam Adra,
Amel Mahgoub, Tigest Seifu, Lana Focic,
Charianne Tomacruz, Nikhil Ameer,
Anuradha Jangam, Reem El Madad,
Aysenur Yavuz, Maeda Solaiman Al Haidar

QM Support
Basant El Razzaz, Khaled AlShebeeb,
Rowond Zarandah, Translation

Thanks also to QM Legal, QM Finance
and QM Procurement Teams

Exhibition Design and Build
Espai-Visual Cultural Projects,
Barcelona, Spain

SPECIAL THANKS TO

Exhibition Lenders
Lusail Museum, Qatar Museums, Doha
General Collection, Qatar Museums, Doha
Mathaf: Arab Museum of Modern Art, Doha
Archaeology Department, Qatar Museums
Qatar National Library, Doha
Abdulrahman AlMulla

Photography and AV Content
Qatar Photography Centre
Abdulaziz Al Kubaisi
Nasser Al Emadi
Jassim Al Malki
Aisha Al-Muhannadi
Layali Al Qahira
Bandar Eden Restaurant
Günaydin
Al Ibtihal Bakery
Qatar Cooking Academy
Aisha al Tamimi
Mehboob Khan
Naveed Alam
Najmieh Batmanglij
Amin Sepehri
Hadiza Ibrahim Ango

THE PUBLICATION

A Seat at the Table:
Food and Feasting in the Islamic World

Book Concept
Tara Desjardins

Authors
Reem Aboughazala
Mounia Chekhab Abudaya
Tara Desjardins
Nicoletta Fazio
Linda Komaroff
Daniel Newman
Teslim Sanni
Simone Struth

Copy Editor
Marika Sardar

Qatar Museum's Publications Department
Randa Takieddine, Director
Tracy Goulding, Editorial

Image Credits
All images © Museum of Islamic Art /
Qatar Museums, Doha

Photography by Chrysovalantis Lamprianidis
front and back covers, pp. 22, 26, 73, 76, 85,
87, 89, 91, 92, 95, 99, 100–101, 103, 104, 111, 112,
115, 116, 118–119, 121, 127, 129, 130–131, 137, 139,
141, 143, 144–145, 156

Samar Kassab pp. 4, 25, 33, 50, 67, 69, 107,
108–109, 125

Marc Pelletreau pp. 10, 14, 42, 54, 59, 80,
82–83

Mohammed Faris Edakkunimal p. 34

Samar Kassab and Christian Sanchez
pp. 71, 75, 79, 97, 133, 134–135

Christian Sanchez pp. 123, 150

Courtesy Qatar National Library pp. 62, 65

PUBLISHING AND DISTRIBUTION

Qatar Museums
Doha, Qatar
www.qm.org.qa

Silvana Editoriale
Milan, Italy
www.silvaneditoriale.it

First published in 2025 by Silvana Editoriale
in collaboration with Qatar Museums

Printed and bound in Italy. First edition

ISBN: 9788836661107 (Silvana Editoriale)
ISBN: 9789927184024 (Qatar Museums)
Qatari Legal Deposit No: 549/2025

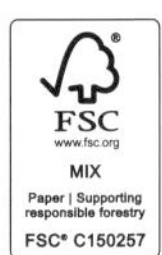